BEST of the BEST
from
IDAHO
COOKBOOK

Selected Recipes from Idaho's
FAVORITE COOKBOOKS

The magnificent Sawtooth Mountains, "America's Alps," dominate the Idaho landscape for nearly 60 miles. Shown here towering above Stanley Lake Creek, the Sawtooth Mountains were named for their jagged profile.

BEST of the BEST
from
IDAHO
COOKBOOK

Selected Recipes from Idaho's
FAVORITE COOKBOOKS

Edited by
GWEN McKEE
and
BARBARA MOSELEY

Illustrated by Tupper England

QUAIL RIDGE PRESS
Preserving America's Food Heritage

Library of Congress Cataloging-in-Publication Data

Best of the best from Idaho cookbook : selected recipes from Idaho's favorite cookbooks / edited
by Gwen McKee and Barbara Moseley ; illustrations by Tupper England.
  p. cm.
Includes index.
ISBN-10: 1-893062-46-5
ISBN-13: 978-1-893062-46-7
  1. Cookery, American 2. Cookery—Idaho. I. McKee, Gwen. II. Moseley, Barbara.

TX715.B4856483 2003
641.59796—dc21   2003043151

QUAIL RIDGE PRESS
P. O. Box 123 • Brandon, MS 39043 • 1-800-343-1583
email: info@quailridge.com • www.quailridge.com

Contents

PHOTO © WILLIAM H. MULLINS OUTDOOR PHOTOGRAPHY

An ocean of low, rolling hills make up the Palouse region of north Idaho. The Palouse is the world's leader in the production of soft white winter wheat.

Preface

Idaho's spectacularly diverse landscape is largely unspoiled, providing a virtual playground where adventure abounds. Among the peaks and valleys, rivers and lakes, you can play in over 19,000 miles of hiking trails, over 14,000 miles of single-track biking trails, over 3,000 miles of white water rivers, and 17 ski areas. And the widest variety of game in the United States—trophy elk, mule deer, two species of bighorn sheep, antelope, bear, moose, cougar, mountain goat, white-tailed deer, waterfowl, and upland game birds—abound freely in these areas. The outdoors always brings on an appetite, and Idahoans have excelled at how to please the palate around the campfire as well as at a suburban table.

When you think of Idaho food, you definitely think of those famous Idaho potatoes. And while they do indeed influence the cuisine—and you will find numerous great recipes utilizing them throughout the book—Idaho offers so much more. Abundant natural resources provide juicy huckleberries, savory lentils, plentiful wild game and fish, and oh, that warm delicious sourdough bread. . . . You'll discover Idaho has a taste all its own when you prepare stick-to-your-ribs dishes like Idaho Buckaroo Beans (page 105) and Mining Camp Spare Ribs (page 148), as well as terrific wild game such as Papa's Favorite Trout (page 195) and the warm and hearty spoon-licking good Thunder Mountain Turkey Soup (page 65). The thing that stood out most characteristically was the use of the Dutch oven for outdoor cooking. Not only do these recipes tell you what to put inside, but they clearly tell you what to do outside the pot in order to heat and cook it properly. Dutch oven favorites like Mountain Man Breakfast (page 52) get you started on the trail, and Camas Creek Carrot Cake (page 208) can be waiting for you when you get back. These recipes and methods are definitely a boon for campers and lovers of the outdoors, and they can also be prepared indoors in your own oven.

Idaho's outdoor cooking goes hand-in-hand with the culinary magic that is performed in the kitchen. Consider the creativity of Spuds Romanoff (page 108) and Idaho Caviar (page 13), in addition to the palate joy of Tenderloin with Shiitake Sauce (page 132) and Sugar-Free Banana Split Cake (page 218). Basque influence and other ethnic cultures add their flavor, too, in typical dishes like Basque Baked Eggs (page 54) and Basque

Wedding Cookies (page 223). You have to love the diversity that leads to delicious eating!

In addition to the hundreds of remarkable recipes, this book catalogs an assortment of Idaho cookbooks. Below each of the 347 recipes is the name of its contributing cookbook. A special Catalog of Contributing Cookbooks Section (see page 261) shows each book's cover, along with a description and ordering information. This section is especially popular with cookbook collectors.

As an added bonus, *Best of the Best from Idaho Cookbook* showcases the beauty and charm of the Gem State with revealing photographs and intriguing state facts. Did you know one of the largest diamonds ever found in the United States, nearly 20 carats, was discovered near McCall? Or that nearly 85% of all the commercial trout sold in the United States is produced in the Hagerman Valley near Twin Falls?

Research and compilation takes a lot of effort, so to everyone who contributed to this cookbook, especially those of you who so generously provided recipes, we extend a big thank you. We sincerely appreciate the food editors and the bookstore and gift shop managers who guided us to the state's most popular cookbooks. Thanks also to the tourism department and many chambers of commerce for providing historic and informative data. To our BEST OF THE BEST artist, Tupper England, we thank you once again for bringing the state to life with your charming illustrations.

We hope you enjoy all the "ins and outs" of Idaho cooking with the *Best of the Best from Idaho Cookbook*. Put on your hiking boots . . . or your apron . . . it's a great trip!

Gwen McKee and Barbara Moseley

Contributing Cookbooks

Another Cookbook

Ashton Area Cookbook

Bacon is not a Vegetable

Basque Cooking and Lore

Be Our Guest

Bound to Please

Caldera Kitchens

Cee Dub's Dutch Oven and Other Camp Cookin'

Cee Dub's Ethnic & Regional Dutch Oven Cookin'

Centennial Cookbook

A Century of Recipes

The Complete Sourdough Cookbook

Cookin' at its Best

Cookin' in Paradise

Cooking for a Crowd

Cooking on the Wild Side

Cooking With Cops, Too

Don Holm's Book of Food Drying, Pickling and Smoke Curing

Down Home Country Cookin'

Elegant Cooking Made Simple

Generations "Coming Home"

Grandma Jane's Cookbook

The Hearty Gourmet

Hey Ma! Come Quick! The Hog's in the Garden Again!!

Huckleberry Haus Cookbook

Idaho Cook Book

The Idaho Table

Idaho's Favorite Bean Recipes

Contributing Cookbooks

Idaho's Wild 100!
Ketchum Cooks
Mackay Heritage Cookbook
Matt Braun's Western Cooking
The Miracle Cookbook
More Cee Dub's Dutch Oven and Other Camp Cookin'
98 Ways to Cook Venison
Northern Lites: Contemporary Cooking with a Twist
Old-Fashioned Dutch Oven Cookbook
Onions Make the Meal Cookbook
The Outdoor Dutch Oven Cookbook
The Pea and Lentil Cookbook
Potatoes Are Not the Only Vegetable!
Quilter's Delight, Busy Day Recipes
Recipes Logged from the Woods of North Idaho
Recipes Stolen from the River of No Return
Recipes Tried and True
The Rocky Mountain Wild Foods Cookbook
Sausage & Jerky Handbook
Sharing Our Best
Sowbelly and Sourdough
Spragg Family Cookbook
A Taste of Heaven
Tastes from the Country
Wapiti Meadow Bakes

(Classic Onion Bloom continued)

together). Cut out 2-inch core from center of onion. This allows petals to separate. Place Dipping Sauce in a small dish and place in center of onion. Serve immediately. One 4-inch onion serves 4.

DIPPING SAUCE:

2 cups mayonnaise	**¹/₂ cup bottled chili sauce**
2 cups sour cream	**¹/₂ teaspoon cayenne pepper**

Combine well; cover and refrigerate until ready to serve.

Onions Make the Meal Cookbook

Onion Sausage Sticks

1¹/₂ cups finely chopped onions (Idaho-Eastern Oregon)	**1 cup buttermilk baking mix**
¹/₂ pound bulk pork sausage, fried and drained	**¹/₂ teaspoon salt**
	4 eggs, beaten
¹/₃ cup sausage drippings or vegetable oil	**1 cup shredded Cheddar cheese**
	2 tablespoons minced parsley

Combine onions with remaining ingredients. Spread into greased 9x13-inch baking pan. Bake at 350° for 20–25 minutes or until golden. Let stand 5 minutes before cutting into sticks. Makes about 4 dozen appetizers.

Onions Make the Meal Cookbook

Stuffed Mushrooms

This tasty mixture works well as a stuffing for wild goose and duck encroûte.

2 pounds Italian sausage
1¼ pounds breakfast sausage
2 tablespoons chopped garlic
¾ cup chopped red onion
2 tablespoons fennel seed
¼ cup chopped fresh basil
1½ tablespoons chopped fresh tarragon
½ tablespoon chopped fresh rosemary
1 tablespoon crushed red pepper flakes
¼ cup chopped red bell pepper
¼ cup chopped yellow bell pepper
1 tablespoon chopped thyme
1 tablespoon chopped Greek oregano
¼ cup chopped fresh parsley
¾ cup finely chopped seasoned bread crumbs
1½ cups Monterey Jack cheese
¾ cup grated Parmesan cheese
Large mushroom caps, as needed
Melted butter

Crumble and mix the two kinds of sausages well; cook in large pan and drain off the fat. While the meat is still hot, add the chopped garlic, red onion, and fennel seed; mix. Add remaining ingredients, except cheeses and mushrooms. After the mixture has cooled a bit, add the Monterey Jack and Parmesan cheeses; mix well and chill.

Take the stems out of the mushrooms and save for something else. Dip the mushrooms into melted butter and drain. Stuff the mushrooms with the chilled stuffing mixture. Bake at 400° for 12 minutes. These can be done a day or two ahead, just store covered in the refrigerator. This mixture works well as a stuffing for wild goose and duck encroûte. Yields 10½ cups stuffing.

Cooking on the Wild Side

Potato Logs

5 medium potatoes
1/4 cup butter

Salt and pepper to taste
3/4 cup grated Cheddar cheese

Wash potatoes thoroughly; microwave or boil until fork pierces easily. Peel and mash, adding butter, seasoning, and cheese. Set aside to cool.

FILLING:
12 Little Sizzlers Pork Sausages

Preheat oven to 400°. Cook sausages thoroughly. Drain on cookie sheet lined with paper towels. While sausages are cooling, on a floured surface, pat potato mixture out to 1/4 inch thick. Divide into 12 equal parts. Place 1 sausage in the center of each piece. Using a spatula or scraper, lift from work surface and mold potato mixture around sausage. Place wrapped sausage in a greased baking dish, being sure to make only 1 layer; do not stack. Bake approximately 20 minutes or until golden brown.

Elegant Cooking Made Simple

Tater Wedges

2 sticks butter
4 large Idaho russet potatoes, cut
    lengthwise into wedges
1/2 cup grated Parmesan cheese

2 teaspoons garlic powder
1 teaspoon seasoned salt
Parsley flakes

Melt butter in 12-inch Dutch oven and add potato wedges. Stir to coat well and arrange in a circular pattern. Mix the grated cheese and spices, and sprinkle over the tater wedges. Sprinkle with parsley flakes. Bake about 40 minutes or until the taters are done with 5 or 6 briquets underneath and 16–18 on the lid. Serve as either an appetizer or as a side dish.

Cee Dub's Ethnic & Regional Dutch Oven Cookin'

Chicken and Spinach Wraps

1½ quarts cooking oil
2 pounds frozen spinach, thawed
  and drained
2 pounds roasted chicken breast
20 egg roll wraps

10 slices of bacon, cut in half and
  fried
10 ounces shredded Cheddar
  cheese
2 ounces vegetable oil

Pour cooking oil into deep fryer; heat to 400°. Meanwhile, steam spinach until tender; set aside to cool. Remove all skin, fat and bones from chicken. Cut into 20 equal pieces.

Lay 1 egg roll wrap at a time on work surface (to prevent drying, keep all other wraps covered). Dip fingers in a cup of water and moisten ½ inch around edges of each wrap.

Place 1 piece of chicken at an angle in center of wrap, then layer 1½ ounces spinach, 1 piece of bacon, ½ ounce cheese. Beginning with corner closest to you, fold corner of wrap over ingredients. Fold right and left corners in, and roll to seal last corner. Place in a long greased baking dish and brush with vegetable oil (this prevents drying). Repeat until all wraps are filled.

Place 3 rolls in fryer basket and lower into hot oil. Cook approximately 1 minute or until golden brown. Place cooked chicken rolls in a warm oven to maintain temperature. Makes 20 appetizers.

Elegant Cooking Made Simple

Smoked Salmon Cheesecake

Different and always a hit! I serve as an appetizer, but could be a luncheon or brunch entrée. Very rich!

WALNUT CRUST:

2 cups bread crumbs
1/2 cup chopped walnuts
1/2 cup butter, softened

1/4 cup shredded Gruyère cheese
1 teaspoon dill

Preheat oven to 350°. Combine bread crumbs, walnuts, butter, cheese, and dill in a bowl. Mix well and press firmly into bottom and sides of a buttered 9-inch springform pan, and chill.

1 medium onion, minced
3 tablespoons butter
1 3/4 pounds cream cheese,
  softened
1/3 cup half-and-half

1/2 cup shredded Gruyère cheese
1/4 teaspoon pepper
4 eggs
1/2 pound smoked salmon, finely
  chopped

Sauté onion in butter until tender. Combine cream cheese and half-and-half, and whip until smooth. Add onion, Gruyère cheese, and pepper. Mix well. Add eggs, one at a time, beating slowly until incorporated in mixture. Stir in salmon and mix well.

Pour into Crust and bake for 1–1 1/2 hours. Unmold and serve with small rye or pumpernickel bread or crackers. Serves 16.

Ketchum Cooks

Flowing 425 miles, the Salmon River is the longest free-flowing river within one state in the lower 48 states.

Cocktail Quiches

PASTRY:

1 (3-ounce) package cream
   cheese, softened

$^1/_3$ cup butter, softened
1 cup flour

In a medium bowl, cream together cream cheese and butter. Mix in flour and chill overnight.

   Form dough into 24 small balls and press into mini-muffin tins.

FILLING:

1 cup milk
1 egg, slightly beaten
$^1/_4$ teaspoon salt
$^1/_4$ teaspoon pepper

$^1/_2$–1 tablespoon chopped chives
1 cup grated sharp Cheddar
   cheese

In a medium bowl, mix together milk, egg, salt, pepper, and chives. Evenly distribute cheese over Pastry in muffin tins. Pour milk and egg mixture gently over grated cheese. Bake at 350° for 30 minutes. Serve warm. Makes 24 servings.

Bound to Please

Dill and Cream Cheese Pastry

1 (4-ounce) can refrigerated
   crescent dinner rolls
1$^1/_2$ teaspoons minced fresh dill
   weed, or $^1/_2$ teaspoon dried
   whole dill weed

1 (8-ounce) package cream cheese,
   softened
1 egg yolk, beaten
Fresh dill weed sprig for garnish
   (optional)

Unroll dough on a lightly floured surface; press seams together to form a 4x12-inch rectangle. Mix the dill weed and cream cheese together and place the cream cheese mixture in the center of the dough. Bring up sides of dough snugly around cheese, pinching to seal. Place seam-side-down, on a lightly greased baking sheet. Brush with egg yolk. Bake at 350° for 20 minutes. Garnish, if desired. Serve warm with crackers. Yields 16 appetizer servings.

Be Our Guest

Spicy Hummus

This hummus variation contains sweet bell peppers and a touch of cayenne.

1 (15-ounce) can chickpeas, drained and rinsed (about 2 cups boiled)
6 tablespoons tahini
6 tablespoons fresh lemon juice
3 tablespoons plain yogurt
2 tablespoons olive oil
4 cloves garlic, crushed (about 2 teaspoons)

1 teaspoon ground cumin
$\frac{1}{4}$ teaspoon cayenne pepper
$\frac{1}{4}$ cup minced jalapeño pepper
$\frac{1}{4}$ cup red bell pepper, seeded and diced
Salt and freshly ground black pepper to taste

In a food processor or blender, purée chickpeas, tahini, lemon juice, yogurt, and oil until smooth, adding water a little at a time as needed to make a creamy mixture. Transfer the purée to a medium bowl. Add garlic, cumin, cayenne, jalapeño, and bell pepper, and mix well. Season with salt and pepper. Cover and chill 2–4 hours to allow the flavors to blend. Garnish with cayenne pepper just before serving. Makes about 4 cups, approximately 16 servings.

The Pea & Lentil Cookbook

Hojun's Tex Mex Dip

1 (16-ounce) can refried beans
1 cup salsa
2 large avocados, peeled and
chopped
1 tablespoon lemon juice
Garlic powder to taste
2 cups sour cream
2 bunches green onions, chopped
1 (15-ounce) can sliced pitted ripe
olives
3 medium to large tomatoes,
chopped
1 (16-ounce) package shredded
Cheddar/Monterey Jack cheese

Mix refried beans and salsa, and spread on jellyroll pan or similar size
pan. Beat avocados, lemon juice, and garlic powder into a sauce.
Spread over the refried beans. (This avocado sauce is optional—just
as good without it). Stir sour cream well and spread over bean or avocado dip. Spread chopped green onions, sliced olives, and chopped
tomatoes evenly over sour cream. Sprinkle cheese over top. Keep in
refrigerator until about an hour before use. Take out to warm up a little for easier dipping. Serve with corn or nacho chips.

Sharing Our Best

Homemade Salsa

This makes a big batch.

1 (106-ounce) can (13 cups)
tomatoes, drained
1 (106-ounce) can (13 cups)
chili sauce
$\frac{1}{2}$ cup lemon juice
$\frac{1}{2}$ cup vinegar
2 teaspoons Tabasco sauce
2 tablespoons salt
2 teaspoons pepper
4 tablespoons Worcestershire
sauce
3 medium onions, chopped
6 green peppers, chopped

Combine all ingredients. Refrigerate in jars. This makes a big batch.

Down Home Country Cookin'

Bread & Breakfast

South of Buhl in the Salmon Falls Creek Canyon stands the world-famous Balanced Rock. Over 48 feet tall and weighing 40 tons, the wind-carved rock balances precariously on a pedestal only 3 feet by 17 inches.

PHOTO © WILLIAM H. MULLINS OUTDOOR PHOTOGRAPHY

Sourdough Starter

Although a starter is simply flour and water, there are a number of ways folks make it—in fact, most sourdough cooks develop their own individual idiosyncrasies about it. Here are a few suggestions:

2 cups flour   **Lukewarm water**
1 package dry yeast

Mix flour with dry yeast and enough lukewarm water to make a thick batter. Stir it only enough to break up the lumps, then let stand in a warm place for at least 24 hours or until the house is filled with a delectable yeasty odor. Starter may be kept in refrigerator between uses.

OR TRY THIS VERSION:

Boil some potatoes for supper, and save the potato water; when lukewarm, mix with flour to make a thick batter without the yeast. This is a good way to make it in camp, where you have no yeast available and want fast results. This is also the way most farm gals made it in the olden days. Let stand a day or so, or until it smells right.

Whichever starter you use, remember that it takes several hours for the yeast to start growing under ideal conditions (75° to about 90°). If the house is cold, try using a mildly warm oven for a few minutes at a time, but be careful it doesn't get too hot and kill the yeast.

If you keep the starter in the refrigerator between uses, take it out several hours in advance, until it is again at room temperature and active. Then, always remember to replenish the starter you remove for cooking purposes. Do this by adding enough flour and lukewarm water to restore the mixture to its original amount and consistency. Let this work for at least a day before storing it in the refrigerator.

The Complete Sourdough Cookbook

In 1953, the engineering prototype of the first nuclear submarine, the Nautilus, was built and tested in the Idaho desert on the Snake River Plain near Arco.

Aunt Cora's Biscuits

See Sourdough Starter recipe on opposite page.

1½ cups sifted flour	3 teaspoons baking powder
1½ cups sourdough starter	1 teaspoon salt
¼ cup shortening, melted	1½ teaspoons baking soda (more,
2 tablespoons sugar	if starter is very sour)

Place flour in bowl; make a well and add starter, then add melted short-ening and remaining dry ingredients. Mix slightly, then turn out onto a lightly floured board and knead until consistency of bread dough, or of a satiny finish. Pat or roll out dough to ½-inch thickness, cut, and put on a greased pan; turn biscuits to coat all sides. Let rise in warm place (over boiling water, if necessary) for ½ hour. Bake at 425° for 15–20 minutes.

The Complete Sourdough Cookbook

Cee Dub's Basic Biscuits
plus Variations

2 cups all-purpose flour	⅓ cup vegetable oil
1 tablespoon baking powder	⅔ cup milk or buttermilk
⅛ teaspoon salt (optional)	

Preheat oven to 425°. Mix dry ingredients. Add liquid ingredients. Stir in bowl. Work with hands in bowl just long enough to form a ball. Pat out on floured board ¾ inch thick. (Do not knead.) Cut into desired size, and bake approximately 20 minutes until brown.

• For herb biscuits, add ⅛ teaspoon celery seed, ⅛ teaspoon sage, and ⅛ teaspoon thyme to above ingredients.
• For plain dumplings, increase milk to 1 cup.
• For chicken dumplings, add ½ teaspoon poultry seasoning to flour.
• For beef or venison dumplings, add 1 heaping tablespoon prepared horseradish to liquids.

Cee Dub's Dutch Oven and Other Camp Cookin'

Buttermilk Biscuits

2 cups flour
3/4 teaspoon salt
3 teaspoons baking powder
1/2 teaspoon baking soda

3 tablespoons soft butter or
  shortening
1 cup buttermilk
Melted butter

Preheat oven to 450°. Sift flour once before measuring. Then sift together into a large bowl the flour, salt, baking powder, and baking soda. Add butter or shortening and beat about 2 minutes or until mixture is the consistency of coarse meal. Add buttermilk and beat about 1 minute, just enough to mix thoroughly. Be certain to scrape sides of bowl while beating.

Turn out onto a lightly floured board and knead gently by folding over 2 or 3 times, until texture is even. Roll out to 1/2-inch thickness. Dip cutter in flour and cut biscuits. Place on ungreased baking pan and brush with melted butter. Bake 12–15 minutes until golden brown. Makes 12 or more biscuits, depending on cutter size.

Matt Braun's Western Cooking

Grandma's 60 Minute Rolls

2 packages dry yeast
1/4 cup warm water
1 1/4 cups milk
2 eggs
1 teaspoon salt

3 tablespoons sugar
2 heaping tablespoons butter or
  margarine, softened
4 cups flour
1/4 cup butter, melted

Dissolve yeast in warm water. Scald milk and let cool to lukewarm. Beat eggs, then add salt, sugar, and butter to eggs. Add yeast and egg mixture to milk. Add flour until a nice soft dough forms. Let rise for 20 minutes, covered. Turn out on floured board, roll and spread with melted butter, and cut for Parker House rolls. Put in buttered pan and let rise until double. Bake in 400° oven for 15–20 minutes.

Mackay Heritage Cookbook

Grandma Jane's Dinner Rolls

$1/3$ cup warm milk	2 eggs, room temperature
$1^1/2$ cups warm water	1 cup margarine, melted divided
$3/4$ cup sugar	1 teaspoon salt
$1/4$ cup yeast	5 cups white flour

Put warm milk, warm water, sugar, and yeast in mixing bowl, set aside. Yeast should start working. Add eggs, slightly beaten, and $3/4$ cup melted margarine; set aside the remainder of the margarine. Mix together. Combine salt and flour. Add to liquid. Mix till stiff. Brush top lightly with melted margarine, leaving some margarine for later. Place in warm plate and let rise till double in size. When doubled, take out of bowl and knead on floured surface till bubbles are gone.

Break apart dough into sections about 2 inches in diameter; work each into round balls and place in greased pans about 2 inches apart. Again brush tops with margarine and let rise till at least double in size. (The more they rise, the fluffier they are, however, too high and they'll fall.) When risen, place in oven at 375° for about 15 minutes or until tops are good and brown. Remove from oven; brush tops with remaining margarine. Best served hot out of the oven, but can be reheated. May freeze after cooling and reheat later. Makes about 2 dozen.

Grandma Jane's Cookbook

China Bar Rolls

1 tablespoon yeast (not quick rising)
1/2 cup plus 1 teaspoon sugar, divided
1/4 cup warm water
1 cup milk

3/4 cup margarine, divided
3 eggs
1 cup cold water
1 teaspoon salt
6 cups flour

The night before, mix yeast, 1 teaspoon sugar, and warm water. Let mixture stand until it is foamy. In a saucepan, scald milk, 1/2 cup margarine, and 1/2 cup sugar. In a separate bowl, mix well-beaten eggs, cold water, and salt. In a large bowl, stir together egg and milk mixtures first. Stir in foamy yeast mixture next. Add and stir exactly 6 level cups of flour. Dough will appear sticky, but this is how it should be. Cover dough and let stand at room temperature for 1 hour. Pat down by poking with finger. Keep covered in a refrigerator or a cool place. Let it sit for at least 3 hours, or best overnight.

Next morning, roll out dough, using a generous amount of flour, to approximately 1/2 inch thick. Cut out rolls into a 3- to 31/2-inch circle (a used 16-ounce vegetable can works great). Dip cut-out rolls in 1/4 cup melted margarine and place close together in cake pan; fold over, pressing a "belly button" on the open side with your finger to hold the rolls together.

Let rise in pan for 11/2 hours. Bake in 425° oven for 15 minutes. Serves 8–10.

Note: This is a great dough for cinnamon rolls as well (sprinkle cinnamon sugar on dough; roll and cut into rolls).

Recipes Stolen from the River of No Return

Flavored Hamburger and Hot Dog Buns

1 package fast-rising yeast
2 tablespoons sugar
1½ teaspoons salt
1 teaspoon garlic powder
4½ cups flour, divided

1 cup milk
½ cup water
¼ cup butter
1 large egg, lightly beaten

In a large mixing bowl, combine yeast, sugar, salt, and garlic powder with 1¾ cups flour. Heat milk, water, and butter to 120°–130°. Stir liquid and egg into flour mixture to form a batter consistency. Incorporate the remaining flour gradually, using only enough to form a firm dough.

Knead 15–20 times or until dough becomes smooth and elastic, adding more flour, if necessary. Cover and let rise until almost double in bulk (30–40 minutes). Divide into 12 equal parts, work into balls, flatten slightly and arrange on 2 greased cookie sheets—6 buns on each. Cover dough to rise again.

Carefully place the 6 raised dough buns from first cookie sheet on top of raised dough buns on second cookie sheet (if you want smaller buns, eliminate this step). Cover and allow to rise for 20 minutes. Bake in preheated 400° oven for 12–14 minutes. Buns should be golden brown.

For hot dog buns, roll dough into desired logs; bake as above.

Elegant Cooking Made Simple

Sage and Olive Focaccia Bread

Focaccia, a mouth-watering Italian delight, is simpler to make than pizza, because it is usually topped with just a coating of olive oil and a sprinkling of spices and/or herbs. Serve as a snack or a bread.

2–4 tablespoons olive oil, divided	1 cup rye flour
2 packages active dry yeast	1 tablespoon sage
1½ cups lukewarm water	2 teaspoons rosemary
3½–4 cups unbleached all-purpose flour	¼ cup chopped kalamata olives

Grease a 12-inch Dutch oven or baking sheet with olive oil. Oil a bowl for rising, and set aside.

In a large bowl, dissolve yeast in water. Add 3 cups all-purpose flour, rye flour, sage, rosemary, and olives, and knead about 5 minutes, gradually working in the rest of the flour. Put dough in oiled bowl, cover with a damp towel or plastic wrap, and let double in size.

Press dough into bottom of Dutch oven or in ½-inch-thick rectangle on baking sheet; cover and let rise until doubled in size.

Brush top of dough with remaining 2 tablespoons olive oil. Put about 10 coals beneath the Dutch oven and a double layer covering the top.

Bake in Dutch oven for 10 minutes, or in 375° conventional oven for 15 minutes, or until brown on top and pulled away from the edges of the pan. Yields 1 loaf.

The Outdoor Dutch Oven Cookbook

Idaho's nickname is "The Gem State." Gems from all around Idaho give credence to its nickname —jasper from Bruneau, opal from Spencer, and jade, topaz, zircon, and tourmaline from around the state. The same geological processes that gave Idaho its mountains also gave it Star Garnets, the state gem. This stone is considered more precious than either Star Rubies or Star Sapphires. The color is usually dark purple or plum and the star seems to glide or float across the dark surface.

Italian Onion Bread

1 package yeast	1 tablespoon cornmeal
½ teaspoon salt	1 medium onion
2 cups white flour	2 tablespoons Parmesan cheese
3+ tablespoons olive oil, divided	1 teaspoon rosemary
1 cup water	¼ teaspoon black pepper
1 cup whole-wheat flour	¼ cup sun-dried tomatoes

Combine yeast, salt, and white flour. Heat 2 tablespoons olive oil and water (125°–130°). Mix into white flour mixture. Stir in whole-wheat flour. Knead dough for 8 minutes. Cover and let rise for 5 minutes. Grease a 9x13-inch pan and sprinkle with cornmeal. Pat the dough out to fit pan, then cover. Let rise for 30 minutes.

Slice onion and cook in a little olive oil until translucent. Make a deep depression in the entire dough and sprinkle with remaining 1 tablespoon olive oil. Bake for 15 minutes in a 400° oven. Remove from oven and top with onion, Parmesan, rosemary, and pepper. Bake for 20–25 minutes, then put on the tomatoes. (You may also put on grated cheese of your choice before the last baking.)

Quilter's Delight, Busy Day Recipes

Bread in an Onion Ring

2 large onions	2 teaspoons sugar
(Idaho-Eastern Oregon)	1½ teaspoons baking powder
¼ cup yellow cornmeal	½ cup milk
½ cup all-purpose flour	1 egg
½ teaspoon salt	¼ cup bacon drippings or
¼ teaspoon cayenne pepper	vegetable oil

Peel onions and cut crosswise into ½-inch slices. Remove centers of slices to leave ½-inch-thick rings. Prepare batter by mixing rest of ingredients in order given. Place onion rings on griddle that has been coated liberally with oil and heated to 350° (medium heat). Fill each onion ring with batter and cook on one side. Turn and cook on other side. Serve hot. Very good with fish and coleslaw.

Onions Make the Meal Cookbook

Sheepherder Bread II

The original Basque sheepherder bread was always made in a Dutch oven . . . on coals, covered with lid, and more coals piled on top. It was then covered with dirt, if one were going to be out in the hills all day.

This one has been adapted for kitchen use, but it has a tangy and delicious open-range taste, just as delectable as those baked out on the high and wild plateaus of the Rockies.

4 cups flour	**¹/₄ teaspoon baking soda**
2 tablespoons sugar	**1¹/₂ cups sourdough starter***
1 teaspoon salt	**2 tablespoons melted shortening**

Into a large bowl, sift the dry ingredients. Dig a well in the center of the sourdough starter. Add melted shortening. Blend the dry mix into the starter from the edges with enough flour to knead until smooth and shiny. Place in greased pan and let rise. Then shape into 2 loaves and place in 2 greased bread pans. Bake at 375° until done, about 45–55 minutes.

*See recipe for Sourdough Starter on page 28.

The Complete Sourdough Cookbook

Lily's Beer Bread

Beer bread used to be made out of necessity rather than as a novelty the way it is today. The beer acted as a yeast and allowed the bread to rise.

4 cups flour	**Pinch salt**
3 teaspoons baking powder	**2 tablespoons butter, softened**
3 tablespoons sugar	**12 ounces beer**
¹/₂ teaspoon baking soda	

Sift dry ingredients together. Add butter and cut in well. Add beer, but make sure it is not cold, even a little warm will help. (The cold will drastically slow down the "rise.") If you need more moisture to make a good dough, add a little warm water.

In a greased bowl, set in a warm place to rise for several hours, covered with a towel. Put in a well-greased bread pan and bake at 350° for approximately an hour.

Note: You can brush the top with butter or egg during the last 15 minutes of baking, and it will make a nice crisp crust.

Sowbelly and Sourdough

Bread on a Stick

Roasting sticks
1 cup Bisquick
½ cup water, divided

Butter or margarine
Honey or jam

With the end of the stick, make a little well in the Bisquick mix. Pour 1 tablespoon water into the well. Place the stick in the well and stir until a small ball of dough (around an inch or so in diameter) forms around the stick. Lift the stick out of the Bisquick and press the dough firmly around the end of the stick. Repeat process until all of the Bisquick is used. Grill the dough on the stick over a bed of hot coals, turning often. When it is golden brown and cooked throughout, spread with butter and slather with honey or jam.

Centennial Cookbook

North Idaho Spoon Bread

3 cups milk, scalded
1 cup white cornmeal
1 teaspoon butter or margarine
1 teaspoon sugar

1 teaspoon salt
3 egg yolks, beaten
3 egg whites, stiffly beaten

Add scalded milk gradually to cornmeal, and cook 5 minutes, stirring constantly. Add butter or margarine, sugar, and salt. Add beaten egg yolks; beat well, then fold in beaten egg whites. Turn into greased baking dish, and bake at 350° for 45–50 minutes. Serve hot from baking dish with plenty of butter. Makes 4–5 servings.

Recipes Logged from the Woods of North Idaho

Located in the north-central part of Idaho, No Return Wilderness Area, with its 2.4 million acres, is the largest wilderness area in the lower 48 states.

Jalapeño Corn Bread

$^1/_2$ cup flour
$1^1/_2$ cups cornmeal
2 teaspoons sugar
1 teaspoon baking soda
1 teaspoon baking powder
$1^1/_2$ cups buttermilk
1 teaspoon salt

1 (7-ounce) can jalapeño peppers
$1^1/_2$ cups minced onions
2 eggs, beaten
1 cup grated sharp Cheddar
  cheese
3 tablespoons bacon drippings

Combine all dry ingredients, except salt, in bowl and set aside. In saucepan, heat milk and salt until hot. Add peppers and onions; cover and cook 30 minutes over low heat. Cool. Mix eggs and cheese. Blend all ingredients together until batter is smooth. Put in well-greased baking pan and bake at 425° for 40–50 minutes.

Wapiti Meadow Bakes

Skillet Corn Bread

3 eggs
$^1/_2$ cup sugar
$1^1/_2$ cups flour, sifted
1 cup cornmeal
$2^1/_2$ teaspoons baking powder

$^1/_2$ teaspoon baking soda
1 teaspoon salt
$1^1/_2$ cups buttermilk
$^1/_3$ cup butter, melted
1 teaspoon butter

Beat eggs with sugar until blended. Sift together flour, cornmeal, baking powder, baking soda, and salt. Add dry ingredients alternately with buttermilk to the egg/sugar mixture. Stir thoroughly after each addition. Stir in melted butter. Melt the 1 teaspoon butter in a 9-inch cast-iron skillet. Pour batter into warm skillet. Bake at 400° for 30 minutes or until top begins to brown. Serve warm in wedges from the skillet.

Ashton Area Cookbook

Onion Shortcake

1¹/₂ cups sliced sweet Spanish
  onions
¹/₄ cup butter or margarine,
  divided
2 packages Jiffy corn muffin mix
2 eggs, beaten

¹/₃ cup milk
1 cup cream-style corn
1 cup sour cream
¹/₄ cup chopped dill
1 cup grated sharp Cheddar
  cheese

Peel, slice, and sauté onions in 2 tablespoons butter until translucent. Combine muffin mix, eggs, milk, and corn. Place in greased 9x13-inch pan or casserole. Evenly distribute the sour cream, dill, Cheddar cheese, and sautéed onions over the top of the batter. Cut remaining butter into the ingredients with 2 butter knives. Do not mix. Bake at 425° for 25–30 minutes. Yields 12 portions.

Cooking on the Wild Side

Oven Apple Butter

5 quarts unsweetened applesauce
10 cups sugar
1 cup vinegar

2 teaspoons cinnamon
1 teaspoon ground cloves

Mix all ingredients together. Put in a large roasting pan. Bake at 350° for 3 hours or until thick. Stir every 20 minutes. Pour into jars and seal. Makes approximately 10–12 pints.

Cookin' in Paradise

Chocolate Chip Banana Nut Bread

4 cups all-purpose flour
2 cups sugar
4 teaspoons baking powder
1 teaspoon salt
4 eggs, lightly beaten
2 cups mashed ripe bananas

²⁄₃ cup vegetable oil
¹⁄₂ cup milk
1 (12-ounce) package chocolate
  chips
1 cup chopped nuts

Mix flour with sugar, baking powder, and salt in a large bowl. Stir eggs, bananas, oil, and milk until well blended. Add to the flour mixture; stir just until moistened. Stir in chocolate chips and nuts. Pour into a well-greased, 12-inch Dutch oven. Bake at 350° for 50 minutes or until a wooden toothpick inserted in the center comes out clean. Cool 5 minutes and remove from pan; finish cooling on a rack. Serve warm or wrap and store overnight.

Bacon is not a Vegetable

Plum Bread

2 (2-pound) cans purple plums,
  drained, or equivalent chopped
  fresh plums (2 cups)
1 stick butter or margarine
2 teaspoons baking soda
2 cups flour

1 cup sugar
¹⁄₂ teaspoon salt
¹⁄₂ teaspoon cinnamon
¹⁄₄ teaspoon ground cloves
1 cup raisins
³⁄₄ cup chopped walnuts

Combine chopped plums and butter in saucepan and heat slowly until butter is melted. Transfer into large mixing bowl; stir in baking soda. Allow mixture to cool. Add all remaining ingredients to plums and mix well. Pour into 2 greased and floured bread pans. Bake at 350° for 40–50 minutes.

Cookin' in Paradise

Huckleberry Muffins

2 cups flour
2 tablespoons sugar
1/2 teaspoon salt
2 teaspoons baking powder
1 scant teaspoon baking soda

1 cup drained but damp, fresh or
    canned huckleberries
1 egg, slightly beaten
2 tablespoons melted butter
3/4 cup buttermilk

Sift dry ingredients together in round-bottomed bowl. Stirring from edge to center, add huckleberries to the dry ingredients. Stir gently until they are all separated and coated with flour. Add beaten egg, butter, and buttermilk to mixture. Stir just enough to dampen all ingredients. The mixture will be thick, more like sticky dough. Fill greased muffin tins half full. Bake at 400° for about 18 minutes. Makes about 1 1/2 dozen.

Caldera Kitchens

Dakota Prairie Muffins

Most of the old sourdoughs in the mining camps, and the chuckwagon pot-bangers on the cattle range, wouldn't have been caught dead making muffins. "A mite too sissified for the like o' them," they'd mutter.

This is one sourdough trick that the ladies came up with, long after the frontier had been tamed—but by then the old-timers didn't know what they were missing anyhow.

1 1/2 cups flour
1 1/2 teaspoons baking powder
1/2 teaspoon baking soda
1/2 teaspoon salt
1 cup whole bran
1 cup buttermilk

1/4 cup shortening
1/3 cup sugar
1 egg
1/2 cup sourdough starter*
1/2 cup raisins (optional)

Sift together the flour, baking powder, baking soda, and salt. To soften the bran, soak in buttermilk. Cream shortening and sugar and beat in the egg. Stir in bran mixture and starter, then fold in dry ingredients until just moist. Add raisins, if desired. Drop into greased muffin pans. Bake at 375° for 35 minutes. Makes 8 muffins.

*See recipe for Sourdough Starter on page 28.

The Complete Sourdough Cookbook

Morning Glory Muffins

2 cups flour
1¼ cups sugar
2 teaspoons baking soda
2 teaspoons cinnamon
1–2 teaspoons salt
2 cups grated carrots
½ cup raisins
½ cup shredded coconut
½ cup chopped pecans or almonds
3 eggs
1 cup vegetable oil
1 apple, peeled, cored and
  shredded
2 teaspoons vanilla extract

In large mixing bowl, combine flour, sugar, baking soda, cinnamon, and salt. Stir in carrots, raisins, coconut, and nuts. In separate bowl, combine eggs, oil, apple, and vanilla. Add to flour mixture. Stir only until combined. Spoon into greased or lined muffin tins. Bake at 350° for 15–18 minutes. Yields about 18 muffins.

A Taste of Heaven

Mocha Vanilla Huckleberry Muffins

1 tablespoon instant coffee
  granules
¼ cup warm milk
1¾ cups flour
2 teaspoons baking powder
½ teaspoon baking soda
½ cup packed brown sugar
½ cup ground walnuts
2 teaspoons pure vanilla extract
1 egg, lightly beaten
1 cup sour cream
½ stick (¼ cup) margarine,
  melted
1¼ cups huckleberries

In a small bowl, dissolve instant coffee in milk. Mix flour, baking powder, baking soda, brown sugar, and walnuts. Add remaining ingredients, except huckleberries, stirring until just moistened. Gently fold in berries. Spoon batter into paper cup-lined muffin pans. Bake at 400° about 20 minutes. Makes a dozen.

Huckleberry Haus Cookbook

Oatmeal Bannocks

Contrary to pulp fiction writers, bannock is not a frontier word, but an old Gaelic word for tea biscuits or big round cakes that have been cut into pie-shaped wedges for serving. Oatmeal bannock is made from yeast dough and enriched with uncooked oatmeal and currants.

2½ cups unsifted flour, divided
⅓ cup sugar
¾ teaspoon salt
1 cup uncooked old-fashioned
  rolled oats
2 packages active dry yeast

½ cup milk
½ cup water
¼ cup (½ stick) margarine
1 egg
1 cup currants (or raisins)

Thoroughly mix about ⅓ of the flour with the sugar, salt, rolled oats, and undissolved yeast in a large bowl. Combine milk, water, and margarine in a saucepan. Heat over low fire until warm. Gradually add liquid to dry ingredients and beat 2 minutes. Add egg and ½ cup flour, or just enough to make a thick batter. Beat vigorously for a couple of minutes. Stir in enough additional flour to make a soft dough.

Turn out onto floured board, and knead until smooth and elastic. Place in greased bowl, turning over to grease all sides. Cover and let rise in a warm place until doubled. Then punch dough down, turn out onto floured board, and knead in currants.

Divide in half, and roll each into an 8-inch circle. Place them in greased 8-inch round cake pans. Cut each into wedges with a sharp knife, but not all the way through to the pan. Cover and let rise until doubled again. Then bake in 375° oven for 20 minutes or until done. Remove and cool. Freeze for later use whatever is not immediately needed.

The Complete Sourdough Cookbook

Five of the pioneer trails traveled somewhere between 1843 to 1869, including the Oregon Trail and the California Trail, cross southern Idaho. Wagon ruts are still visible all along the rugged terrain.

Potato Scones

2 cups flour
1 tablespoon baking powder
1 teaspoon salt
3 tablespoons cold butter

1 cup mashed potatoes (prepared
  with milk and butter)
5 tablespoons plus 1 teaspoon milk
1 egg

In a bowl, combine flour, baking powder, and salt. Cut in butter until mixture looks like coarse crumbs. Combine potatoes, milk, and egg; stir into crumb mixture until a soft dough forms. Turn onto a floured surface; knead gently 10–12 times or until no longer sticky. Gently pat or roll dough into a 9-inch circle about ¾ inch thick. Cut into 10–12 wedges; separate wedges and place on an ungreased baking sheet. Bake at 400° for 15–18 minutes or until golden brown. Good with butter, honey, and jam, or as base for creamed dishes. Makes 10–12 servings.

Mackay Heritage Cookbook

Victory Baked Apple Rolls

APPLE LAYER:
3 apples, peeled and thinly
  sliced

¼ cup sugar

Combine apples and sugar; set aside.

DOUGH:
1 cup flour
3 teaspoons baking powder
1 teaspoon salt

3 tablespoons shortening
½ cup milk
1 tablespoon butter

Mix first 3 ingredients, cut in shortening; mix in milk. Roll out on floured board. Spread with Apple Layer, dot with butter, and roll jellyroll-style; cut into rolls.

SAUCE:
¾ cup sugar
½ cup brown sugar
½ teaspoon nutmeg

⅛ teaspoon salt
1 teaspoon cinnamon
2 cups water

Bring ingredients to boil and pour into 9x13-inch pan. Place cut rolls in hot Sauce. Bake at 400° for 30 minutes.

Quilter's Delight, Busy Day Recipes

Frosted Orange Rolls

CREAMY ORANGE FILLING:

3 tablespoons soft butter

1 tablespoon grated orange rind

2 tablespoons orange juice

$1^1/_2$ cups sifted, powdered sugar

Combine all ingredients and beat until creamy and smooth. Set aside.

60-MINUTE SWEET DOUGH:

$^1/_2$ cup milk

1 teaspoon salt

1 tablespoon sugar

1 cake yeast or dry yeast

1 egg

2 tablespoons soft shortening

$2–2^1/_2$ cups sifted flour

Heat milk to lukewarm; remove from heat and add salt and sugar. Crumble yeast into mixture; stir until dissolved. Stir in egg and shortening. Add flour. Mix just enough to handle easily and knead until smooth. Roll dough into 12x17-inch rectangle. Spread surface with $^1/_2$ of Creamy Orange Filling.

Roll up dough as for cinnamon rolls; cut into 12 slices. Grease round 9-inch pan. Let rise until double in size. Bake at 375° or 400° (depending on oven) for 10–15 minutes. Watch closely. Remove from pan. Spread remaining Creamy Orange Filling over top.

Can double or quadruple the recipe. If small tea rolls are preferred, use half the amount of dough, and cut the same amount of slices (12). Double the recipe will fill a jellyroll-size pan.

Be Our Guest

Coffee Cake

This isn't the kind that "nester ladies" nibble on while drinking tea from china cups. This was made from the leftover coffee, as opposed to throwing it out.

1 cup molasses	1 tablespoon cinnamon
1 cup of coffee with grounds strained out	4 cups flour
	1 pound raisins
1 cup brown sugar	Chopped nuts (optional)
1/2 cup butter, softened	

Mix together molasses, coffee, sugar, butter, and cinnamon; then mix in the flour. Add raisins and nuts, if desired. Bake at 375° for 45 minutes, or until done. Dot the top with butter while still warm, and sprinkle with white sugar.

Note: The coffee used in this recipe is true "cowboy coffee"—the kind that can float a horseshoe.

Sowbelly and Sourdough

Myrtle's Applesauce Doughnuts

Here's a superb creation, a sample of which Myrtle sent next door to a neighbor who is a professional baker. He called them the best doughnuts he'd ever tasted.

2²/₃ cups flour	2 tablespoons shortening
1/2 cup sourdough starter*	1/2 cup sugar
1¹/₂ teaspoons baking powder	2 egg yolks
1/2 teaspoon baking soda	1/2 teaspoon vanilla
1 teaspoon salt	1/2 cup applesauce
1/2 teaspoon nutmeg	1/4 cup buttermilk
1/2 teaspoon cinnamon	

Mix all ingredients and knead well. Roll out and cut into doughnuts. Let stand. Heat cooking oil to 390°. Drop doughnuts into hot oil and fry till done. These take slightly longer to cook. Makes about 2 dozen.

Note: You can substitute 1 tablespoon sour cream for part buttermilk. Myrtle says to tell you that for a variation, you can use 1 whole egg instead of 2 egg yolks; instead of vanilla, add 1/4 teaspoon mace.

*See recipe for Sourdough Starter on page 28.

The Complete Sourdough Cookbook

Pecan Pancakes

³/₄ cup milk or buttermilk
1 egg, beaten
1 cup whole-wheat biscuit mix
¹/₂ teaspoon ginger

¹/₂ teaspoon cinnamon
¹/₄ cup honey
¹/₂ cup chopped pecans

Combine milk and beaten egg to biscuit mix along with ginger and cinnamon. Stir with wire whisk. Add honey and nuts. Spray hot griddle or skillet with nonstick spray. Pour ladle of batter onto hot griddle or skillet; let cook until bubbles break, then turn and brown on other side. Serve hot with maple syrup and butter. Serves 6.

Note: If cakes brown before bubbles break, turn down griddle, it's too hot.

Grandma Jane's Cookbook

Swedish Pancake

¹/₂ stick butter
3 eggs
2 tablespoons sugar
1 cup flour

¹/₂ teaspoon salt
¹/₂ teaspoon baking powder
2 cups milk

Preheat oven to 400°. Place butter in 9x13-inch pan. Place in oven to melt the butter.

In a mixer, beat eggs well. Mix all dry ingredients together, and add to eggs alternately with milk. Pour into pan with the melted butter. Bake for 30 minutes. Pancake will be high like a soufflé but will fall when taken out of the oven. Do not worry—this is normal. Serve hot with syrup or sprinkle with powdered sugar. Serves 4.

Recipes Stolen from the River of No Return

President Abraham Lincoln signed the Territorial Act on March 4, 1863, to make Idaho a territory. It wasn't until July 3, 1890, that President Benjamin Harrison signed the Act making Idaho the 43rd state of the Union.

Whole Grain Pancake and Waffle Mix

PANCAKE AND WAFFLE MIX:

6 cups white flour

2 cups whole-wheat flour

1 cup cornmeal

²/₃ cup sugar

6 tablespoons baking powder

2 teaspoons salt

Combine all ingredients in a very large bowl and store, covered, until ready to make pancakes or waffles.

TO MAKE PANCAKES OR WAFFLES:

2 cups Pancake and Waffle Mix

2 cups milk

2 eggs

¹/₄ cup oil

Mix just until smooth (do not over-mix the batter, as it will make them tough). Bake on griddle or waffle iron.

Another Cookbook

Huckleberry Waffles

1¹/₂ cups cake flour

¹/₄ cup oat bran

2 teaspoons baking powder

1 tablespoon sugar

3 eggs, separated

¹/₄ cup butter, melted

1¹/₂ cups milk

1¹/₂ cups huckleberries

Sift together flour, bran, baking powder, and sugar. Beat egg yolks. Add to butter. Stir into dry ingredients until dry particles are just moistened. Beat egg whites stiff. Fold into batter along with huckleberries. Bake on preheated waffle iron. Serves 4.

The Rocky Mountain Wild Foods Cookbook

Stuffed French Toast

1 (8-ounce) package cream cheese,
   softened
4 teaspoons vanilla extract,
   divided

8 slices sourdough bread
8 eggs
1 tablespoon cinnamon
1½ cups milk

Preheat griddle to 250° about 45 minutes before cooking. Stir together well the cream cheese and 2 teaspoons vanilla. Spread thickly on 4 pieces of bread, then place another piece of bread on top of each. Beat together eggs, cinnamon, and other 2 teaspoons of vanilla. Add milk and whisk together until well mixed. Pour ⅔ of milk/egg mixture in 9x13-inch pan (or sided cookie sheet) and place stuffed bread on top. Allow to soak at least 15 minutes. Turn stuffed bread over, adding remainder of milk/egg mixture to dish, and allow to soak another 15 minutes. Butter griddle well; cook 10–15 minutes per side, or until bread is cooked through, and is medium to dark brown on surface.

CARAMEL SAUCE:
2 cups butter
1 pound dark brown sugar
1 pint whipping cream

4 tablespoons good quality dark
   rum

Melt butter; add sugar and cream. Bring to slow boil and cook just until sugar is dissolved (sometimes doesn't even need to boil). Whisk in rum and serve warm.

Note: Keeps well in refrigerator. Just microwave to reheat and stir. Amaretto makes a good substitute for rum.

The Hearty Gourmet

Italian Breakfast Frittata

1/2 cup finely minced onion
2 tablespoons olive oil
2 basil leaves, minced
4 Roma tomatoes, diced, or
  1 (16-ounce) can diced
  tomatoes, drained
8 large eggs

1/2 cup ricotta cheese or small
  curd cottage cheese
1/4 cup grated Parmesan cheese
2 tablespoons butter or margarine
1 sprig fresh parsley, minced
Salt and pepper

In a skillet, brown onion in olive oil until golden brown; add basil and tomatoes, and cook for 5 minutes over medium heat. With a wire whisk, beat the eggs well, adding ricotta and Parmesan cheeses. While preparing this recipe, preheat the Dutch oven over 5 or 6 briquets and load the lid with 20–24 briquets. Melt the butter in the Dutch oven, then pour in the egg mixture. (The Dutch oven should be hot enough that a couple drops of the egg mixture will sizzle.)

Spoon the onion, basil, and tomato mixture over the eggs and place the Dutch oven in the firepan over 5 or 6 briquets. Put the preheated lid on and bake for 15–20 minutes. Every few minutes, give the Dutch oven a quarter turn to evenly brown the bottom. The eggs will be well set when done. Serve in wedges and garnish with minced parsley.

Cee Dub's Ethnic & Regional Dutch Oven Cookin'

Edward Pulaski of Idaho, invented the Pulaski axe after surviving the great fire of 1910 that burned 3 million acres of Idaho and Montana in 48 hours. The Pulaski is a combination tool: axe and mattock (a digging tool). Pulaski is also well known for one of the most famous escapes from the wildfire of 1910. Trapped in Placer Creek Canyon by approaching fire, Pulaski led 45 men through the inferno to an old mine shaft where they fought the fire and miraculously survived the night.

Breakfast in One

12 eggs, beaten
2 cups milk
6 slices bread, cubed
1 cup grated American cheese
1/2 cup shredded pepper cheese
1 1/2 pounds cooked sausage, or 1
   pound cubed ham
1 (4-ounce) can chopped green
   chiles
1/2 teaspoon salt
Dash Worcestershire
1/2 teaspoon dry mustard

Combine all ingredients well; place in greased baking dish. Cover; leave in refrigerator overnight.

Bake in 350° oven for 1 hour or until golden brown on top.

Cooking with Cops, Too

Breakfast in the Skillet

6 bacon slices
2 tomatoes, diced
1/2 cup grated cheese
6 eggs, beaten
1 tablespoon snipped chives
1 tablespoon snipped parsley
1 tablespoon Worcestershire
   sauce
Salt and pepper

In large skillet, cook bacon until crisp, then drain on paper towels. To bacon fat, add tomatoes; sauté 3 minutes. With a wooden spoon, blend in grated cheese, then pour eggs into skillet. Cook mixture over low heat, lifting it occasionally from bottom of skillet with pancake turner, until eggs are set but still very soft. Break bacon into small pieces and add to eggs along with chives, parsley, Worcestershire sauce, and salt and pepper. Toss lightly. Makes 2 generous servings.

Mackay Heritage Cookbook

Mountain Man Breakfast

18 eggs
1 pound bacon, diced
1 large onion, diced
1 pound sausage
1 (32-ounce) package frozen hash browns

1 (13-ounce) can sliced mushrooms
1 (7-ounce) can diced green chiles
Salt and pepper to taste
1 (8-ounce) jar salsa
24 ounces shredded Cheddar cheese

Break eggs into a large bowl, mix with a fork, then cover and set aside.

Brown bacon in bottom of 14-inch Dutch oven. Add onion and sauté until tender. Remove bacon and onion and place on paper towel to drain. Drain excess grease from pan. Brown sausage; remove from oven, drain grease, and set aside. Place $\frac{1}{2}$ the bacon/onion mixture in bottom of Dutch oven. Add hash browns and fry until golden brown. Turn as little as possible. When hash browns are done, add remaining bacon/onion mixture and sausage.

Add drained and chopped mushrooms and diced chiles to beaten eggs, then pour over ingredients in oven. Add salt and pepper, if desired. Cover oven with lid and place a ring of 22 charcoals on the top, and 14 under the oven, spaced evenly in a ring design. Check every few minutes until eggs are almost set. Then cover with salsa and grated cheese, and continue cooking until eggs are set and cheese has melted. Serve with fresh hot homemade buttermilk biscuits. Enjoy.

Potatoes Are Not the Only Vegetable!

Editor's Extra: As a rule of thumb, most Dutch oven recipes can be baked in a 350° oven for allotted time.

Soups, Chilies, & Stews

Sun Valley, America's first ski resort, opened in 1936 and has entertained world champion skiers and Hollywood royalty. Sun Valley now boasts 78 ski runs and world-renowned lodges, such as Seattle Ridge on Bald Mountain (shown here).

Potato Soup

12 potatoes, peeled and diced
2 stalks celery, chopped
2 carrots, chopped
2 onions, chopped
½ pound bacon, cooked and
   crumbled

1 (12-ounce) can evaporated milk
Salt and pepper to taste
Grated cheese for garnish
Chopped green onions for
   garnish

Cook the potatoes, celery, carrots, and onions in a little water until tender. Add crumbled bacon along with drippings to the potato mixture. Add evaporated milk, salt and pepper to taste. Heat thoroughly. Serve garnished with grated cheese and chopped green onions.

Spragg Family Cookbook

Very Creamy Potato Soup

2 cups chopped onions
1 large garlic clove, minced or
   pressed
3–4 tablespoons butter
2 large potatoes, unpeeled and
   coarsely chopped
1 large carrot, unpeeled and
   coarsely chopped
3 cups vegetable stock or water

1 teaspoon dried dill, or
   2 tablespoons fresh dill
4 ounces cream cheese
1½ cups milk or part cream
Salt and pepper to taste
1 cup grated sharp Cheddar
   cheese
Chopped fresh parsley

In a large soup pot, sauté onions and garlic in butter until the onions are translucent. Add potatoes and carrot and sauté for 5–10 minutes longer. Add the stock or water and dill. Simmer until all the vegetables are tender. Purée the vegetables with cream cheese and milk in a blender or food processor. Return the purée to the soup pot. Season with salt and pepper. Stir in the Cheddar cheese and reheat gently. Serve each cup or bowl garnished with chopped fresh parsley. Serves 4–6.

Cookin' in Paradise

Potato and Carrot Soup

2 pounds ground beef
4 (14-ounce) cans chicken broth
2 (8-ounce) cans tomato sauce
2 (14½-ounce) cans peeled,
   diced tomatoes
Salt and pepper to taste

Red cayenne pepper
2 medium to large onions
1 (16-ounce) bag baby carrots
4–5 large potatoes
2 cups uncooked macaroni noodles

Brown ground beef in large Dutch oven. Add chicken broth, tomato sauce, and diced tomatoes. Add salt, pepper, and cayenne to taste. Bring to a boil, then lower heat and simmer.

Meanwhile peel and dice onions and place in pot with carrots. Bring to a boil and let cook until tender, but not soft. Drain. Peel and dice potatoes into 1-inch squares. Boil in salted water until tender, but not soft. Drain. Add vegetables and macaroni to soup; bring soup to boil, then lower heat and let simmer again. When macaroni is done, the soup is ready to serve. Yields 24 servings.

Cooking for a Crowd

Old-Fashioned Vegetable Soup

2 quarts soup stock, or 3 pounds
   shin of beef
2 small onions, sliced
1½ cups diced potatoes
¾ cup sliced celery

½ cup fresh peas
1½ cups sliced carrots
1½ cups canned tomatoes
Salt and pepper
2 teaspoons parsley

Heat stock (or cook fresh meat in 3 quarts water till tender). Add vegetables and seasonings and cook gently until vegetables are tender. Add chopped parsley and serve.

Recipes Logged from the Woods of North Idaho

 The Idaho potato, also called the Russet Burbank potato, was first developed by Luther Burbank in 1871.

Mixed Bean Soup

$1/3$ heaping cup pinto beans
$1/3$ heaping cup Great Northern
  beans
$1/3$ heaping cup red beans
$1/8$ cup kidney beans
$1/8$ cup small white beans
1 tablespoon black beans
$1/4$ scant cup garbanzo beans
1 tablespoon black-eyed peas
2 tablespoons split peas

$1/3$ cup lentils
2 quarts water
$1/2$ pound cubed lean ham
1 large onion, chopped
1 (28-ounce) can tomatoes
1 teaspoon chili powder
1 garlic clove, chopped
Salt and pepper to taste
$1/2$ cup red wine
$1/2$ cup chopped parsley

Place all dry beans and peas in large pan; cover with water. Soak, rinse well, then add 2 quarts water and ham. Simmer slowly $2^{1/2}$ hours. Add onion, tomatoes, chili powder, garlic, salt and pepper to taste. Simmer another hour or until done. Before serving, add wine and parsley. Yields 10 servings.

A Century of Recipes

Cathy's Black Bean Soup

4 tablespoons olive oil
2 pounds chicken, cubed
1 onion, chopped
4–6 cloves garlic, minced
2–3 cups prepared chicken
  bouillon
2 (16-ounce) cans black beans,
  rinsed

2 (16-ounce) cans Mexican diced
  tomatoes
Cumin to taste
Salt and pepper to taste
Water, if needed

Heat olive oil in a 12-inch Dutch oven and brown chicken on all sides. Add onion and garlic and continue cooking for a few more minutes. Add prepared bouillon, black beans, diced tomatoes, cumin, and other seasonings. More bouillon or water can be added to reach desired consistency. Simmer on low heat for 30 minutes or longer. Serve with hot tortillas. Serves 6.

Cee Dub's Ethnic & Regional Dutch Oven Cookin'

Mexican Split Pea Soup

Yellow split peas make a particularly pretty background for the red tomatoes and green peppers. A generous sprinkling of cheese and a dash of red pepper bring out the best in this soup.

1 large onion, chopped
2 tablespoons vegetable oil
4 cloves garlic, minced
2 teaspoons ground cumin
2 teaspoons dried oregano
1 cup dry green or yellow split
   peas, rinsed
1 quart water
1 (4-ounce) can chopped green
   chiles
1 (14½-ounce) can whole or diced
   tomatoes

1 (10-ounce) box frozen corn
   kernels, or 1 (15-ounce) can
   corn, drained
1 large green bell pepper, seeded
   and chopped
Salt to taste
1 cup shredded Cheddar or
   Monterey Jack cheese (optional)
Crushed red pepper (optional)

In a large sauce pan or Dutch oven over medium-high heat, cook onion in oil until tender, stirring frequently, about 5 minutes. Add garlic and cook 2 minutes longer. Add cumin and cook, stirring for 1 minute. Add oregano and split peas; stir to coat peas with oil, then add water and chiles. Heat to boiling, then reduce heat, cover, and simmer 35–45 minutes, or until peas are just tender.

Add tomatoes, corn, and bell pepper, and simmer another 15–20 minutes. Add salt to taste. Sprinkle each serving with shredded cheese and crushed red pepper, if desired. Makes 6 servings.

The Pea & Lentil Cookbook

Gutzon Borglum, the sculptor who carved Mt. Rushmore National Memorial in South Dakota, was born near Bear Lake. Borglum spent 14 years on the massive sculpture, removing more than 400,000 tons of granite from the 6,200-foot cliff.

Pen's Lentil Soup

Lentils abound here in North Central Idaho. The Palouse region, which encompasses parts of Idaho and eastern Washington, is billed the "Lentil Capitol of the World." Whether that's actually true or not, I don't know. What I do know is this: we enjoy a great variety of locally produced lentils. My wife created this recipe one winter day, and it's become a favorite, especially on those cool, gloomy days when fog banks hang halfway down the timbered ridges, and the best spot in the house is being backed up to the woodstove.

1 cup brown lentils
6 slices bacon, diced into $^1/_4$-inch
   pieces
4–6 cloves garlic, minced
1 large onion, minced
4–6 ribs celery, diced or chopped
   fine
1 (15-ounce) can garlic and herb
   tomato sauce
2 cups chopped fresh spinach

$1^1/_2$ teaspoons coarsely ground
   pepper
$^3/_4$ teaspoon garlic salt
4 teaspoons sun-dried tomato
   mustard, if available, or
   3 teaspoons ketchup
1 teaspoon yellow mustard
$1^1/_2$ teaspoons horseradish or
   creamed horseradish

Soak lentils for several hours or overnight, then rinse thoroughly.

Bring soaked lentils to a boil in Dutch oven with twice the water to cover; add remaining ingredients. Add water to cover ingredients, and simmer until all fresh vegetables are cooked.

More Cee Dub's Dutch Oven and Other Camp Cookin'

Italian Sausage Soup with Tortellini

1 pound Italian sausage
1 cup coarsely chopped onions
2 garlic cloves sliced
5 cups beef broth
1/2 cup water
1/2 cup dry red wine
2 cups (4 medium) chopped,
    seeded, peeled tomatoes
1 cup thinly sliced carrots
1 (8-ounce) can tomato sauce

1/2 teaspoon basil leaves
1/2 teaspoon oregano leaves
1 1/2 cups sliced zucchini
8 ounces frozen (or fresh) meat- or
    cheese-filled tortellini or very
    small ravioli
3 tablespoons fresh parsley
1 medium green pepper, cut into
    1/2-inch pieces
Grated Parmesan cheese

If sausage comes in casing, remove casing. In 5-quart Dutch oven, brown sausage. Remove sausage from Dutch oven; drain, reserving 1 tablespoon drippings. Sauté onions and garlic in reserved drippings until onions are tender. Add beef broth, water, wine, tomatoes, carrots, tomato sauce, basil, oregano, and sausage. Bring to a boil. Reduce heat and simmer, uncovered, for 30 minutes.

Skim fat from soup. Stir in zucchini, tortellini, parsley, and green pepper. Simmer, covered, an additional 35–40 minutes or until tortellini are tender. Sprinkle Parmesan cheese on top of each serving. Makes 6 (1/2-cup) servings.

Note: If tortellini or small ravioli are not available, 2 cups bow-tie egg noodles or spiral macaroni can be substituted. Simmer, covered, an additional 20–25 minutes or until tender. Serve with lots of sourdough French bread and wine.

Be Our Guest

The world's first alpine skiing chairlift was first used in Sun Valley in 1936. Built by Union Pacific Railroad engineers, its design was adapted from a machine used to load bananas onto cargo ships. It is still in use. Sun Valley Village, America's first ski resort, was built in 1936 by Union Pacific tycoon Averell Harriman.

Zesty Pumpkin Soup

1/4 cup butter
1 cup chopped onion
1 garlic clove, crushed
1 teaspoon curry powder
1/2 teaspoon salt
1/8–1/4 teaspoon ground coriander
1/8 teaspoon crushed red pepper

3 cups chicken broth
1 (16-ounce) can solid-pack
  pumpkin
1 cup half-and-half
Sour cream
Chives (optional)

In a large saucepan, melt butter; sauté onion and garlic until soft. Add curry powder, salt, coriander, and red pepper; cook 1 minute. Add broth; boil gently, uncovered 15–20 minutes. Stir in pumpkin and half-and-half; cook 5 minutes. Pour into blender and blend until creamy. Serve warm to hot. Top with sour cream and chives, if desired.

Centennial Cookbook

Cheatin' Chicken Chowder

2 boneless chicken breasts
  or thighs
2 tablespoons vegetable oil
4 tablespoons soy sauce
6 medium potatoes

3 (10¾-ounce) cans cream of
  mushroom soup
1 (10¾-ounce) can cream of
  chicken soup
1 cup milk

Cut chicken into 1/2-inch cubes; stir-fry in oil and soy sauce until solid white inside. Cut potatoes into 1/2-inch cubes; boil for 10 minutes; drain. Mix soups, milk, chicken, and potatoes in soup pot. Cook on low heat for 1/2 hour, stirring frequently.

Tastes from the Country

Thunder Mountain Turkey Soup

4 quarts water
1 turkey carcass with some meat
   still attached
1 cup butter
3 onions, finely chopped
1 cup flour

2 (3½-ounce) packages
   boil-in-bag rice
2 large carrots, shredded
2 teaspoons salt
¾ teaspoon coarsely ground black
   pepper

Bring water and turkey carcass to boil in very large stockpot, then reduce heat, cover, and simmer for 3 hours or more. Cool; remove carcass and pick off all the meat, returning it to the broth. Heat butter and sauté onions for 5 minutes. Add flour to the onion and cook 2 minutes more. Add some broth and stir to make a smooth medium paste, then add more to make roux runny. Add roux to the turkey stock and stir until well mixed. Add rice, carrots, and salt and pepper. Bring to boil, then reduce heat and simmer until rice is tender and soup is somewhat thickened. Serve hot.

Note: You may need to add more water to the stock at some point to make texture right, but end product should be thick and stew-like. I call it "Stoup."

Recipes Tried and True

Chicken Gumbo

2 pounds okra
4 tablespoons cooking oil
   or olive oil
3 tablespoons flour
2 medium onions, chopped
2 bell peppers, chopped

2 cloves garlic, chopped
1 quart water
$^1/_2$ cup chopped celery
3 medium tomatoes, chopped
2 pounds chicken breast, cubed

Slice okra into $^1/_4$-inch-thick slices and fry in oil until the edges are golden brown. Set aside. Heat oil in Dutch oven, and stir in the flour. Stir until a golden-brown roux appears. Add chopped onions, peppers, and garlic. Stir in water and the remaining vegetables; cover, and simmer for 30 minutes. Increase heat and add cubed chicken; cook until cubes are done (about 30 minutes more). Serve with Lemon Garlic Rice.

LEMON GARLIC RICE:
4 cups water
2 cups long-grain rice

1 clove garlic, crushed
1 lemon, sliced

Combine water and rice in Dutch oven. Cook until water level falls below the rice. Sprinkle garlic on top and squeeze lemon slices into rice, laying them on top afterwards. Cook until done.

Hey Ma! Come Quick! The Hog's in the Garden Again!!

 Butch Cassidy, a.k.a. George Leroy Parker, robbed the bank in Montpelier, Idaho, on August 13, 1896. He got away with $7,165, allegedly to hire a lawyer for his partner Matt Warner, who was awaiting trial for murder in Ogden, Utah.

Turkey Gumbo

1 turkey carcass
8 cups water
½ cup butter or margarine
1 cup chopped onion
1 cup chopped celery
⅓ cup flour
1 (28-ounce) can tomatoes
3 cups sliced okra

4–5 bay leaves
⅛ teaspoon thyme
⅛ teaspoon marjoram
2 tablespoons chopped parsley
2 teaspoons gumbo filé
Salt and pepper
Steamed rice

Boil turkey carcass in water until meat falls away from the bones, about 2–3 hours. Remove meat from bones and set aside. Reserve broth.

In a large soup kettle, melt butter or margarine and sauté onion and celery. Add flour and stir mixture over medium heat until golden, the color of caramel. Stir in reserved broth, then add tomatoes, okra, bay leaves, thyme, marjoram, parsley, gumbo filé, and reserved turkey meat. Heat to boiling and simmer 30 minutes. Add salt and pepper to taste. To serve, put ½ cup rice in each bowl. Ladle gumbo over rice. Makes 10–12 servings.

Bound to Please

Northwest Chili

At the core of this chili are the Northwest's chickpeas and lentils.

1 cup chopped onion
2 large garlic cloves, minced
1 1/2 tablespoons canola oil
1 cup dry lentils, rinsed
1 cup diced potatoes
1/2 cup shredded carrots
1 green bell pepper, seeded and
 chopped
1 tablespoon chili powder, or to
 taste
2 1/2 cups water

2 teaspoons beef bouillon granules,
 or 2 beef bouillon cubes
1 (14 1/2-ounce) can tomatoes
1 (8-ounce) can tomato sauce
1 (15-ounce) can chickpeas,
 drained and rinsed, or about 2
 cups boiled
1/4 teaspoon crushed red pepper,
 or to taste
Salt and freshly ground black
 pepper to taste

In a large, heavy saucepan, cook onion and garlic in oil for 3–4 minutes. Add lentils, and stir to coat them with oil. Add potatoes, carrots, bell pepper, chili powder, water, and bouillon. Bring to a boil. Reduce heat, cover, and simmer about 25 minutes, or until lentils are tender.

Add tomatoes, breaking them up as you do, and tomato sauce, chickpeas, and red pepper. Simmer for another 15 minutes. Season to taste with red pepper, salt, and black pepper. Serves 6–8.

The Pea & Lentil Cookbook

In the late 1940s, an isolated U.S. Navy weapons test range in the Upper Snake River Plain of Idaho was chosen as the site for a nuclear research facility. On December 20, 1951, the world's first nuclear power plant, Experimental Breeder Reactor I (EBR-I), became fully operational. This facility earned its place in scientific history as the first reactor to generate useable electricity from atomic power. The site is now known as the Idaho National Engineering and Environmental Laboratory.

Gunsmoke Chili

4 pounds venison, elk or beef,
    ground
2 large onions, minced
1½ teaspoons salt
1 teaspoon coarsely ground
    black pepper
2 tablespoons parsley flakes

1 teaspoon seasoned salt
1½ teaspoons basil
1½ teaspoons oregano
1 teaspoon cayenne pepper
4 tablespoons chili powder
4 cups strong beef bouillon
4 cups tomato sauce

Brown meat and onions together; add remaining ingredients and simmer 2½–3 hours. Serve with Jalapeño Corn Bread (page 28). Serves 10.

Recipes Tried and True

Red Hot Tortilla Chili

1 pound lean ground beef
1 large Texas sweet onion,
    chopped
1 (10-ounce) can cream of
    asparagus soup
1 (14-ounce) can condensed milk
1 (4-ounce) small can green
    chiles, drained and rinsed

1 habanero pepper, chopped
½ clove garlic, chopped
¼ teaspoon oregano
2 cups grated sharp Cheddar,
    divided
1 (5-ounce) jar processed Cheddar
    cheese spread
4 cups corn tortilla chips

Preheat 12-inch Dutch oven over coals. Sauté beef and onion. Mix in and simmer for a few minutes the soup, milk, green chiles, habanero pepper, and seasonings. Stir in ½ sharp Cheddar cheese and the jar of cheese. Crush and stir in tortilla chips. Cover with lid. Remove from coals after 5 minutes and let stand for a few minutes more. Serve with remaining grated cheese sprinkled on top. Have a glass of cold milk handy to put out the fire.

Note: The habanero pepper is said to be 100 times hotter than a jalapeño.

Old-Fashioned Dutch Oven Cookbook

Chili and Cornbread

CHILI:

2 pounds ground beef
2 (10¾-ounce) cans tomato soup
1 large onion, chopped
1 (2-pound) can red kidney beans, undrained
4 cloves garlic, minced

½–1 red Fresno pepper, chopped
1–2 jalapeño peppers, chopped
1–2 green peppers, chopped
At least 2 tablespoons chili powder
Salt and pepper to taste

In the bottom of the 14-inch Dutch oven, brown ground beef. Then add all of the other ingredients into the Dutch oven and mix.

CORNBREAD:

2 boxes corn muffin mix (Jiffy)
2 eggs

⅔ cup milk

Mix corn muffin mix with eggs and milk, then add to the top of the chili mix. Cook 25–30 minutes at 400°.

Potatoes Are Not the Only Vegetable!

"Go-fast" Chili

I used to make this chili for my son, Kris, when he was on the United States Biathlon Development Team. It would make him "go-fast" in his races!

1 pound ground chicken or turkey
1 large onion, chopped
1–2 cloves garlic, chopped
2 tablespoons olive oil
1 large green pepper, chopped
1 stalk celery, chopped
1 (28-ounce) can whole tomatoes
1 (15-ounce) can tomato sauce

1 (16-ounce) can pork and beans (remove fat pieces)
1 (16-ounce) can kidney beans, drained and rinsed
1 (16-ounce) can black beans, drained and rinsed
1 (16-ounce) can chili beans, drained
4 tablespoons chili powder
Pepper and Tabasco to taste

Brown meat, onion, and garlic in olive oil. Add green pepper and celery. Sauté for 10 minutes longer. Add remaining ingredients and simmer for 45 minutes, covered. Serve with crackers or a fresh loaf of French bread. Serves 6.

Ketchum Cooks

Mouse River Chili Con Carne

Years ago, as a nineteen-year-old lad roamin' around the world, I worked a spell for a man who had retired after making a fortune with a chain of lunch counters down on the Texican border. Even retired, he could not help looking for good dishes. This was one of them, which I copied down on the back of the first Social Security card the New Deal issued me. It's the best chili I've ever tasted before or since.

1/4 cup cubed beef suet	1 teaspoon paprika
1 pound ground round or chuck	1 tablespoon salt
1/8 cup olive oil	Fresh ground black pepper
1/2 cup chopped onion	1 small red pepper, crushed
1 clove garlic, minced	1 tablespoon oregano
1 tablespoon chili powder	1 cup hot water

Put into Dutch oven the suet, ground meat, and olive oil. Cook until meat is brown. To this add chopped onion, garlic, chili powder, paprika, salt, pepper, red pepper, oregano, and water, cooking about 3 minutes while stirring well. Simmer until done.

If you like frijoles con chili con carne, add a small can of puréed tomatoes to the pot and dish up over cooked kidney beans. Only a peasant would mix beans into a chili pot.

Old-Fashioned Dutch Oven Cookbook

Shepherd's Stew

Back then cowboys had no time for sheep or sheepherders. But more than one cowboy sat down at a sheep camp to fill his belly. I'm sure they wouldn't have ever admitted it in front of anyone. It is also said that a few cooks stole a sheep or two to feed the cowhands so they wouldn't have to use any of their own beef. So it only seemed right to throw in a lamb recipe.

2 pounds lamb shoulder, cubed in 1-inch pieces	4–5 carrots, sliced
2 tablespoons fat or butter	4–5 potatoes, cubed
Flour	1 onion, chopped
2 quarts water	3–4 ears of corn, cut off
Garlic, parsley, salt, pepper, and bay leaf to taste	1 cup green peas
	2 tablespoons flour

In a Dutch oven, brown the meat in hot fat after it has been dredged in flour. Add the water and seasonings and simmer about 2 hours. Add carrots, potatoes, onion, and corn, and cook another 30 minutes. Add the peas and cook for 15 minutes. Thicken stew with flour and water.

Sowbelly and Sourdough

From 1881 to 1917, the sheep ranching industry boomed in Ketchum. Many say it was second only to Sydney, Australia, as the sheep shipping capital of the world. Over the years, several million sheep have trailed through the valley and have been shipped from various points along the railway. The sheep drive way, which parallels the railroad in many places, is still maintained. Sheepherders today still trail their sheep through the Wood River Valley during their annual migrations to and from summer pastures in the northern mountains, and in October 1997, the first annual "Trailing of the Sheep" celebration was held.

Wyoming Beef Stew

This recipe is from a hotel in Cheyenne, Wyoming, from the late 1800s.

½ cup flour
Salt and pepper
2–3 pounds beef chuck, cubed in
    1-inch pieces
2 tablespoons shortening
1 large onion, chopped
1 (16-ounce) can chopped
    tomatoes
3 cups water

2 beef bouillon cubes
2 cloves garlic, crushed
1 tablespoon molasses
½ teaspoon celery salt
3 peppercorns
2 pounds sliced potatoes
1 handful sliced carrots
1 handful chopped celery
¼ cup water, if necessary

Season flour with salt and pepper. Dredge beef in flour, then brown in shortening in Dutch oven over medium-high heat. Remove when evenly browned. In same Dutch oven, cook onion for a few minutes, then add remaining flour and stir. While still stirring, slowly add the tomatoes with liquid. Add 3 cups water and browned meat. Stir in beef bouillon, garlic, molasses, celery salt, and peppercorns. Bring to a boil, then cover and simmer over low heat for 2–3 hours.

Add sliced potatoes, carrots, celery, and more water, if needed. Cook an additional hour. Top with potato dumplings, if desired.

Sowbelly and Sourdough

Dad's Beef Stew

This was my father's favorite stew recipe. He learned it from a chuck-house cook on a ranch in western Oklahoma. Over the years, he added and refined, until he got it just right.

3 tablespoons shortening
1 pound beef chuck, round, or
  rump, cut in 1½-inch cubes
1 medium onion, coarsely
  chopped
2 cups water
1 beef bouillon cube
⅓ clove garlic, finely chopped
¾ tablespoon chopped fresh
  parsley

½ bay leaf
1/16 teaspoon dried thyme
  leaves
½ teaspoon salt
⅛ teaspoon pepper
3–4 small white onions
2 medium potatoes, chopped
2 medium carrots, chopped
1 stalk celery, chopped
1 medium green pepper, chopped

Over medium heat, slowly melt shortening in Dutch oven. Add meat cubes and brown well, turning on all sides. Remove and set aside. In Dutch oven, sauté the onion until tender. Return meat to pan; add 2 cups water, bouillon cube, garlic, parsley, bay leaf, thyme, salt and pepper. Cover and simmer 1½ hours.

When meat has cooked 1½ hours, add vegetables, except green pepper. Cook 40 minutes. Then add the green pepper; cook for 20 minutes more. Serves 4.

Matt Braun's Western Cooking

What makes Idaho potatoes different? Idaho's clean air, climate, rich volcanic soil, and fresh water from melting snow in nearby mountains create ideal conditions for potato growing. The mountains collect snow all winter, which melts and flows crystal clear into large surface and underground reservoirs. That water is then used to irrigate the potatoes. Look for the "Grown in Idaho" seal as assurance that you are getting Genuine Idaho Potatoes.

Basque Bean Stew

1 pound Idaho Great Northern
  beans
5 cups water
Meaty ham bone or ham hocks
3 bay leaves, divided
1 large onion, quartered
4 potatoes

4 carrots
2 cloves garlic, minced
1 teaspoon thyme
$\frac{1}{2}$ pound fully cooked sausage
Salt and pepper
Chopped parsley

Soak beans overnight in water. Or, for quick-soak method, add beans to boiling water, boil 2 minutes and let stand 1 hour. Measure soaking liquid and add water to make 4 cups. Cook beans, ham bone or hocks, 2 bay leaves, and onion in reserved liquid about 2 hours or until beans are tender. Drain, reserving liquid. Peel and coarsely dice potatoes and carrots. Cook in bean liquid with garlic, thyme, and 1 bay leaf until tender.

Add beans, meat from ham bone, and sausages, thickly sliced. Cook just until heated through. Add salt and pepper to taste. Remove bay leaf. Before serving, sprinkle with chopped parsley.

Idaho's Favorite Bean Recipes

Rattlesnake Stew

For less adventurous souls, substitute stew meat, cubed steak, or cubed roast for the rattlesnake meat.

1 large rattlesnake, skinned,
   cooled and cubed
1/3+ cup flour, divided
1 tablespoon oil
1 large onion, chopped
5 cups water, divided
1 teaspoon seasoned salt

1/2 teaspoon pepper
2–3 teaspoons salt, or to taste
6 medium potatoes, peeled and
   cubed
2 carrots, peeled and sliced
1 cup sliced celery
2 teaspoons browning sauce

Coat meat lightly with flour (reserve 1/3 cup) and brown lightly in oil in a large pan. Cover meat with 4 cups water and add chopped onion and seasonings. Bring to a boil and turn down to simmer until meat is tender, between 1 and 2 hours, then add vegetables. Bring to a boil and turn down to simmer until the vegetables are tender, about 30 minutes. Combine 1/3 cup flour, 1 cup cold water, and browning sauce together until smooth. Stir into the stew and continue stirring until stew thickens slightly.

Sharing Our Best

Salads

*Built between 1848 and 1853, the Old Mission (Mission of the Sacred Heart),
located in Cataldo, is the oldest standing building in Idaho.*

Chinese Chicken Salad

1–1½ pounds cooked chicken
   breasts
1 medium head cabbage
¼ cup sesame seeds, roasted
1 cup sliced almonds
2 tablespoons minced onion

½ package Ramen noodles,
   crushed
½ cup sweet rice vinegar
½ cup olive oil
2 teaspoons dry mustard
¼ teaspoon black pepper

The seasoning you use to cook chicken changes the taste of the salad. Use five-spice or seasoned salt and garlic. Either bake whole breasts in oven or cut in small pieces and fry in hot oil. Cool chicken before placing in salad.

Cut cabbage in thin slices as in a slaw; place in bowl, and add sliced chicken, sesame seeds, almonds, minced onion, and crushed Ramen noodles.

Make dressing with vinegar, oil, mustard, and pepper. Whisk and pour over salad. Stir and place in refrigerator for at least 4 hours.

Caldera Kitchens

Oriental Chicken Salad with Lentils

Garlic chili paste gives this salad a satisfying kick.

2 cups dry lentils, rinsed
1 quart water
2 tablespoons minced scallions
2 cups seeded and julienned
    cucumber
2 teaspoons minced garlic
2 tablespoons minced fresh
    ginger
2 tablespoons rice vinegar

3 tablespoons soy sauce
2 teaspoons sugar
2 tablespoons garlic chili paste
2 tablespoons dark sesame oil
Salt and freshly ground black
    pepper to taste
Romaine lettuce leaves
4 cups cooked chicken breast,
    julienned

In a medium saucepan, combine lentils and water and bring to a boil. Reduce heat, cover, and simmer until lentils are tender, about 20 minutes. Drain, cover, and chill.

Combine scallions, cucumber, garlic, ginger, vinegar, soy sauce, sugar, chili paste, and sesame oil in a bowl. Mix well. Add dressing mixture to lentils. Mix well. Season with salt and pepper.

Arrange lettuce leaves on serving plates. Arrange the chicken over lettuce, then spoon lentils over chicken. Serves 16.

The Pea & Lentil Cookbook

Known as the City of Trees, Boise (pronounced boy-see) is the capital of Idaho. The first new world adventurers to come to the Boise Valley were French missionaries who had traveled through the high-mountain desert of the Snake River plain. When they came out of the hills to Boise's east, they saw the trees and exclaimed "les bois, les bois," ("the trees, the trees"), giving Boise its name.

Garden Fresh Chicken Pasta Salad

When you're grilling chicken breasts for another recipe, do three to four extra and try this dish for a change of pace. It makes a quick dish when you want a "lite" dinner or lunch.

1 (12-ounce) package vegetable rotini
$^1/_2$ (15-ounce) can black olives, sliced
$^1/_2$ cup green olives, sliced (optional)
$^1/_2$ small purple onion, diced
1 cucumber or zucchini, diced into $^1/_2$-inch cubes
3–4 large mushrooms, sliced

2 Roma tomatoes, diced
$^1/_2$ green or red bell pepper, diced
1 teaspoon salt
4–6 tablespoons olive oil
$^1/_2$ cup vinegar
Ground black pepper to taste
3–4 chicken breasts, grilled and seasoned to taste, cut into 1-inch squares

Cook pasta according to package directions; rinse, and chill in fridge or cooler. Put veggies in a bowl, add salt, and toss. Let veggies rest for 15–20 minutes. Add oil, vinegar, pasta, pepper, and chicken. Gently toss. Let salad rest for about 30 minutes, stirring occasionally. Serve with a side of garlic or French bread.

More Cee Dub's Dutch Oven and Other Camp Cookin'

Tuna on a Shoestring

1 (6¹/₂-ounce) can tuna, drained
1 cup shredded carrots
1 cup sliced celery
¹/₄ cup minced onion
³/₄–1 cup mayonnaise

1 (14-ounce) can shoestring
  potatoes
Fresh parsley for garnish
  (optional)
Carrot curls for garnish (optional)

In a large bowl, separate tuna into chunks. Add carrots, celery, onion, and mayonnaise. Toss until tuna is well coated. Cover and chill. Just before serving, fold in shoestring potatoes. To add a bright touch, garnish with parsley and carrot curls, if desired. Yields 4–6 servings.

A Century of Recipes

Editor's Extra: Carrot curls are easy to make by running a vegetable peeler down the length of a peeled carrot.

Tuna and Dandelion Green Salad

1¹/₂ quarts shredded young
  dandelion greens
1 can tuna in spring water, well
  drained
8 anchovy fillets
¹/₂ cup sliced green olives with
  pimento

1 hard-cooked egg, chopped
¹/₂ cup diced Swiss cheese
¹/₂ cup diced green pepper
1¹/₂ tablespoons finely chopped
  fresh basil
Vinaigrette dressing

Combine all ingredients, except dressing, and toss well. Add dressing just prior to serving. Serves 4.

The Rocky Mountain Wild Foods Cookbook

Ham and Cabbage Salad

1 (12-ounce) can spiced ham,
  or 2 cups cooked ham
1 cucumber
1 Bermuda onion
4 cups shredded cabbage

1 green pepper, diced
2 tomatoes, cut in wedges
1/2 cup French Dressing
1/4 cup mayonnaise

Cut meat in match-like strips. Peel cucumber and slice. Slice onion thin and separate rings. Toss all ingredients lightly with the French Dressing mixed with mayonnaise. Serves 8.

FRENCH DRESSING:
1 teaspoon salt
1/4 teaspoon pepper
1 teaspoon paprika

1/3 cup vinegar
1 cup oil
1 clove garlic, grated

Combine all ingredients in a jar and shake well.

Recipes Logged from the Woods of North Idaho

Gwen's Macaroni Salad

1 (16-ounce) package elbow
  macaroni, cooked
1 slice ham, cut 1/2 inch thick,
  cubed
1 cup cubed Cheddar cheese
1/2 cup sliced carrots
1/2 cup sliced celery
1/4 cup diced onion

1/2 cup diced sweet pickles
1 (4-ounce) can sliced black olives
1 1/2 cups mayonnaise
1/3 cup milk
1/4 cup sweet pickle juice
1/2 teaspoon salt
1/4 teaspoon pepper
1/8 teaspoon chili powder

In a large bowl, mix macaroni, ham, cheese, carrots, celery, onion, sweet pickles, and olives. In a medium bowl, mix mayonnaise, milk, pickle juice, salt, pepper, and chili powder. Pour mayonnaise mixture over macaroni and vegetable mixture. Stir well until all macaroni and vegetables are well coated. Refrigerate for 1 hour.

The Miracle Cookbook

Roasted Pepper Salad

2 large green bell peppers
2 large yellow bell peppers
2 large red bell peppers
2 tablespoons red wine vinegar

Dash salt
Freshly ground pepper
6 tablespoons Spanish olive oil

Char peppers over gas flame or in broiler, turning occasionally, until skin blackens. Place in plastic bag; let stand for 19 minutes to steam. Peel and seed peppers, then cut into 1/2-inch-wide strips and place in bowl. Mix together vinegar, salt and pepper. Whisk in oil in a slow steady stream. Stir into peppers. Allow to stand at least 2 hours, and up to 24 hours, stirring occasionally. Serve at room temperature. Serves 4.

Basque Cooking and Lore

Avocado Citrus Toss

6 cups torn salad greens
2 medium grapefruits, peeled and
   sectioned

3 oranges, peeled and sectioned
1 ripe avocado, peeled and sliced
1/4 cup slivered almonds, toasted

In a large salad bowl, toss the salad greens, grapefruits, oranges, avocado, and almonds.

DRESSING:
1/2 cup vegetable oil
1/3 cup sugar
3 tablespoons vinegar
2 teaspoons poppy seeds

1 teaspoon finely chopped onion
1/2 teaspoon dry mustard
1/2 teaspoon salt

In a jar with a tight-fitting lid, combine the Dressing ingredients; shake well. Pour over salad and toss. Serve. Makes 6 servings.

Another Cookbook

Emma Edwards designed the Great Seal of Idaho in 1891. She is the only woman in history to design the Great Seal of any state.

Marinated Onion-Tomato Salad

2 large onions
  (Idaho-Eastern Oregon)
2 large, ripe tomatoes
2 tablespoons chopped parsley
1/2 cup olive oil
2 tablespoons red wine vinegar

1 clove garlic, minced
1 1/2 teaspoons crushed basil leaves
1 teaspoon sugar
1/2 teaspoon each salt and black
  pepper

Cut onions and tomatoes in 1/4-inch slices. Combine remaining ingredients except parsley to make marinade. Make a layer of onions and tomatoes and parsley on a platter; drizzle with half of marinade; repeat layers. Cover tightly with plastic wrap and refrigerate overnight. Serves 8.

Onions Make the Meal Cookbook

Marinated Sweet and Sour Carrot Salad

1 1/2 pounds carrots, pared and
  thinly sliced
1 medium onion, chopped
1 medium sweet green pepper,
  chopped
1 (10 3/4-ounce) can tomato soup

3/4 cup sugar
1/2 cup vegetable oil
1/2 cup red wine vinegar
1 teaspoon Worcestershire sauce
1/2 teaspoon salt

Cook carrots in boiling salted water until crisp-tender, about 5 minutes. Drain. Cool. Combine carrots, onion, and green pepper in bowl. Combine soup, sugar, oil, vinegar, Worcestershire sauce, and salt in small bowl. Pour the marinade over the vegetables; stir gently to combine. Cover, and refrigerate at least 24 hours to blend flavors.

Recipes Logged from the Woods of North Idaho

Bean Salad Francaise

The pleasures of serving bean salads are unlimited, for they are such good eating, so adaptable to occasions, so accommodating as to time, and so economical. And, as a bonus, there's nourishing goodness in every mouthful!

1/2 cup Idaho red beans	1/4 cup olive or salad oil
1/2 cup Idaho pinto beans	2 tablespoons lemon juice
1/2 cup Idaho Great Northern beans	1 tablespoon tarragon vinegar
3/4 cup sliced celery	1 clove garlic, minced
1/2 cup sliced radishes	1/2 teaspoon salt
1/2 cup diced cucumber	Freshly ground black pepper
1/4 cup sliced green onions	Lettuce

Soak and cook beans according to directions. Drain and cool beans. Combine beans and vegetables. Beat together oil, lemon juice, vinegar, garlic, and seasonings. Pour dressing over beans and toss to coat thoroughly. Chill for 2 hours. Serve on lettuce-lined plate. May garnish with skewered cold meat and vegetables, if desired.

Idaho's Favorite Bean Recipes

Coleslaw

1 medium cabbage	1 pint salad dressing
2 raw carrots	(mayonnaise-style)
1 medium green pepper	1 tablespoon salt
1 medium onion	1 tablespoon pepper
½ cup sugar	¼ cup vinegar

Grate the vegetables in medium bowl. Combine remaining ingredients for dressing and pour over vegetables. Refrigerate.

Quilter's Delight, Busy Day Recipes

Grandmother's Mayonnaise

This was my great-grandmother's recipe from about 1905. My mother made this and kept a jar in the refrigerator for salads with fresh lettuce from the garden, and to go with fruits as well.

2 cups sugar	1½ cups hot water
2 tablespoons flour	2 eggs
1 teaspoon dry mustard	1 cup vinegar
½ teaspoon white pepper	1 tablespoon melted butter
(optional)	1 cup milk
1 teaspoon salt	

In the top of a double boiler, mix together sugar, flour, mustard, pepper, and salt. Add hot water and cook till smooth. Beat eggs and add half of the cooked mixture. Beat, then add the other half and mix well. Add vinegar, butter, and milk. Heat through and pour in jar with good cover and keep in the refrigerator.

A Century of Recipes

"Some-Buddy's" Salad Dressing

Much like "Buddy's" salad dressing at a famous Pocatello restaurant known for having "Buddy's Breath."

2 cups olive oil
1¼ cups red wine vinegar
1 pound blue cheese
1 tablespoon garlic powder
1 tablespoon onion powder

2 teaspoons salt
2 teaspoons pepper
1 teaspoon parsley flakes
1 teaspoon oregano

Mix all together; add to lettuce and let sit.

Sharing Our Best

Cucumber Sauce

Excellent served with cold poached salmon or as a topping for a crisp salad.

1 cup sour cream
2 teaspoons fresh lemon juice
1 teaspoon prepared mustard
½ teaspoon dill weed

1 teaspoon finely minced onion
1 large cucumber, peeled, seeded,
 and finely chopped
3 drops Tabasco sauce

Combine all ingredients in a small bowl. Blend well; cover and refrigerate overnight. Makes 2 cups.

Bound to Please

The 1988 legislature designated the Hagerman Horse Fossil as the official state fossil. Discovered in 1928, the Hagerman horse is the oldest known representative of the modern horse genus Equus (includes horses, donkeys, and zebras) and is believed to be more closely related to the living Grevy's zebra in Africa.

Raspberry Pretzel Salad

2 cups crushed pretzels
3 tablespoons sugar
1/4 cup butter, melted
1 (8-ounce) package cream
  cheese, softened
1/2 cup confectioners' sugar
2 cups miniature marshmallows

1 1/2 cups whipped topping
2 (3-ounce) packages raspberry
  Jell-O
2 cups boiling water
2 (10-ounce) packages frozen
  raspberries

Mix pretzels with sugar and butter. Press into a 9x13-inch baking dish. Bake at 350° for 15 minutes. Set aside to cool.

Cream softened cream cheese with confectioners' sugar; beat well. Fold in marshmallows and whipped topping. Spread this mixture over cooled crust. Dissolve Jell-O in water and stir in raspberries; chill until thick. Spread this over cream cheese layer. Chill until ready to serve. Garnish with mint leaves and raspberries. Can also be served as a dessert.

Cooking with Cops, Too

Shrimp Aspic

2 tablespoons unflavored gelatin
1/2 cup cold water
1 cup tomato soup, undiluted
1 (8-ounce) package cream
  cheese, softened
1 cucumber, finely chopped
1 cup chopped celery
4 cups salad shrimp

1 teaspoon salt
3 teaspoons minced onion
1 cup mayonnaise
Juice of 1/2 lemon
Dash cayenne
Garnishes: crisp salad greens,
  artichoke hearts, deviled eggs,
  asparagus tips

In a large bowl, soften gelatin in cold water. Heat soup to boiling, remove from heat and add to gelatin mixture. Blend in cream cheese and allow to cool. Stir in remaining ingredients, except garnishes. Pour into a 2-quart mold and chill overnight or for several hours.

To serve, unmold on a serving plate lined with salad greens. Garnish with artichoke hearts, deviled eggs, or asparagus tips. Makes 12 servings.

Bound to Please

Daiquiri Mold

2 envelopes unflavored gelatin
1/2 cup lime juice
1 (14-ounce) can pineapple tidbits,
  undrained
Water
1 1/2 teaspoons grated lime peel

1/2 cup sugar
1/4 teaspoon salt
1 cup orange juice
1/2 cup light rum
1 avocado, cut into balls

In a small bowl, soften gelatin in lime juice; set aside. Drain syrup from pineapple and combine with enough water to make 2 cups.

In a medium saucepan, stir grated lime peel, sugar, and salt into syrup-water mixture. Heat, stirring to dissolve sugar. Add softened gelatin; continue cooking and stirring until dissolved. Cool.

Stir in orange juice and rum. Chill until mixture begins to thicken. Fold in drained pineapple and avocado balls; turn into a 1 1/2-quart mold. Chill until ready to serve.

Bound to Please

Cookie Salad

1 (3-ounce) package vanilla
  instant pudding
1 cup buttermilk
1 (8-ounce) container whipped
  topping
1 can mandarin oranges,
  drained

1 (8-ounce) can pineapple tidbits,
  drained
1 (11½-ounce) package fudge
  stripes cookies, broken up

Mix pudding and buttermilk. Add whipped topping, fruit, and cookies.
Mix together. Need to double for a big crowd.

Ashton Area Cookbook

Vegetables

PHOTO © WILLIAM H. MULLINS OUTDOOR PHOTOGRAPHY

Idaho's higher elevations, ideal climate, and light, volcanic soil tend to produce superior potatoes. It is no surprise that Idaho leads the nation in potato production with more than 30% of potatoes grown. Washington ranks second.

Asparagus Menestra

2 pounds asparagus tips
2 tablespoons Spanish olive oil
1/2 cup chopped onion
2 ounces chorizo, cut into thin
  rounds

1/4 cup diced salt pork
1 1/2 tablespoons flour
1 cup dry white wine
1/2 cup liquid from asparagus

Steam asparagus tips until tender but not over-cooked. Reserve 1/2 cup liquid from steaming.

Heat oil in heavy skillet over moderate heat until light haze forms. Add onion, chorizo, and salt pork. When onion is translucent, add flour and stir gently. Add wine and reserved asparagus liquid. Bring to a boil, then pour over asparagus. Serves 6.

Basque Cooking and Lore

Asparagus Casserole

1 sleeve saltine crackers
1 cup grated Cheddar cheese
1/2 cup butter or margarine,
  melted

1 (14 1/2-ounce) can cut asparagus
1 (10 3/4-ounce) can cream of
  mushroom soup
1/2 cup chopped pecans

Crush crackers and mix together with grated cheese and melted butter. In a separate bowl mix together asparagus and soup. In a 9x13-inch baking dish, layer soup and asparagus mixture with cheese mixture, ending with cheese mixture on top. Sprinkle pecans over the casserole. Bake at 350° for 20 minutes. Serves 6–8.

Be Our Guest

Movies made in Idaho: "Told in the Hills" 1919; "Northwest Passage" 1939; "Bus Stop" 1956; "Breakheart Pass" 1976; "Bronco Billy" 1979; "Heaven's Gate" 1979; "Pale Rider" 1984; "Talent for the Game" 1991; "Dark Horse" 1992; and "Dante's Peak" 1996.

Mushrooms Supreme

2 pounds fresh mushrooms,
  quartered
6+ tablespoons melted butter
2 tablespoons beef bouillon base
1 cup hot water
1/2 cup butter

4 tablespoons flour
1/4–1 teaspoon pepper
1 cup whipping cream
Sour cream to taste and texture
Fine dry bread crumbs to cover
Grated Parmesan cheese to cover

Sauté mushrooms in 6 tablespoons melted butter until just giving off liquid. Dissolve bouillon in hot water and set aside. Melt 1/2 cup butter in large, nonstick pan. Add flour and stir until smooth. Blend in pepper, cream, and bouillon. Stir in sour cream. Stir in mushrooms. Leave in pan to bake, or transfer to a baking dish. Top with bread crumbs and cheese. Bake, uncovered, at 350° for 30–45 minutes. Serves 8.

The Hearty Gourmet

Company Carrots

2 pounds baby carrots
1/4 cup reserved carrot liquid
1/2 cup mayonnaise
1 tablespoon instant onion

1 tablespoon horseradish
1/3 cup bread crumbs
1/2 teaspoon paprika
1 tablespoon dried parsley

Boil carrots in salted water until done; reserve 1/4 cup liquid, then drain. Cool; cut in strips. Place in shallow dish. Mix together reserved 1/4 cup carrot liquid, mayonnaise, instant onion, and horseradish. Pour over cooked carrots. Top with bread crumbs, paprika, and parsley. Bake in a 350° oven for 30 minutes.

Be Our Guest

Cauliflower Curry

2 pounds cauliflower (2 medium
   heads)
3 tablespoons butter
$^1/_4$ teaspoon cinnamon
$^1/_2$ teaspoon cayenne
$^1/_2$ teaspoon turmeric
$^1/_2$ teaspoon salt
$^1/_2$ teaspoon ground ginger

$^1/_2$ teaspoon coriander
$^1/_2$ teaspoon mustard seed
$^1/_2$ teaspoon cumin seeds
1 clove garlic, put through press
$^1/_2$ cup water
2 tablespoons torn cilantro leaves
$1^1/_2$ cups fresh peas
2 tomatoes, diced

Clean cauliflower and break into small flowerets. Add all the spices to
the heated butter in large skillet. Stir mixture, then add cauliflower and
water when the spices are thoroughly warmed. Stir again and cover
tightly, letting cauliflower steam till almost tender. Add cilantro and
peas and cook another 5 minutes, stirring gently from time to time.
Add tomatoes at last moment, and when they are hot, it's time to serve.
Serves 4–6.

Caldera Kitchens

Dandelion Greens

$^1/_2$ pound young dandelion
   greens
$^1/_2$ cup water
$^1/_4$ teaspoon salt

Dash pepper
$2^1/_2$ tablespoons butter
1 lime, quartered

Cook greens in water over medium heat for 12 minutes. Drain. Add
salt, pepper, and butter, and heat with greens until butter melts. Serve
hot with wedges of lime. Serves 4.

The Rocky Mountain Wild Foods Cookbook

Spinach and Feta Pie

2 pounds fresh spinach
7 ounces olive oil, divided
2 large onions, finely chopped
9 ounces feta cheese, crumbled
2 eggs, beaten
2 tablespoons finely chopped
  fresh parsley

1 tablespoon finely chopped
  fresh dill
Salt and pepper to taste
10 sheets filo pastry dough

Preheat 12-inch Dutch oven to 350°. Pick through the spinach, removing any large stalks, then wash, drain, and roughly chop. Heat 2 tablespoons olive oil in a pan, and fry the onions until soft and golden. Add spinach and cook for 5 minutes, or until tender. Remove from pan, drain thoroughly in a colander, then place in a large bowl with the feta, eggs, parsley, and dill. Mix well; season and let cool.

Brush the Dutch oven with olive oil. Line with 1 sheet of filo dough, brush with oil, and continue with 4 more sheets of dough, covering the last sheet with the spinach mixture. Add the remaining filo dough in the same way and score the top of the pie with a sharp knife. Bake for 40 minutes until golden brown. Serve hot or cold.

Bacon is not a Vegetable

Calabacitas

6–10 zucchini squash, depending
  on size
2 green peppers
1 large onion
2 pounds pork
2 pounds beef
2 green chiles, or 2 small cans
  green chiles
2 tablespoons oil

4 ears corn, cut off the cob
Salt and pepper
$1\frac{1}{2}$ bay leaves
$\frac{1}{2}$ teaspoon oregano
$\frac{1}{4}$–$\frac{1}{2}$ teaspoon cumin
$\frac{1}{4}$ teaspoon garlic powder, or 1
  clove, chopped fine
1 teaspoon paprika
2 cups water

Cut squash, peppers, onion, pork, beef, and chiles into bite-size pieces. Brown meat well in oil in large skillet or saucepan; drain. Add all vegetables and seasonings, plus water to browned meat. Cook at medium heat for about 1 hour, maybe more. You might need more water after it boils awhile. Makes 4 quarts.

Spragg Family Cookbook

Zucchini Enchiladas

Make filling first, then cook enchiladas in the Dutch, but if you're the adventurous type, the entire dish could be prepared in the Dutch.

MEXICAN HOT SAUCE:

2 cups chopped onion
Several cloves garlic, crushed
2 teaspoons salt
4 tablespoons olive oil
2 teaspoons cumin
1 teaspoon cayenne
1 teaspoon chili powder
$^1/_2$ teaspoon ground coriander
$^1/_2$ teaspoon black pepper
6 cups chopped tomatoes
2 cups water
4 tablespoons tomato paste
3 tablespoons dry red wine

In 10-inch Dutch oven sauté onion, garlic, and salt in olive oil until the onion is clear. Add spices and mix. Add tomatoes, water, tomato paste, and wine. Simmer for 30 minutes or longer; several hours is best. Hot spices tend to get hotter as they cook.

1 cup uncooked rice
2 cups water
Garlic cloves, crushed, divided
1 large onion, minced
4 tablespoons olive oil
1 teaspoon salt
2 red (or green) bell peppers, minced
10 small zucchini, shredded and squeezed out
1 teaspoon each: cumin, oregano, basil, cayenne, black pepper
$^1/_2$ cup unsalted sunflower seeds
1 cup slivered almonds
2 cups grated sharp Cheddar cheese, divided
14 burrito-size flour tortillas
Mexican Hot Sauce

Wash rice; cook in water with a few crushed garlic cloves. Once boiling, reduce heat and simmer for 25–30 minutes. *Do Not Remove The Lid Until Done!* In a large, heavy skillet, sauté additional garlic cloves (to taste) and onion in olive oil and salt. When the onion is soft, add peppers, zucchini, and herbs. Stir and continue to cook over medium heat another 8 minutes; stir in sunflower seeds and almonds; cook 2 more minutes. Remove from heat and stir in the cooked rice and 1 cup cheese. Allow to cool to room temperature.

Assemble enchiladas by placing 1–2 heaping spoonfuls of filling on one side of tortilla, then roll up. Pour a small amount of Mexican Hot Sauce into 14-inch Dutch oven; place enchiladas on top, then sauce, and $^1/_2$ cup cheese; repeat, making 2 layers. Preheat the lid; cook for about 30 minutes.

Bacon is not a Vegetable

Zucchini Pie

4 cups thinly sliced zucchini
1 cup chopped onion
$^1/_2$ cup margarine
$^1/_2$ cup chopped parsley, or
 2 tablespoons parsley flakes
$^1/_2$ teaspoon salt
$^1/_2$ teaspoon pepper
$^1/_4$ teaspoon garlic powder
$^1/_4$ teaspoon basil

$^1/_4$ teaspoon oregano leaves
2 eggs, beaten
4 ounces (1 cup) shredded
 mozzarella cheese
4 ounces (1 cup) shredded sharp
 Cheddar cheese
1 (8-ounce) can crescent rolls
2 teaspoons prepared mustard

Cook and stir zucchini and onion in margarine for 10 minutes. Stir in parsley (or flakes), salt, pepper, garlic powder, basil, and oregano. Combine eggs and cheeses; stir into zucchini mixture. Separate crescent rolls into 8 triangles. Place in ungreased 10-inch pie pan (or 12x8-inch pan; just separate rolls into rectangles to form crust). Press over bottom and up sides to form crust. Spread crust with mustard. Pour vegetable mixture into crust. Bake at 375° for 18–20 minutes, or until center is set. Cover crust with foil last 10 minutes. Let stand a few minutes before slicing. Serves 6.

Cookin' in Paradise

Dave's Eggplant Parmesan

1 eggplant, peeled
2 eggs, beaten
1/2 cup milk
2 cups seasoned Italian bread
   crumbs
1/2+ cup olive oil, divided
4–6 cloves garlic, minced
1 pound bulk Italian sausage,
   casing removed
1 onion, chopped
1 (26-ounce) can spaghetti sauce

1 (14 1/2-ounce) can stewed
   tomatoes
1/2 pound fresh mushrooms,
   sliced
2–3 tablespoons chopped fresh
   basil
1 pound grated Parmesan cheese

(or mozzarella, Romano, or
combo)

Slice peeled eggplant. Mix beaten eggs and milk in a bowl. Dip eggplant in egg wash, then coat slices with bread crumbs. Fry slices in olive oil until brown. Drain and set aside.

In a separate pan or Dutch oven, brown garlic in a small amount of olive oil. Crumble Italian sausage into garlic and brown. Add onion. When onion is translucent, add spaghetti sauce, tomatoes, mushrooms, and basil. Bring to a boil and simmer for 15–20 minutes.

In a 12-inch or 12-inch-deep Dutch oven, make layers using about 1/3 of the sauce, 1/3 eggplant slices, then 1/3 grated cheese. Continue the layers 2 more times. Cover and bake for about an hour using 6–8 briquets under the oven and 18–20 briquets on the lid.

Cee Dub's Ethnic & Regional Dutch Oven Cookin'

Triple Corn Casserole

1 egg, slightly beaten
1 cup sour cream
1/2 cup butter or margarine, melted
1 (15-ounce) can cream-style corn

1 (15-ounce) can whole-kernel corn, undrained
1 small package corn bread mix

Put into mixing bowl in order given; mix well. Pour into greased casserole dish. Bake at 350°, uncovered, for 1 hour.

Quilter's Delight, Busy Day Recipes

Tomato Primavera

1 tablespoon olive oil
1 small onion, finely chopped
1 large garlic clove, finely chopped
1 small carrot, cut into 1/4-inch cubes
1 (14 1/2-ounce) can whole tomatoes
1 small zucchini, cut into 1/4-inch cubes

1 small yellow squash, cut into 1/4-inch cubes
8 medium mushrooms, halved or quartered, if large enough
1 teaspoon double-concentrated tomato paste
3/4 teaspoon dried oregano
1/2 teaspoon dried basil
1/2 teaspoon sugar
1/2 teaspoon salt

In a large skillet, heat oil over moderate heat. Add onion and garlic and sauté 2–3 minutes. Add carrot and tomatoes, breaking the latter up with your hands. Allow to simmer until carrots are just crisp-tender. Stir in remaining ingredients. Raise the heat slightly and simmer sauce until thick, about 10 minutes. Spoon over cooked pasta or serve at side. Serves 4.

The Hearty Gourmet

Sweet and Sour Green Beans

4 slices bacon
2 medium onions, sliced thin
1 tablespoon dry mustard
1 teaspoon salt
2 tablespoons brown sugar

2 tablespoons white sugar
1/4 cup vinegar
1 (16-ounce) bag frozen cut green
   beans (or fresh)

Cook bacon until crisp; remove and crumble. Sauté onions in bacon drippings, stir in mustard, then the remainder of the ingredients, except beans. Boil and thicken. Cook beans in water until just done. Drain and add beans and bacon to onion and heat through.

Recipes Tried and True

Green Beans with Swiss Cheese

1 tablespoon butter
1 tablespoon flour
1/2 teaspoon pepper
1/4 cup milk
1/2 teaspoon grated onion
1/2 cup sour cream

2 (16-ounce) cans green beans,
   drained
1 1/2 cups grated Swiss cheese
1/3 cup cornflake crumbs
2 tablespoons melted butter

Heat oven to 400°. Melt 1 tablespoon butter in saucepan and blend in flour and pepper; cook, stirring until bubbling. Blend in milk. Remove from heat and stir in onion and sour cream. Combine sauce with green beans and cheese. Turn into buttered 1 1/2-quart casserole. Combine cornflakes with melted butter and spread on top. Bake 20 minutes. Yields 6–8 servings.

Ashton Area Cookbook

 One of the largest diamonds ever found in the United States, nearly 20 carats, was discovered near McCall.

Baked Beans

½ pound bacon, fried crisp and
   drained
1 pound ground beef, browned
   and drained
1 onion, chopped, sautéed
2 teaspoons liquid smoke
1 (16-ounce) can kidney beans
1 (16-ounce) can butter beans

1 (16-ounce) can lima beans
1 (16-ounce) can pork and beans
1 (16-ounce) can baked beans
   (Bush's Original)
1½ cups ketchup
1 cup brown sugar
Salt and pepper

Combine all ingredients and slow bake (300°) in Dutch oven 2 hours.
Refrigerate and cool overnight. Re-bake at least 1 hour before serving.

Ashton Area Cookbook

Chuck Wagon Bean Pot

*This savory "stew" featuring ham and beans borrows its robust seasonings from
the chuck wagon cooks of the old western cattle ranges. The secret is long, slow
cooking, and your electric slow-cooker is ideal for the job. Just follow the directions that come with your particular model. If you don't have one, slow-cook the
mixture on top of the stove in a heavy pot with lid.*

1 pound (any variety) dried beans
1 ham hock or shank
1 large onion, chopped
6 cups water
1 teaspoon salt

1 (7- to 10-ounce) can green chile
   salsa, or 1 (8-ounce) can tomato
   sauce, or 2 cups canned or
   stewed tomatoes

Rinse and sort beans. If using an electric slow-cooker, put in all ingredients, cover, set temperature at LOW, and forget for at least 10 hours.
If you have only ½ day, cook the mixture 5 or more hours on high.

For top-of-stove cooking, heat all ingredients to boiling with pot
uncovered. Turn down heat, cover, and simmer gently, adding enough
boiling water to keep beans well covered. Most varieties will be done
in 2–3 hours.

When beans are done, take out ham bone, cut meat off the bone, and
put meat back into pot. Serve hot with corn bread or muffins.

Idaho's Favorite Bean Recipes

Calico Beans

1 pound ground beef
1/2 package bacon, diced
1 onion, chopped
1 (16-ounce) can pork and beans,
   with liquid
1 (16-ounce) can lima beans,
   drained
1 (16-ounce) can kidney beans,
   with liquid

3/4 cup brown sugar
2 tablespoons white vinegar
1 tablespoon dry mustard
1/2 cup ketchup
1 teaspoon onion salt
1 teaspoon garlic powder
2 teaspoons beef bouillon

Brown ground beef, bacon, and onion in skillet. Mix together the beans and seasonings. Add meat mixture to bean mixture, and simmer for 1/2 hour on stove, or in a crockpot on LOW for 3 hours.

A Taste of Heaven

Cowboy Beans

Great with grilled hamburgers or hot dogs and fresh corn on the cob.

1 pound ground beef
1 (16-ounce) can baked beans
1 (16-ounce) can kidney beans
2 cups chopped onions
3/4 cup brown sugar

1 cup catsup
2 tablespoons dry mustard
1/4 teaspoon salt
2 teaspoons vinegar

Brown and drain meat. Mix all of the ingredients together in a crockpot. Cook on HIGH 1–2 hours or until thoroughly heated.

Down Home Country Cookin'

Idaho Buckaroo Beans

1 pound (2 cups) pink, red, or
  pinto beans, soaked overnight
  in 6 cups water
$^1/_2$ pound smoked ham, salt pork,
  or slab bacon, cut up
1 large onion, coarsely chopped
2 garlic cloves, sliced
1 small bay leaf
2 cups solid-pack or fresh-peeled
  tomatoes

$^1/_2$ cup chopped green pepper
2 teaspoons chili powder
2 tablespoons brown sugar
$^1/_2$ teaspoon dry mustard
$^1/_4$ teaspoon crushed oregano
  leaves
Salt (optional)

Drain beans and add fresh water to 2 inches above beans. Add meat, onion, garlic, and bay leaf. Heat to boiling and cover tightly. Cook over low heat for $1^1/_2$ hours or until beans are almost tender.

Add all remaining ingredients, except salt, and more water if necessary. Simmer, uncovered, for 2 hours, stirring once or twice. Taste and add salt, if necessary. There should be enough liquid left on the beans to resemble a medium-thick gravy.

If desired, the beans may be baked, covered, at 325° after the first step is completed. Makes 8–10 servings.

Note: Long, slow cooking helps to give a rich, full flavor. May be made ahead and refrigerated, then reheated, even on a barbecue grill.

Bound to Please

Jack Straw

1 cup flour
1/2 teaspoon salt
1 egg, beaten
1 cup milk
1 tablespoon oil
3 medium zucchini, or 12 ounces
  mushrooms, or 1 pound broccoli
  florets, or 1 eggplant

Oil for deep frying
Freshly grated Parmesan cheese
Salt to taste

Combine flour and salt. Mix together egg, milk, and oil and add to dry ingredients.

Slice zucchini lengthwise into several long fingers, similar to large french fries; slice large mushrooms or leave small mushrooms whole; peel eggplant and cut like zucchini. Dip vegetables into fritter batter and deep fry until golden. Sprinkle with cheese and salt. Serves 4.

Bound to Please

Heavenly Sour Cream Potatoes

2 cups mashed Idaho potatoes
1 1/2 cups creamed cottage
  cheese
1/2 cup sour cream
3/4 tablespoon grated onion

1 1/4 teaspoons salt
Pepper to taste
2 tablespoons butter, melted
1/4 cup chopped almonds

Mix potatoes and cottage cheese. Add sour cream, onion, salt, and pepper. Spoon into a buttered 1-quart casserole. Brush surface with melted butter. Bake at 350° for 30 minutes. Sprinkle with almonds. Place under broiler to brown lightly. Makes 6 servings.

Bound to Please

Never buy potatoes that are soft or have excessive cuts, cracks, bruises or discoloration and decay. If your potatoes have any green spots, pare them off before cooking because they could taste bitter.

Spuds and Onions au Gratin

Olive or vegetable oil
2–3 pounds russet spuds, sliced
   as thin as you can
2–3 tablespoons melted butter
   or margarine
Salt and pepper or seasoning to
   taste

2–3 medium yellow onions,
   sliced thin
1 ($10^3/4$-ounce) can cheese soup
$1/4$ cup milk
$1/2$ cup cracker or bread crumbs
   (seasoned, if you wish)
1 cup grated Cheddar cheese

Take a paper towel and wipe a 12-inch Dutch oven with a little olive or vegetable oil. Layer spuds in the Dutch oven and brush each layer with melted margarine and a little seasoning. Then put in a layer of onions and keep layering spuds brushed with butter till you've used all your spuds and onions. Thin the soup with a little milk and pour over the top. Sprinkle bread or cracker crumbs over and add any additional seasoning. Set the Dutch in the firepan with 4–6 briquets underneath and 16–18 on the top. Bake for 40–45 minutes. Remove the Dutch oven from the firepan and sprinkle the grated cheese over the top and let set for 5 minutes or so before serving. Serves 6–8.

Cee Dub's Dutch Oven and Other Camp Cookin'

Cabbage & Bacon Mashed Potatoes

4 slices thick-sliced bacon
2 pounds cabbage, shredded or
   diced

$1/2$ cup water
4 cups leftover mashed potatoes

Cook bacon until crisp and remove from Dutch oven or skillet. Fry cabbage in bacon grease for about 5 minutes. Add water and simmer until the liquid is reduced by half. Stir in leftover mashed potatoes and crumble bacon into the mixture. Bake for 15–20 minutes with 5 or 6 briquets underneath and 14–16 on top.

Cee Dub's Ethnic & Regional Dutch Oven Cookin'

Spuds Romanoff

8 medium russet potatoes
3 tablespoons butter or
  margarine
1/4 cup milk
1 (10 3/4-ounce) can cream of
  mushroom soup
1 bunch green onions, chopped

1 pint sour cream
1 pound sharp Cheddar cheese,
  grated
1 cup bread or cracker crumbs
Salt and pepper to taste
Paprika

Boil potatoes for about 20 minutes, then drain and cool. When cool, grate them and set aside in a large bowl. In a skillet, melt the butter, stir in the milk and soup, and mix well over low heat for a few minutes. Add all remaining ingredients, except paprika and bread crumbs to the grated potatoes; season to taste with salt and pepper then stir to mix.

Pour this into a 12-inch Dutch oven and bake with 6–8 briquets underneath and 16–18 on the lid for about 30 minutes. Lift the lid off, sprinkle bread crumbs over the top, and bake for another 15 minutes. Dust with paprika before serving.

Cee Dub's Ethnic & Regional Dutch Oven Cookin'

Ham and Potato Scallops

5 cups sliced potatoes
2 slices ham, chopped
1 (10 3/4-ounce) can cream of
  mushroom soup
1/4 cup milk

1/2 cup chopped onion
1/4 cup chopped green pepper
1/2 teaspoon salt
Dash pepper
Butter

Place potatoes in greased casserole dish. Combine chopped ham, soup, milk, onion, and green pepper; add seasonings. Pour mixture over potatoes; dot with butter. Cover. Bake at 350° for 1 hour. Remove from oven; uncover and bake 45 minutes longer or till potatoes are done.

Down Home Country Cookin'

Herb Potatoes

HERB BUTTER:
1/2 cup butter
1 teaspoon dried parsley
1/2 teaspoon dried basil

1/2 teaspoon garlic powder
1/4 teaspoon each: dried oregano, marjoram, thyme, rosemary

Place butter in a medium mixing bowl; allow to reach room temperature. Work butter with a fork or a wire whisk until softened. Add herbs and mix thoroughly. This mixture can be refrigerated and will keep up to 3 weeks, if tightly covered.

4 large potatoes
1/2 cup Herb Butter, room temperature

Salt and pepper to taste

Preheat oven to 375°. Thoroughly wash potatoes and cut into 1-inch cubes. Soften Herb Butter with wire whip or fork in a large bowl. Stir in potatoes until fully covered with butter mixture. Pour ingredients into baking dish/pan (scrape bowl with spatula to get all of butter mixture). Season with salt and pepper to taste. Cover and bake in preheated 375° oven for 30 minutes or until done. For browned potatoes, remove cover and bake another 15 minutes or until golden brown.

Note: To use Herb Butter as a spread, reduce herbs by half.

Elegant Cooking Made Simple

Navajo Potatoes

8 medium Idaho potatoes, firm-cooked and grated
1 1/2 cups grated Cheddar cheese
1 (10 3/4-ounce) can cream of chicken soup
1/2 cup chopped onion

1/2 teaspoon each salt and pepper
1 1/2 cups sour cream
1/4 cup butter, melted
1/2 cup crushed cornflakes or potato chips

Combine all ingredients except butter and cornflakes. Place in 9x13-inch pan; drizzle melted butter over top; sprinkle cornflakes last. Bake at 350° for 30 minutes.

Idaho Cook Book

Onion Roasted Potatoes

1 envelope onion soup mix
2 pounds all-purpose potatoes,
   cut into large chunks

$^1/_3$ cup olive or vegetable oil
Chopped parsley for garnish
   (optional)

Preheat oven to 450°. In large plastic bag, add soup mix, potatoes, and oil. Close bag and shake until potatoes are evenly coated. Empty potatoes into greased shallow baking or roasting pan. Discard bag. Bake, stirring occasionally, 40 minutes, or until potatoes are tender and golden brown. Garnish, if desired, with chopped parsley. Makes 8 servings.

Spragg Family Cookbook

Puffy Coated Onion Rings

2 large onions
   (Idaho-Eastern Oregon)
2 eggs, separated
$1^1/_4$ cups buttermilk

$1^1/_2$ tablespoons oil
$1^1/_4$ cups all-purpose flour
1 teaspoon salt
$1^1/_4$ teaspoons baking powder

Peel and slice onions $^1/_4$ inch thick. Separate into rings. Beat egg yolks. Add buttermilk, oil, and sifted dry ingredients. Beat egg whites until stiff. Fold into buttermilk mixture. Dip onion rings into batter. Fry, a few at a time, in deep fat (375°). Drain thoroughly on paper towels and sprinkle with salt. Keep in warm oven. Serves 4.

Note: May be frozen. When ready to serve, place frozen onion rings on baking sheet and heat at 450° for 5 minutes.

Onions Make the Meal Cookbook

 The city of Arco was the first in the world to receive all of its electricity from a nuclear power plant.

Microwave Creamed Onions

2 medium onions
(Idaho-Eastern Oregon)
2 tablespoons water
2 tablespoons flour
$\frac{1}{2}$ teaspoon salt

$\frac{1}{2}$ teaspoon dill weed
$\frac{1}{8}$ teaspoon ground white pepper
$\frac{1}{2}$ cup skimmed milk
$\frac{1}{2}$ cup chicken broth
2 tablespoons minced parsley

Peel and slice onions $\frac{1}{4}$ inch thick. Combine onions and water in a
$1\frac{1}{2}$-quart casserole. Microwave on HIGH, $3\frac{1}{2}$ minutes. Stir and
microwave $3\frac{1}{2}$ minutes more, or until onions are tender; drain off liquid. Combine remaining ingredients in a microwave bowl and mix
well. Microwave on HIGH for $1\frac{1}{2}$ minutes; stir and microwave $1\frac{1}{2}$
minutes more or until thickened. Pour sauce over onions, toss to coat,
and microwave on MEDIUM 2–3 minutes or until thoroughly heated.
Serves 4.

Onions Make the Meal Cookbook

Onion Harvest Medley

2 large onions
(Idaho-Eastern Oregon)
3 medium tomatoes, quartered
3 medium zucchini, cut in 1-inch
slices

$\frac{1}{4}$ cup chopped fresh basil, or
1 teaspoon dried basil
$\frac{1}{2}$ teaspoon salt
$\frac{1}{4}$ teaspoon pepper
3 tablespoons vegetable oil

Peel and cut onions into wedges. Arrange in microwave-proof baking
dish with tomatoes and zucchini. Sprinkle with seasonings. Drizzle
oil over vegetables. Cover with plastic wrap and microwave on HIGH
10–12 minutes, or until onions are tender, rotating dish $\frac{1}{4}$ turn every
4 minutes. Serves 6.

Onions Make the Meal Cookbook

One Pot Bachelor Cookout

Many a lonely cowpoke in a remote line camp thirty miles from town will appreciate this simple rugged feast. Next time the cow boss comes around, have him bring all the necessary fixin's.

10–12 Idaho spuds, peeled
1 pound thick-sliced bacon
3 onions (Walla Walla Sweets),
  chopped
Salt, pepper, and Tabasco to taste
2 tablespoons all-purpose
  seasoning
1 small clove garlic, minced

1 bay leaf
1 green pepper, chopped
1 red pepper, chopped
1 small yellow squash, sliced
4 carrots, sliced
1 zucchini, sliced
10 slices cheese

Cut potatoes into 1-inch chunks. In Dutch oven, fry bacon crisp, then crumble; add onions, and cook until onions are transparent. Add potatoes and seasonings. Place vegetables on top. Cook 30–40 minutes until done. Remove from heat; add cheese slices on top. Cover and let cheese melt over the mess.

Old-Fashioned Dutch Oven Cookbook

Lamb's Quarters with Basil

$^{1}/_{3}$ cup water
2 pounds lamb's quarters
3 green onions, chopped

$^{1}/_{2}$ cup chopped fresh basil
2 tablespoons butter

In large saucepan, add water to lamb's quarters and onions. Cover and steam for 10 minutes. Drain. Add basil and butter. Toss to mix. Serve at once.

The Rocky Mountain Wild Foods Cookbook

Pasta, Rice, Etc.

White water plunges over 212 feet at the spectacular horseshoe rim of Shoshone Falls on the Snake River—52 feet further than Niagara Falls. October through April are the best times to view the falls, located near Twin Falls, Idaho.

Basque Style Paella

4 whole chicken breasts, halved
Salt and freshly ground pepper
1/4 cup butter, melted
1/4 teaspoon ground coriander
  seed
1/3 cup cooking sherry
4 cloves garlic, minced
1 medium onion, chopped
1 1/2 cups long-grain white rice
1/3 cup Spanish olive oil
1 green pepper, cut in 1/2-inch
  strips

2 cups clam broth
1 cup chicken broth
1 pound ripe tomatoes, chopped
1/2 teaspoon salt
1 1/2 teaspoons sugar
1 pound medium-size shrimp,
  shelled and deveined
1 dozen clams
Dash cayenne pepper
3/4 cup pimento-stuffed green
  olives

Place chicken breasts, skin-side-up, in greased 9x13x2-inch baking pan. Season with salt and pepper. Brush with melted butter. Sprinkle with coriander, cover with foil, and bake at 350° for 40 minutes. Uncover, sprinkle with sherry, and bake 20 minutes longer, basting occasionally with pan drippings.

Cook garlic, onion, and rice in hot olive oil in large skillet until golden. Add green pepper, broths, tomatoes, salt, and sugar. Cover and simmer gently for 25 minutes. Stir occasionally.

Stir in chicken, shrimp, clams, cayenne, and olives. Cover and continue cooking 5 minutes, or until clams pop open and liquid is absorbed. Serves 6–8.

Basque Cooking and Lore

In the late 1800s, a large number of Basque immigrants came to Idaho from Spain to work mainly as sheepherders. Today, Boise, Idaho's capital, has the largest Basque community in the United States as well as the country's only Basque Museum.

Arroz Amarillo Con Pollo

2 cloves garlic, minced
1 large onion, chopped
1 large green pepper, chopped
1/4 cup olive oil
1 chicken, cut up
Paprika
2 cups chicken broth
1/2 (10-ounce) box frozen peas
1 pint tomatoes, fresh or canned
4 ounces diced pimiento
1/4 teaspoon saffron, crumbled (or few drops yellow food coloring)
2 chicken bouillon cubes (optional)
1 cup uncooked white rice

In a cast-iron chicken fryer, sauté garlic, onion, and green pepper in olive oil until soft. Do not brown. Remove from oil and set aside. Sprinkle the chicken generously with paprika. Brown chicken pieces in oil in pan. Remove chicken; set aside. Drain oil from pan.

Add broth, peas, tomatoes, pimiento, saffron, bouillon cubes, and rice to pan. Stir in onion mixture. Lay chicken pieces on top, skin-side-up. Bake, covered, at 325° for at least 1 1/2 hours without stirring. Check to see if rice (just under chicken pieces) is done and liquid is absorbed.

Quilter's Delight, Busy Day Recipes

Rainbow Rice

1 bag pre-measured rice for 4, prepared
2 tablespoons oil
1 (4-ounce) can sliced black olives
1 red pepper, sliced and diced
1 green pepper, sliced and diced
1 purple onion, sliced and diced
2 Roma tomatoes, sliced and diced
Seasoned rice vinegar
Olive oil

Prepare rice with oil. Rinse thoroughly in a strainer to prevent lumping, and cool. In a large bowl, place cooled rice. Fold in olives, red and green peppers, onion, and tomatoes. Dress with seasoned rice vinegar and olive oil.

Cee Dub's Dutch Oven and Other Camp Cookin'

Brown Rice and Lentils

Havarti cheese tops off this flavorful lentil and rice pilaf.

2 tablespoons butter, margarine, or vegetable oil
1 small onion, chopped
2 large cloves garlic, minced or pressed through a garlic press
¼ cup dry lentils, rinsed
¼ cup brown rice
1 teaspoon Italian seasoning

2 cups water
1 teaspoon salt
¼ teaspoon hot red pepper sauce, or more to taste
1 medium green bell pepper, seeded and coarsely chopped
¼ cup shredded Havarti cheese with herbs

Melt butter in a 2-quart saucepan over medium heat. Add onion and garlic and cook about 3 minutes, stirring until onion is tender. Stir in lentils and rice, and continue cooking, stirring constantly, for another 3–5 minutes. Stir in Italian seasoning.

Add water, salt, and pepper sauce and heat to boiling. Reduce heat, cover, and simmer about 50 minutes, adding water, if necessary, until rice is tender and liquid is absorbed. Stir in bell pepper and sprinkle top with cheese. Serves 4.

The Pea & Lentil Cookbook

Turkey and Brown Rice Casserole

3 cups cooked turkey or chicken, cut in large chunks
3½ cups cooked brown rice
1 cup chopped onion
1 cup sliced celery
1 cup chopped green pepper
3 tablespoons margarine, divided
1 (10¾-ounce) cream of mushroom soup
½ cup dry white wine or chicken broth
1 (4-ounce) can sliced mushrooms, undrained
1 teaspoon dried sage leaves, crumbled
¼ teaspoon dried thyme leaves
½ teaspoon salt
Dash pepper
1 (4-ounce) can pimientos, drained and chopped
1 cup herb-seasoned croutons

Combine turkey and rice in Dutch oven or a 2½-quart casserole. Set aside.

Sauté onion, celery, and green pepper in 2 tablespoons of the margarine for 8 minutes, stirring frequently, until tender-crisp. Stir in soup, wine or broth, mushrooms, sage, thyme, salt, pepper, and pimientos. Pour mushroom-vegetable mixture over turkey and rice in casserole or Dutch oven. Stir with large spoon to combine.

Heat remaining 1 tablespoon margarine until melted. Toss croutons in melted margarine. Spoon around edge of Dutch oven. Bake with coals on top and underneath Dutch oven for 35–40 minutes, or in 350° conventional oven for 40–45 minutes, until bubbly. Yields 8 servings.

The Outdoor Dutch Oven Cookbook

 Running 400 miles long, the Main Salmon River is the longest undammed river in the lower 48 states.

Rice with Ham and Shrimp

$^1/_2$ cup Spanish olive oil
$^1/_4$ pound chorizo, thinly sliced
2 medium onions, finely chopped
4 cloves garlic, minced
3 cups chicken broth
3 medium tomatoes, finely
chopped
2 medium green peppers, seeded
and cut into strips
3 tablespoons chopped Italian
parsley

2 teaspoons sugar
$^1/_2$ teaspoon salt
1 teaspoon ground cumin
$^1/_2$ teaspoon freshly ground
pepper
2 cups uncooked short-grain
white rice
1 pound medium shrimp, cleaned
$^1/_2$ pound lean ham, cut into
1$^1/_2$-inch cubes

Heat oil in Dutch oven until light haze forms. Add chorizo, onion, and garlic, and cook until chorizo is browned and onions are soft (approximately 5 minutes). Stir in remaining ingredients except rice, shrimp, and ham. Cook, covered, over medium heat until almost tender (approximately 12 minutes). Stir in rice, shrimp, and ham. Cook for 8–10 minutes, or until all liquid has been absorbed. Serve as an entrée with a hearty loaf of bread. Serves 6.

Basque Cooking and Lore

Becky's Jambalaya

RICE:

2 cups long-grain rice
1 tablespoon olive oil
4 cups water

$^1/_2$ teaspoon red pepper
$^3/_4$ teaspoon salt

Put all ingredients into appropriate pot and bring to boil. Cook 15 minutes. Fluff. Set aside to cool.

ROUX:

$^1/_2$ cup olive oil

6–8 tablespoons flour

In an iron skillet (the only way to get authenticity), heat olive oil on medium-low heat until vapors rise. Incorporate 6–8 tablespoons flour into oil with a wire whip. Reduce to low, stirring constantly until Roux becomes a nice brown and has a faint fragrance of popcorn. If you burn the roux, even a little, throw it out and start over. Set aside.

MAIN INGREDIENTS:

$^1/_2$ cup olive oil
2 medium onions, chopped
2 bunches green onions, chopped
$^1/_2$ cup chopped celery
$^1/_2$ small bell pepper, chopped
4 large garlic cloves, minced
2–3 cups chicken broth
2 cups meat of your choice
   (chicken, shrimp, coon, crab,
   etc., or a combo)

$1^1/_2$ pounds smoked sausage
$^1/_2$ teaspoon red pepper
$^1/_2$ teaspoon white pepper
$^1/_2$ teaspoon black pepper
$^3/_4$ teaspoon MSG (optional)
$^1/_2$ teaspoon paprika
$^1/_2$ teaspoon filé (optional)
1 tablespoon dry parsley
Salt to taste

In a large pot, heat olive oil. Toss in both types of onions, celery, bell pepper, and garlic. Cook until onions are clear. Pour in chicken broth. Add meats, except shrimp, crab, and any meats which only take a few minutes to cook. Add peppers, MSG, paprika, filé, parsley, and salt. Cook over medium heat for 30 minutes. Turn heat up a little and add Roux, stirring constantly until thickening begins. If too thick, add a little water.

Add all seafoods now and cook 10–15 minutes more. Now add cooled rice until no longer soupy. The moment the whole thing is hot again, turn it off. Excellent with good garlic bread and a tossed salad.

Note: Don't leave any shells on any seafood. Add more pepper if you like it hot!

Caldera Kitchens

Bohemian Stuffed Shells

2 (26-ounce) jars of spaghetti
  sauce
1½ teaspoons cinnamon
2 (10-ounce) packages frozen
  spinach
2 large cloves garlic, crushed
2 tablespoons oil
16 ounces firm tofu (optional)
½ teaspoon nutmeg
½ cup sunflower seeds
¼ cup grated ginger

1 cup raisins
2 teaspoons sugar
24 ounces cottage cheese
2 eggs, slightly beaten
1 cup chopped hazelnuts, toasted
2 (4-ounce) cans chopped black
  olives
16 ounces mozzarella cheese,
  shredded
½ cup Parmesan cheese
2 packages jumbo pasta shells

Heat spaghetti sauce and stir in cinnamon; set aside.

Cook spinach according to box instructions; squeeze out water. Sauté garlic in oil. Squeeze out the water from tofu; add tofu to garlic and cook for 10 minutes. Add spinach, nutmeg, and sunflower seeds; cook additional 5 minutes.

Mix remaining ingredients except pasta; add to spinach mixture. Pour ½ of sauce on bottom of 14-inch Dutch oven. Prepare pasta as directed on package; drain and put shells in bowl of cold water. Fill shells with spinach mixture and arrange a layer in the Dutch oven. Pour a layer of sauce over; add another layer of stuffed shells and remaining sauce. Bake at 350° for 30– 45 minutes. Serves 8–12.

Potatoes Are Not the Only Vegetable!

When blowing or drifting snow piles up on a roadway, it can take hours to clear the snow and reopen the road. Idaho uses snow fences to block blowing snow from the road, reducing maintenance cost substantially in comparison to snow plowing.

Fettuccine with Gorgonzola and Pecans

1 cup heavy cream
3 ounces Gorgonzola (or other
  creamy blue cheese), crumbled
1/4 cup grated mozzarella cheese
1/2 cup grated Parmesan cheese,
  divided

5 tablespoons butter
1/2 cup chopped pecans
Salt and black pepper to taste
1 pound fettuccine

Bring cream to boil and cook until reduced by half. Whisk in Gorgonzola, and simmer gently until melted. Working over lowest heat, whisk in mozzarella, half the Parmesan, butter, pecans, and seasoning. Remove from heat. Cook pasta, drain, and toss with sauce. Sprinkle rest of Parmesan on top. Serves 4.

Recipes Tried and True

Pasta Primavera

1 sweet onion, thinly sliced
6 garlic cloves, minced, or
  to taste
1 tablespoon olive oil
1/4 cup pine nuts
2 cups sliced mushrooms
8 basil leaves, chopped

1/4 cup white wine or
  vegetable broth
4 Roma tomatoes, cut in
  bite-size wedges
Salt and pepper to taste
1 pound fresh linguine
1/2 cup Parmesan

Sauté garlic and onions in olive oil until onions become slightly translucent. Toast pine nuts until golden brown. Set aside. Add mushrooms, basil, and wine to garlic-onion mixture. Sauté until mushrooms are tender.

Gently stir in tomatoes and toasted pine nuts. Season with salt and pepper. Meanwhile, add separate strands of linguine to lightly salted boiling water and cook 7–10 minutes, or until al dente. Do not overcook. Drain.

Add linguine to sauté pan and gently toss with vegetables. Toss with Parmesan. Serve immediately. Serves 4.

Northern Lites: Contemporary Cooking with a Twist

Angel Hair Florentine

1 egg, beaten
1 cup sour cream
2 cups heavy cream
4 tablespoons Parmesan cheese
1/2 medium-large onion, minced
1/2 teaspoon salt
1/2 teaspoon coarsely ground
  black pepper

1 (10-ounce) package chopped
  spinach, thawed and drained
1 1/2 cups shredded Monterey Jack
  cheese
1 1/2 cups shredded sharp Cheddar
  cheese
4 ounces angel hair pasta, cooked,
  drained

Combine egg, sour cream, heavy cream, Parmesan, onion, salt and pepper. Add spinach and blend well. Add Jack and Cheddar and mix well. Fold in pasta. Put in oven-proof casserole, sprinkle with more Parmesan, cover with tin foil, and bake at 350° for 45 minutes to 1 hour, or until set. Remove tin foil last 10 minutes of cooking.

Note: A very full baking dish will usually take 1 1/2 hours to bake.

The Hearty Gourmet

Baked Spaghetti

1 cup chopped onion
1 cup chopped green pepper
1 tablespoon margarine
1 (28-ounce) can tomatoes with
  liquid
1 (4-ounce) can mushrooms,
  drained
1 (2 1/3-ounce) can sliced ripe
  olives, drained
2 teaspoons dried oregano

1 pound ground beef, cooked
  and drained
1 (8-ounce) package spaghetti,
  cooked
2 cups (8 ounces) shredded
  Cheddar cheese
1 (10 3/4-ounce) can cream of
  mushroom soup
1/4 cup water
1/4 cup grated Parmesan cheese

In large skillet, sauté onion and green pepper in margarine until tender. Add tomatoes, mushrooms, olives, and oregano. Add ground beef. Simmer, uncovered, 10 minutes. Place half the spaghetti in greased 9x13-inch pan. Top with half of the vegetable mixture. Sprinkle with 1 cup Cheddar cheese. Repeat layers. Mix the soup and water until smooth. Pour over casserole; sprinkle with Parmesan cheese. Bake, uncovered, at 350° for 30–35 minutes or until heated through.

Cookin' at Its Best

Creamy Garden Spaghetti

$^1/_2$ pound fresh broccoli, broken into florets
$1^1/_2$ cups sliced zucchini
$1^1/_2$ cups sliced fresh mushrooms
1 large carrot, sliced
1 tablespoon olive or vegetable oil
8 ounces uncooked spaghetti
$^1/_4$ cup chopped onion
3 garlic cloves, minced
2 tablespoons butter or margarine

3 tablespoons flour
2 teaspoons chicken bouillon granules
$^1/_2$ teaspoon dried thyme
2 cups milk
$^1/_4$ cup white wine, or $^1/_4$ cup more milk
$^1/_2$ cup shredded Swiss cheese
$^1/_2$ cup shredded mozzarella cheese

In a large skillet, sauté the broccoli, zucchini, mushrooms, and carrot in oil until crisp-tender. Remove from heat and set aside.

Cook spaghetti according to package directions. In another saucepan, sauté onion and garlic in butter until tender. Stir in the flour, bouillon and thyme until blended. Gradually add the milk and wine. Bring to a boil; cook and stir for 2 minutes or until thickened.

Reduce heat to low; stir in cheeses until melted. Do not boil. Add vegetables; heat through. Drain spaghetti; toss with vegetable mixture. Serves 4.

Another Cookbook

Sundance Ziti

1 (16-ounce) package ziti (or rigatoni) noodles
4 quarts water
4 tablespoons olive oil, divided
1 onion, diced
1/2 green pepper, diced
10 mushrooms, quartered
4 cloves garlic, crushed
Oregano, basil, and pepper to taste
1 yellow squash, quartered and sliced
2 (15-ounce) cans tomato sauce
1/2 block tofu, drained and squeezed
1 (8-ounce) carton ricotta
1 (8-ounce) package grated mozzarella, divided
4 ounces grated Cheddar
1 tomato, sliced

Boil noodles in water and 1 tablespoon olive oil until tender. Drain. In pan, sauté onion, green pepper, mushrooms, and garlic in 3 tablespoons olive oil. Spice to taste with oregano, basil, and pepper. Sauté until onions are tender. Add yellow squash and tomato sauce. Reduce heat and simmer.

In a large bowl, combine tofu, ricotta, and 1/2 the mozzarella. Add sauce mixture and noodles. Pour into 12-inch Dutch oven and sprinkle with remaining mozzarella and Cheddar. Top with tomato slices and sprinkle with additional oregano and basil. Bake in 350° oven for 45 minutes to 1 hour.

Bacon is not a Vegetable

Country Pasta with Mozzarella

8 ounces uncooked rigatoni
8 slices bacon, cut into 1-inch
  pieces
2 cups broccoli florets
1/2 teaspoon minced fresh garlic

2 cups (8 ounces) shredded
  mozzarella cheese
1/4 cup grated Parmesan cheese
Pinch cayenne pepper
1/4 cup chopped fresh parsley

Cook rigatoni according to package directions; drain. Meanwhile, in 10-inch skillet, cook bacon over medium-high heat, stirring occasionally, until bacon is browned (6–8 minutes). Reduce heat to medium. Add broccoli and garlic. Cook, stirring occasionally, until broccoli is crisply tender (4–5 minutes). Add rigatoni and remaining ingredients except parsley. Continue cooking, stirring occasionally, until cheese is melted (3–5 minutes). Sprinkle with parsley.

Cooking with Cops, Too

Spinach-Black Bean Lasagna

2 large eggs, lightly beaten
1 (15-ounce) container ricotta
  cheese
1 (10-ounce) package frozen
  chopped spinach, thawed and
  drained
1/4 cup chopped fresh cilantro
1/2 teaspoon salt

4 cups shredded Monterey Jack
  cheese with peppers, divided
2 (16-ounce) cans black beans,
  rinsed and drained
1 (26-ounce) jar pasta sauce
1/2 teaspoon ground cumin
9 precooked lasagna noodles

Stir together eggs, ricotta cheese, spinach, cilantro, and salt. Add 1 cup Monterey Jack cheese; set aside. Mash beans with a potato masher or fork in a large bowl; stir in pasta sauce and cumin. Spread 1/3 of bean mixture on bottom of a lightly greased 9x13-inch baking dish. Layer with 3 noodles, half of the spinach mixture and 1 cup Monterey Jack cheese; repeat layers. Spread with 1/3 bean mixture; top with remaining 3 noodles and remaining bean mixture. Bake, uncovered, at 350° for 1 hour; uncover and top with remaining cheese. Bake 5 more minutes, or until cheese melts.

The Miracle Cookbook

Some-Like-It-Hot
Mexican Chukar Lasagna

This recipe was invented during a rigorous chukar hunt near Brownlee Reservoir.

1 (14-ounce) can whole-kernel corn

4 medium fresh tomatoes, sliced or diced

3–4 jalapeño peppers, or 3–4 fresh serrano peppers, to taste

3 cloves garlic, minced

1 (15-ounce) can sliced ripe olives

1 (19-ounce) can hot enchilada sauce (Las Palmas)

1 pound shredded Monterey Jack cheese, divided

1 pound shredded Cheddar cheese, divided

2 chukars, diced

In 12-inch Dutch oven, layer all of the ingredients until 2 inches from the top. Sprinkle a light layer of cheese on top. Use 6 briquets on the bottom and 10 on top and cook for 1 hour. Add 5 or 6 briquets on top the last 10–15 minutes to weld.

More Cee Dub's Dutch Oven and Other Camp Cookin'

Meats

Southern Idaho near Bruneau is home to a unique desert formed in the middle of a natural basin. The Bruneau dunes contain the largest single sand dune in North America. The two most prominent dunes cover about 600 acres.

PHOTO COURTESY OF IDAHO DEPARTMENT OF COMMERCE

Silver Plated Pot Roast

1 (4-pound) roast
Salt and pepper
3 teaspoons flour
3 teaspoons brown sugar
1 teaspoon salt
1 teaspoon vinegar
$^1/_2$ teaspoon mustard

$^3/_4$ cup catsup
1$^1/_2$ teaspoons Worcestershire
  sauce
2 stalks celery, sliced
2 carrots, sliced
1 onion, sliced

Season meat with salt and pepper; brown in small amount of oil. Line a baking pan with foil to wrap meat in. Mix remaining ingredients together, except vegetables, and place half on foil. Put meat on top of sauce; place vegetables on and around meat. Top with remaining sauce and seal foil. Place a little water in bottom of pan. Bake at 250° for 8–12 hours (depending on size of meat).

Be Our Guest

Spicy Brisket of Beef

1 envelope onion soup mix
3 pounds lean brisket of beef
2 tablespoons brown sugar
1 teaspoon cinnamon
1 teaspoon pepper
$^3/_4$ teaspoon ground ginger
1 tablespoon grated lemon rind
$^1/_4$ cup honey

2 tablespoons orange marmalade
1 tablespoon fresh lemon juice
1 tablespoon brandy
$^1/_2$ teaspoon Worcestershire sauce
1 (12-ounce) can beer
1 (8-ounce) package dried apricots
1 cup pitted prunes
7 medium-size baking potatoes

Place heavy-duty foil (18x26-inches) in the center of a large roasting pan. Sprinkle $^1/_2$ package onion soup in bottom, place brisket in pan, and sprinkle remaining onion mix over meat. Close and seal foil around the brisket and bake at 350° for 3 hours.

Combine brown sugar, cinnamon, pepper, ginger, lemon rind, honey, marmalade, lemon juice, brandy, Worcestershire sauce, and beer in a large bowl. Add apricots and prunes; cover with foil and reserve.

Remove meat from oven. Carefully open and turn back foil. Pour apricot and prune mixture over meat and reseal. Return meat to oven; place potatoes on rack (to serve alongside). Bake another hour or until meat is tender and potatoes are soft. Serves 8.

Matt Braun's Western Cooking

Beef Tenderloin en Croûte

1 (3- to 4-pound) beef tenderloin
1 package frozen ready-to-bake
  pastry sheets
1/2 pound mushrooms, finely
  chopped
2 tablespoons butter
1 (8-ounce) carton cream cheese
  with garlic and herbs

1/4 cup seasoned bread crumbs
2 tablespoons Madeira wine
1 tablespoon fresh chives
1/4 teaspoon salt
1 egg, beaten
1 tablespoon cold water

Heat oven to 425°. Tie meat with string at 1-inch intervals, if necessary. Place meat on rack in baking dish. Roast tenderloin 45–50 minutes or until meat reaches 135°. Remove from oven; cool in refrigerator for 30 minutes. Remove string.

Thaw pastry sheets according to directions. In a large skillet, cook and stir mushrooms in butter for 10 minutes or until liquid evaporates. Add cream cheese, bread crumbs, wine, chives, and salt. Mix well and let cool.

On lightly floured surface, overlap pastry sheets 1/2 inch to form a 12x14-inch rectangle; press edges firmly together. Trim length of pastry 2 1/2 inches longer than the tenderloin. Spread mushroom mixture over top and sides of tenderloin. Place in center of pastry sheet. Fold pastry over meat; press edges together to seal. Decorate with trimmings, if desired. Brush pastry with egg mixed with water; place meat in greased jellyroll pan. Bake 20–25 minutes or until pastry is golden brown. Let stand 10 minutes before slicing. Serves 8–10.

The Miracle Cookbook

Famous Idaho actresses: Born Julia Jean Mildred Frances Turner in Wallace, Lana Turner changed her name when she became a movie star. Marjorie Reynolds was born Marjorie Goodspeed in Buhl.

Tenderloin with Shiitake Sauce

1 tablespoon cracked black
  pepper
4 (6-ounce) beef tenderloins
2 cups fresh shiitake mushrooms,
  washed and sliced
1 tablespoon flour

½ cup nonfat beef broth
½ cup red wine
1 tablespoon Worcestershire sauce
½ teaspoon salt
6 fresh parsley sprigs for garnish

Press cracked pepper into both sides of tenderloins. Set aside. Cook mushrooms in nonstick pan until soft. Stir flour into mushrooms until all slices are coated. Add broth, red wine, Worcestershire sauce, and salt. Stir until thickened. Heat nonstick pan to medium high. Add tenderloins; sear quickly on each side. Lower heat and add mushroom sauce. Cook over low heat until tenderloins are cooked as desired. Remove tenderloins to warm plates and top with sauce. Garnish with parsley. Serves 4.

Note: If you like your meat cooked rare, the internal temperature would be 130°, medium rare, 135°–140°, medium, 145°–150°, and well-done, 160°. Or test doneness by making small slit in middle of steak and twisting knife to give a look at inside. Tenderloin will be medium rare if center is pink.

Northern Lites: Contemporary Cooking with a Twist

Harriet's Company Beef Bourguignonne

This has to be the easiest party dish I have ever served!

10 pounds chuck steak, cut into
  1-inch cubes
2 (16-ounce) jars pearl onions
2 (10¾-ounce) cans onion soup
2 (10¾-ounce) cans cream of
  tomato soup
2 (10¾-ounce) cans beef bouillon
3 cloves garlic, minced
4 cups Burgundy wine
4 (3-ounce) cans whole
  mushrooms, drained
¼–½ cup water
¼ cup cognac
Sour cream

Preheat oven to 325°. Put all ingredients, except cognac and sour cream, in a large covered Dutch oven, and cook for 5 hours. The last 15 minutes, add the cognac and continue to simmer. Serve with a dollop of sour cream on top of each serving. Serves 15.

Ketchum Cooks

Pepper Steaks

½ pound flank steak per person
1 onion
1 medium green pepper
1 tablespoon shortening or
  bacon fat
Salt and pepper to taste

Cut flank steak against the grain in about ¼-inch-thick slices. Peel and slice onion. Quarter green pepper, remove seeds, and cut into ½-inch strips. Melt shortening or bacon fat in Dutch oven. Fry onion until brown. Add meat slices and brown. Put in pepper slices and cover oven with lid. Heap coals on top of lid. Cook until meat is tender. Season to taste.

Old-Fashioned Dutch Oven Cookbook

Scrumptious Flank Steak

Need to start this two or three days ahead.

1/4 cup soy sauce
1 1/2 tablespoons garlic powder
1 1/2 tablespoons powdered
  ginger

1 small onion, chopped
2 tablespoons honey
3/4 cup oil
2 pounds flank steak

Combine soy sauce, garlic powder, ginger, onion, honey, and oil, and pour over flank steak in a large zip-lock bag. Marinate in refrigerator for 1–3 days. Turn daily.

Bring the steak to room temperature and barbecue 5–7 minutes per side. Slice thinly on the diagonal. Serve with Sauce Béarnaise and/or a creamy horseradish sauce.

SAUCE BÉARNAISE:

1/2 cup dry white wine
1/4 cup white vinegar
2 shallots, chopped
4 peppercorns, crushed
3 egg yolks

3/4 cup butter (1 1/2 sticks),
  divided
1/2 teaspoon salt
1/2 teaspoon dried tarragon leaves
1/2 teaspoon finely chopped parsley

In small, heavy saucepan, combine wine, vinegar, shallots, and peppercorns. Cook over brisk flame until liquid is reduced to approximately 2 tablespoons. In top of double boiler, combine egg yolks, 1 tablespoon butter, salt, and tarragon. Strain liquid from saucepan through a fine sieve into top of double boiler. Mix well. Place top over hot (but not boiling) water, and cook, whipping constantly, until creamy. Gradually add remaining butter, cut into small pieces, whipping constantly until smooth and well blended. Add parsley. Serve warm.

Note: Béarnaise cannot be served hot, because heating would cause it to curdle. It should be the consistency of thick mayonnaise. It should be whisked briskly all the time. The pan should not be heated to boiling point; the butter should be added in small pieces and thoroughly blended each time before adding another piece.

Recipes Stolen from the River of No Return

Chicken-Fried Steak

A western mainstay that shows hints of southern cookery. Great numbers of Southerners homesteaded land or established ranches throughout Texas and Oklahoma. Their method of cooking round steak spread to every corner of the West.

2 pounds top round steak
Salt and pepper
2 cups flour

Shortening or cooking oil
2 tablespoons water

Slice steak $1/3$ inch thick and cut into serving pieces. Pound pieces on both sides with a meat hammer until about $1/4$ inch thick. Salt and pepper pieces and thoroughly dredge both sides in flour. (A modern variation is to first dip the steak slices in well-beaten egg and then dredge in flour.)

Heat $1/4$ inch of shortening or cooking oil in a black skillet. Shortening is hot enough when a pinch of flour will sizzle when dropped into the skillet. Place steak in skillet and allow to slowly brown; do not turn until flour has browned to the point where it won't stick to skillet. Then turn the pieces and brown on other side. Cover skillet with tight-fitting lid, turn heat to low, and cook 10 minutes. Add 2 tablespoons water, cover with lid, and cook another 10 minutes. Remove to serving plate and place in low-heat oven to keep warm. Serves 4–6.

True chicken-fried steak must always be served with Cream Gravy. At the table, generously ladle gravy over homemade biscuits and even certain vegetables, such as green beans. Try it and see how you like it!

CREAM GRAVY:
3 tablespoons pan drippings
2 tablespoons flour
2 cups milk

Salt
Freshly ground pepper

Scrape up brown bits in skillet and heat the pan drippings. Stir in flour and blend thoroughly, cooking over low heat until lightly browned. Slowly add milk, stirring constantly until smooth. Add salt and pepper to taste, and cook 5–7 minutes, depending on desired thickness.

Matt Braun's Western Cooking

Beef Roll-Ups

BEEF FILLING:

2 pounds ground beef
$3/4$ cup chopped onion
$1/2$ cup finely diced celery
$1/2$ teaspoon salt
$1/4$ teaspoon pepper
1 (15-ounce) can tomato sauce,
  divided

Cook ground beef, onion, and celery in a frying pan until ground beef is brown and celery and onion are lightly cooked. Add salt, pepper, and $1/2$ cups scant tomato sauce (reserve $1/2$ cup for Dough). Cook slowly until thick. Cool.

DOUGH:

3 cups flour
4 teaspoons baking powder
1 teaspoon salt
$1/4$ teaspoon marjoram
$1/8$ teaspoon sage
6 tablespoons shortening
$1/2$ cup reserved tomato sauce
$1/2$ cup water

Sift together flour, baking powder, salt, and spices. Cut shortening into mixture until it resembles coarse cornmeal. Combine tomato sauce and water. Add to flour mixture and mix until moist. Turn onto a lightly floured surface and knead 3 or 4 times. Roll into a 9x13-inch rectangle. Spread meat mixture on Dough and roll like a jellyroll. Bake at 375° for 30–35 minutes.

SAUCE:

1 ($10^3/4$-ounce) can cream of
  mushroom soup
$1/3$ cup milk
$1/2$ cup shredded Cheddar cheese

Combine soup, milk, and cheese. Cook slowly, stirring occasionally, until cheese melts. Pour over slices of beef roll-ups. Makes 8 servings.

Down Home Country Cookin'

Stuffed Cabbage Rolls

1 egg, beaten
1/2 cup milk
1/4 cup finely chopped onion
1 teaspoon Worcestershire sauce
3/4 teaspoon salt
Dash of pepper
1 pound ground beef, or 1/2 beef
  and 1/2 pork, cooked

3/4 cup cooked rice
6 large or 12 medium cabbage
  leaves
1 (10 3/4-ounce) can condensed
  tomato soup
1 tablespoon brown sugar
1 tablespoon lemon juice

In mixing bowl, combine egg, milk, onion, Worcestershire sauce, salt, and pepper. Mix well. Add cooked meat and cooked rice. Mix thoroughly. Remove center vein of cabbage leaves, keeping each leaf in one piece. Immerse each leaf in boiling water until limp (3 minutes). Drain. Put cabbage leaf on waxed paper. Place 1/4–1/2 cup mixture on each cabbage leaf. Make sure you fold in sides of each leaf, then roll. Arrange each roll in a 7 1/2x12x2-inch baking pan or dish.

Stir together tomato soup, brown sugar, and lemon juice. Pour sauce over cabbage rolls. Bake, uncovered, at 350° for 1 1/4 hours, basting once or twice with sauce. Makes 6–8 servings.

Generations "Coming Home"

The City of Rocks in Southern Idaho is an eerie, granite landscape where rock spires reach six stories high. Some of the oldest rocks in the nation can be found in this area. Geologists say the Green River Complex found in the City of Rocks is some 2.5 billion years old. Once buried under the Earth's surface, the rocks were eventually exposed. Once exposed, wind, water and the elements began eroding the rock—chipping, cracking and molding the rock into an eerie landscape.

Beef Pot Pie

PASTRY CRUST:

3½ cups flour
1 teaspoon salt
1 tablespoon dried cilantro
1 teaspoon garlic powder

½ cup shortening
¼ cup butter or margarine
¼ cup ice water

Sift dry ingredients together. Cut in shortening and butter with fork or pastry cutter until crumbly. Add water 1 tablespoon at a time until dough forms a firm ball. Chill in refrigerator for 20–30 minutes.

1 pound beef stew meat
2 large potatoes, peeled and
  diced
½ (8-ounce) package baby
  carrots, sliced

1 (8-ounce) package frozen peas
1 small onion, diced
2 (10¾-ounce) cans cream of
  mushroom soup
½ cup beef broth

Brown stew meat in preheated oiled skillet over medium heat. Stir in vegetables and cook for 2 minutes, stirring constantly. Set aside to cool.

Meantime, divide Pastry Crust in ½; cover and refrigerate ½, then roll out other ½ to fit a 9x13-inch baking pan or dish. Place 1 portion of rolled dough in baking dish. Spread mixture of meat and all vegetables inside. Thoroughly mix soup and broth and pour over meat and vegetables.

Roll out second portion of dough to ¼-inch thickness; cut into 1-inch strips. Lay strips diagonally, 2 inches apart, over baking dish. Lay remaining strips on opposite diagonal; cut excess dough from edges and secure ends of strips to bottom dough. Bake in 400° oven for 15 minutes; reduce heat and continue baking for 45 minutes or until filling is bubbly and crust is golden brown.

Elegant Cooking Made Simple

Beef Patties with Noodles and Gravy

¹/₄ cup ketchup
3 tablespoons milk
1 cup soft bread crumbs
1¹/₂ tablespoons chopped onion
Salt and pepper
¹/₂ pound ground beef

2 tablespoons fat
1 (10-ounce) can beef gravy
1 (8-ounce) package medium
 noodles
2 tablespoons parsley

Combine ketchup, milk, and bread crumbs. Add onion, salt, pepper, and beef; mix well. Shape into 4 (¹/₂-inch-thick) patties. Heat fat in skillet, add patties, and cook over medium heat about 10 minutes, turning once. Pour gravy over patties; heat to boiling. Cook noodles as directed on package; drain, then arrange on hot platter with patties and gravy. Sprinkle parsley over noodles. Serves 4.

Mackay Heritage Cookbook

Beef Taquitos

3/4 pound ground chuck
1/4 cup minced onion
1/4 teaspoon minced garlic
1/2 cup tomato sauce
1 1/2 teaspoons cumin
1/2 cup (canned) mild green
 chiles, chopped

12 corn tortillas
Oil
Salsa
Sour cream
Guacamole

Brown beef and drain. Add onion and garlic; cook until soft. Add tomato sauce, cumin, and chiles. Simmer for 5 minutes. Set aside.

Briefly heat each tortilla in a pan with a little oil until soft enough to roll. Fill each tortilla with some of the meat mixture. Roll tightly (into the shape of a medium-size cigar). Set aside. Heat 1/3 inch of oil. Quickly brown each taquito, about 1 minute. Serve warm with sides of salsa, sour cream, and guacamole. Makes about 12.

Cookin' in Paradise

Tamale Pie

1 medium onion, chopped
1 clove garlic, minced
2 tablespoons peanut oil
1 1/2 pounds ground beef
1 1/2 cups canned tomatoes
2 teaspoons salt

1/4 teaspoon pepper
1 teaspoon ground cumin
4 teaspoons chili powder
3 cups cornmeal mush (per
 package directions)
Shredded cheese

Sauté onion and garlic in hot oil until browned. Add ground beef and cook until brown. Add tomatoes, salt, pepper, and spices; simmer on low heat for 10 minutes. Remove and set aside.

Follow package directions and mix 3 cups cornmeal mush. Line bottom and sides of casserole dish with cornmeal mixture, reserving about 1/3. Pour cooked meat filling into casserole. Spread remainder of cornmeal mixture over top of pie. Preheat oven and bake for 30 minutes at 425°. Sprinkle with shredded cheese and serve hot. Serves 6–8.

Matt Braun's Western Cooking

Marvelous Meat Loaf

1½ pounds ground beef
1 egg, beaten
¼ cup tomato sauce
¾ cup dry bread crumbs

½ onion, chopped
½ cup ketchup
½ cup brown sugar

In large bowl, combine all ingredients, except ketchup and brown sugar. Mix well. Press into loaf pan. Mix ketchup and brown sugar; spread evenly over meat mixture. Bake at 350° for 45–60 minutes.

Cookin' at Its Best

Swedish Meat Balls with Red Wine Sauce

1 cup fine dry bread crumbs
1 teaspoon cornstarch
1 teaspoon salt
¼ teaspoon pepper
Dash of allspice or mace
1 egg, beaten
1 cup rich milk or cream
1 pound twice-ground beef

1 small onion, minced
Fat or oil
3 tablespoons flour
2 cups water
⅔ cup burgundy or any red
  wine
Salt and pepper

Add bread crumbs, cornstarch, salt, pepper, allspice or mace, beaten egg, and milk to the ground beef. Sauté onion lightly in fat or oil. Mix with ground meat mixture. Blend ingredients thoroughly. Shape into tiny balls—40 to 42 in all. Brown lightly in a little oil or fat. Remove meat balls from pan.

Make gravy by slowly blending the flour into the fat in pan, and then slowly adding water and wine. Add salt and pepper to gravy, to taste. Return meat balls to pan; simmer 20 minutes.

Sharing Our Best

Meatballs in Dill Cream Sauce

8 ounces ground beef
8 ounces ground pork
1 small onion, chopped
$1/2$ teaspoon salt
$1/2$ teaspoon pepper
$1/4$ teaspoon thyme
$1/4$ teaspoon marjoram
$1/4$ teaspoon nutmeg
$1^1/2$ cups fresh bread crumbs

$1/2$ cup water
2 tablespoons butter
2 tablespoons flour
$1^1/2$ cups beef broth
2 tablespoons fresh dill, or
   1 teaspoon dried dill
$1/2$ cup half-and-half cream
Cooked noodles or rice

Combine beef, pork, onion, seasonings, crumbs, and water. Shape into balls $1^1/4$ inch in diameter. Bake at 400° for 20 minutes.

Melt butter in skillet; blend in flour. Cook, stirring constantly, for 2–3 minutes. Add broth, stirring until thickened. Stir in dill and meatballs. Reduce heat to low and simmer 15 minutes. Pour in cream and continue stirring until thick and smooth, about 15 minutes. Serve over noodles or rice.

Centennial Cookbook

Porcupine Meatballs

12 cups water
2 ($10^3/4$-ounce) cans tomato soup
1 pound sausage
2 pounds ground beef

1 cup rice
Salt and pepper to taste
Red cayenne pepper to taste

Bring water and tomato soup to boil in large Dutch oven. Mix sausage, ground beef, and rice in a large mixing bowl. Season to taste with salt, pepper, and cayenne. Roll into 1-inch balls. Add balls to water/soup mixture (may divide into 2 pots) and let cook for approximately 3–4 hours. Mixture should begin to thicken. Yields 24 servings.

Cooking for a Crowd

Liver and Onions

½ pound bacon	1 pound baby beef liver
1 pound sliced onions	1 cup flour

Preheat oven to lowest temperature. Fry bacon and drain on paper towels. Place on oven-proof plate in warm oven to maintain temperature. Pour bacon grease from skillet and set aside; return 2 tablespoons to skillet, and return skillet to medium-high heat. Place onions in skillet; fry until golden brown, stirring occasionally and adding bacon grease 1 tablespoon at a time, if needed. Place onions on heat-proof platter and set in oven to keep warm.

Return remaining bacon grease to skillet and heat to medium high. Dredge liver in flour and place in skillet; watch carefully. As soon as liquid seeps through top of meat, turn over and cook 2 more minutes. To serve, arrange liver over onions and bacon on top of liver. Discard any remaining flour, or use for gravy for this recipe only.

GRAVY:

1½ cups beef broth	Remaining flour

Have beef broth ready and sitting close at hand. Sprinkle remaining flour into hot skillet, stirring constantly with long-handled meat fork. As soon as flour begins to turn brown, add broth. (Do this very carefully, as steam will rise, and can burn you. This is the reason for using a long-handled fork.) Bring to a boil for 1 minute, then reduce heat and simmer for 1 minute longer.

Elegant Cooking Made Simple

 Bones and artifacts carbon-dated to be 14,500 years old were found during a 1959 excavation of Wilson Butte Cave, near Twin Falls. These are among the oldest indisputably dated artifacts in the New World.

Czech Goulash

2 pounds beef	2 tablespoons minced garlic
2 pounds pork	1 1/2 teaspoons paprika
2 tablespoons fat	4 bay leaves
1 teaspoon salt, or to taste	1 quart canned tomatoes (save
1/2 cup chopped onions	juice)
1/2 cup chopped carrots	2 cups liquid—water and/or
2 tablespoons celery flakes	tomato juice
1 1/2 teaspoons caraway seeds	1 tablespoon vinegar
1 teaspoon pepper	4 tablespoons flour

Cut meat into 1-inch cubes; brown well in fat, using a deep 12-inch Dutch oven. Add all other ingredients except tomatoes, liquid, vinegar, and flour. Cook until meat is tender, adding a little water, if necessary. A pressure cooker can also be used.

Measure and reserve 1/2 cup tomato juice; use remaining juice to make 2 cups liquid. Add tomatoes, plus 2 cups of liquid. Make a paste of the reserved tomato juice, vinegar, and flour. Add to above mixture. Cover and cook until thick, stirring occasionally, for 1 1/2 hours. Use 8–10 briquets under the oven and 18–20 briquets on the lid. Serve hot with potato dumplings or mashed potatoes.

Cee Dub's Ethnic & Regional Dutch Oven Cookin'

Kurt's Killer Pork Ribs

1 large package of pork ribs	3/4 (1-pound) package brown
1 (18-ounce) bottle barbecue sauce	sugar
(Bull's Eye)	

Place ribs in 14-inch Dutch oven, taking care not to stack ribs. Cook for 1 1/2 hours in 350° oven, covered, or until the ribs are close to being done. While the ribs are cooking, pour the whole bottle of sauce in a bowl. Add 3/4 package brown sugar to the sauce. Drain juice from ribs and pour sauce over the ribs. Continue to simmer for 1/2 hour, uncovered, so the ribs can absorb the sauce.

Hey Ma! Come Quick! The Hog's in the Garden Again!!

146

Short Ribs with Dumplings

3–4 pounds elk, moose, or beef
  short ribs (cut boneless plate
  or brisket in 2-inch chunks)
Salt, pepper, and/or any other
  seasoning you wish
Olive oil
3–4 cloves garlic, sliced thin
2–3 onions, cut in wedges,
  divided

4–5 bay leaves
2–3 cups water, beef stock, or
  beer
6–8 carrots, scrubbed and cut in
  1-inch chunks
2–3 Idaho taters, cut in
  quarters
Dumplings*

This works best in a deep 12-inch or 14-inch Dutch oven, which gives your dumplings room to fluff up. Season the meat to taste while you sauté the garlic in olive oil. Add the meat and fry for 5–10 minutes, stirring several times. Put in about ¹/₂ the onion wedges and bay leaves when you pour in the water (or stock or beer). Set the Dutch oven in your firepan over 12–14 briquets, and let simmer for a couple of hours.

Since you're using a fairly tough cut of meat, the longer you cook it, the easier it will be on the older folks' dentures. Add remaining onions, vegetables, and more liquid, if needed; cook for 20 minutes while you mix your dumplings. Spoon dumplings in with a large kitchen spoon; cover and let simmer for another 20 minutes. Serves 4–6.

*See page 29 for dumpling variation of Cee Dub's Basic Biscuits.

Cee Dub's Dutch Oven and Other Camp Cookin'

Mining Camp Spare Ribs

One of my cousins worked the mines in Globe, Arizona. At a local eatery, he got this recipe off the "Chinaman" cook. That was in the early 1930s, and nothing's changed since. These are the best ribs you'll ever eat!

2 tablespoons molasses	1 cup applesauce
1 cup soy sauce	5 cloves garlic, minced
3 tablespoons sugar	1/2 cup rice wine
5 tablespoons honey	6 pounds spare ribs, cut

To prepare marinade, mix together all ingredients, except spare ribs. Arrange spare ribs in a large pan in a single layer. Pour marinade over the ribs, cover, and refrigerate for a minimum of 2 hours or overnight. Bake 1 hour (first 1/2 hour covered) in a 450° oven. Allow 1 pound plus per person. Serves 4–6.

Note: The secret of oven-cooked ribs is to cut them first, rather than cooking them in a slab. By first cutting them, each individual rib soaks up the marinade. The meat thus becomes more flavorful and tender. For ribs cooked over a pit or on an outdoor grill, the traditional method of cooking the ribs in a slab works best. The barbecue sauce can then be basted across the entire slab with ease.

Matt Braun's Western Cooking

Swiss Ribs

Spare ribs or short ribs	2 bay leaves
1/4 cup flour	2 teaspoons salt
2 green peppers, chopped	1/4 teaspoon pepper
1/4 cup chopped parsley	1/2 cup chili sauce
1 cup finely chopped celery	1 tablespoon brown sugar
4 onions, chopped	1 cup water

Remove fat from ribs; flour lightly and brown on both sides in skillet. Remove ribs from pan and place in baking dish. To pan drippings, add chopped green peppers, parsley, celery, and onions. Simmer on low heat till onions are clear, then add all other ingredients. Pour sauce over ribs and cover. Bake at 350° for 1 hour.

Cookin' at Its Best

Dutch Oven Pork Chops

Here is an old favorite of ours, good for a whole family meal—a favorite especially of mine, since I have always been a pork chop man.

2 pounds pork chops
1/2 cup dry sherry
1/4 cup soy sauce
2 tablespoons sugar
1 egg yolk
1/4 teaspoon rosemary
1/4 teaspoon oregano
1/4 teaspoon basil
Flour
1/3 cup plus 2 tablespoons
  vegetable oil, divided
1 large onion (Texas Sweet)

1 red pepper
1 ounce mushrooms
1 cucumber
1 stalk celery
8 green onions
1 can pineapple chunks, drained;
  reserve syrup
1/4 cup white vinegar
3 tablespoons tomato sauce
1 cup water
3 tablespoons cornstarch

Marinate pork chops in pot with sherry, soy sauce, sugar, egg yolk, and condiments for an hour or so. Drain pork chops and coat with flour. Heat 2 tablespoons vegetable oil in Dutch oven. Cook the pork until brown.

Slice the onion into thin slices. Cut and chop red pepper. Cut mushrooms in quarters. Slice cucumber into 1/4-inch-thick pieces. Cut celery into chunks and add some of the tops along with green onions. Remove and drain pork chops.

Add 1/3 cup vegetable oil as needed, and heat over hot fire. Stir-fry vegetables 5 minutes. To drained vegetables, add pineapple syrup, vinegar, and tomato sauce. Combine water and cornstarch. Add pineapple chunks and pork chops. Cook and stir thoroughly. Serves 6.

Old-Fashioned Dutch Oven Cookbook

Silver Valley's Morning Star is one of the deepest mines in America at over a mile and a half deep.

Orange Glazed Stuffed Pork Chops

STUFFING:

½ cup butter
½ cup diced celery
¾ cup diced onion
1 apple, peeled and diced
1 cup fresh bread cubes
1 tablespoon parsley
1 teaspoon pepper
½ teaspoon rosemary

1 teaspoon salt
½ teaspoon paprika
½ teaspoon allspice
10 (8-ounce) pork chops, with
    pocket cut in each
2 ounces olive oil
¾ cup water

Melt butter in 14-inch Dutch oven. Sauté celery and onion until tender. Add apple, bread cubes, parsley, and seasonings. Add a small amount of water, if necessary, to moisten the dressing. Stuff the mixture into the slit in the pork chops. Seal the pockets with toothpicks and tie with butcher string. Brown the chops in olive oil on each side. Stand the chops on their sides and pour the water around them. Cover and bake at 350° for 50–55 minutes.

GLAZE:

1 cup sugar
2 tablespoons cornstarch
Zest and juice of 2 oranges

1 teaspoon cinnamon
14 whole cloves
½ teaspoon salt

While the chops are cooking, prepare Glaze by combining sugar and cornstarch in a 10-inch Dutch oven. Stir in the orange zest and juice. Add cinnamon, cloves, and salt. Cook over medium heat until sauce is thick and clear. Pour sauce over chops. Garnish with parsley and orange slices.

Hey Ma! Come Quick! The Hog's in the Garden Again!!

McAllister's Pork Scallops

When you return to camp from a day's deer hunt on the Malheur breaks, the greatest virtue of a Dutch oven is that "instant dinner" which is then unearthed. Stews and roasts are standbys, but the family favorite is scalloped potatoes and pork chops. I learned about this as a boy in Billy Berry's sheep camp in the Jackass Mountains and never forgot.

Slice enough raw potatoes to more than half fill the Dutch oven, and include some onion slices. Before placing the potatoes and onions in the oven, brown a dozen pork chops and remove them, but leave the grease. Cut off some of the pork fat and leave several chunks of this in the bottom of the oven, too.

Then layer the onion and potato slices, and sprinkle with salt and flour. Nearly cover the potatoes with milk, until it can be seen through the top layer. Place the pork chops in a layer on top.

In the meantime, the crew should have dug a hole for the oven and had hot coals ready to shovel into the bottom of the hole, and more to put on top of the lid. When all this is done, and the lid covered with coals, cover with dirt and tamp down firmly.

If this has been done in the morning, the Dutch oven may have cooled somewhat during the day. So when you remove it from the hole, pour some soup cream over the top of the chops and reheat them over the fire. During this all-day cooking process, the chops have dripped and mingled their flavor all the way through the potatoes and onions. The result is all the heavenly virtues, rolled into one pot— Dutch oven, that is.

Old-Fashioned Dutch Oven Cookbook

The Statehouse in Boise and dozens of other buildings in the city are geothermally heated from underground hot springs. In fact, Idaho is well sprinkled with public and private hot springs.

Apple Baked Pork Chops with Sherry

6 boneless pork chops	1/2 teaspoon ground cinnamon
3 large apples, peeled, cored, and sliced	2 tablespoons butter
	1 pinch each salt and pepper
1/4 cup packed brown sugar	1/2 cup dry sherry

In a large skillet, brown chops about 2 minutes on each side. Preheat oven to 350°. Arrange apple slices in bottom of a 9x13-inch baking dish. Sprinkle with brown sugar and cinnamon. Dot with butter. Top with the browned pork chops and season with salt and pepper to taste. Pour sherry over all; cover and bake for 1 hour or until internal temperature of pork has reached 160°.

The Miracle Cookbook

Rolled Pork Loin Stuffed with Feta, Raisins and Spinach

This is great hot or at room temperature for a picnic lunch!

2 tablespoons olive oil	Salt and pepper to taste
4 garlic cloves, minced	1/4 teaspoon ground sage
2 shallots, peeled and minced	1/4 teaspoon cayenne
2 cups cooked spinach	2 pork loins, laid out and flattened
8 ounces feta cheese	with a meat mallet
1/4 cup raisins	

Preheat oven to 350°. Heat oil in skillet and sauté minced garlic and shallots. Cook until tender and set aside.

Cook and drain all moisture from spinach and add remaining ingredients, except pork. Add shallots and garlic and mix well. Lay out flattened pork loins on a work surface. Spread cheese-spinach mixture over flattened pork. Begin rolling pork, as tightly as possible, and tie with string. Repeat for the other loin.

Bake in oven for 30 minutes. Remove from oven and cover to keep warm. Allow the loins to rest for 10 minutes. Slice 1/2 inch thick and serve. Serves 8.

Note: Cover with foil and refrigerate, if taking on a picnic. Wonderful as a cold lunch.

Ketchum Cooks

Pork Loin with Apricot and Pistachio

1 (3- to 4-pound) pork loin roast
¹/₂ cup chopped dried apricots
¹/₂ cup chopped pistachios
¹/₄ teaspoon pepper

1 teaspoon cardamom
¹/₄ teaspoon garlic salt
¹/₄ cup apricot juice
¹/₄ cup apricot preserves

Cut the roast approximately ¹/₂ inch thick in a rolling method, so that the roast will lay out flat. Open the meat flat and sprinkle remaining ingredients, except juice, evenly over the meat. Roll the meat up tightly and secure with toothpicks, or tie with a string. Using a fork, poke holes in the roast. Brush the surface with the apricot juice. Cover and place in the refrigerator for 2 hours. To cook, place the roast in a 12-inch Dutch oven with the fat side up. Cook at 350° for 1¹/₂ hours.

Brush the roast with the apricot preserves and sprinkle on the Crunchy Topping. Roast until internal temperature reaches 160°. While the roast is cooking, prepare the topping.

CRUNCHY TOPPING:
1 tablespoon butter
¹/₄ teaspoon garlic salt

¹/₄ cup coarsely crushed crackers
2 tablespoons chopped pistachios

Melt butter, then mix in garlic salt, crushed crackers, and pistachios and cook over low heat until completely coated with the butter.

Bacon is not a Vegetable

Tangy Glazed Hams

GLAZE:

1 (8-ounce) jar orange marmalade
6 ounces amaretto

½ teaspoon Tabasco or other hot
  pepper sauce

Mix ingredients together and let sit while you're getting the charcoal ready.

3 (2-pound) boneless canned
  hams
1 (15-ounce) can pineapple rings
  (save juice)

1 cup water
1 (4-ounce) bottle maraschino
  cherries (save juice)

Place hams in 12-inch Dutch oven along with juices from the cans and the water. Brush each ham with the Glaze and any other seasoning you wish to add. Place pineapple rings on each ham with a maraschino cherry in the center of each ring.

Set the Dutch oven in a firepan with 8–10 briquets underneath and 12–14 around the outside of the lid, and cook for an hour. Brush each ham with the remaining Glaze 2–3 times.

Cee Dub's Dutch Oven and Other Camp Cookin'

Moussaka

This is a great dish to serve for a large group because it is easily doubled and the flavors actually improve if you bake it, then allow it to sit several hours or overnight. Reheat before serving.

3 small eggplants	1 cup nonfat cottage cheese
1/2 cup egg substitute	1/2 cup dry bread crumbs, divided
1/2 teaspoon nutmeg	3/4 cup nonfat Parmesan, divided

Peel eggplants and cut lengthwise into 1/2-inch-thick slices. Place slices on baking sheet and spray with cooking spray. Broil on both sides until brown. Set aside.

MEAT SAUCE:

3/4 pound extra lean ground lamb or beef	1/4 cup red wine
	1/4 cup chopped parsley
1 1/2 onions, chopped	1/4 teaspoon each: cinnamon, salt,
3 ounces tomato paste	and pepper

Cook ground meat in a large sauté pan over medium heat until meat is brown and juices run clear. Add onions and continue to cook until onions are tender. Combine remaining Meat Sauce ingredients and stir into meat mixture. Simmer, stirring frequently, until liquid is absorbed (about 15 minutes).

WHITE SAUCE:

3 tablespoons flour	1 1/2 cups nonfat evaporated milk
2 tablespoons reduced-fat butter	1/2 cup skim milk

Combine ingredients in small saucepan; cook until thickened. Cool. Beat egg substitute until frothy; stir into White Sauce with nutmeg and cottage cheese.

Spray bottom of an 8x8x3-inch baking dish. Sprinkle with 1/2 the bread crumbs. Arrange 2 alternate layers of eggplant and Meat Sauce, sprinkling each meat layer with Parmesan and bread crumbs. Pour White Sauce over top and bake 60 minutes, or until top is golden and the topping is completely set. (If the sides are getting too brown and the center isn't set, place foil around edges, leaving the center exposed, and continue baking.) Remove from oven and cool 20 minutes before serving. Serve warm, not hot. Serves 6.

Northern Lites: Contemporary Cooking with a Twist

Casserole of Lamb, Lemon, and Wine

4 pounds lamb shoulder steaks
  with bone
Coarse salt
10 peppercorns, crushed
4 medium onions, sliced
2 small lemons, thinly sliced

4 cloves garlic, crushed
$^1/_4$ cup fresh cilantro leaves
$1^1/_2$ cups dry white wine
1 cup water
$^1/_4$ cup Spanish olive oil

Rub meat with mixture of salt and pepper. Layer onions, lamb, and lemon in large casserole. Sprinkle with garlic and cilantro. Add wine, water, and olive oil. Bake, covered, at 300° for 2 hours. Serves 4.

Basque Cooking and Lore

Blue Cheese Lamb Chops

4 lamb chops
Crushed garlic
Salt and pepper to taste

2–3 tablespoons heavy cream
Chunk of blue cheese

Season chops with crushed garlic, salt and pepper. Place on a grill and cook until thoroughly brown. Turn over and cook other side. Mix cream and blue cheese together to make a paste. When second side of chops are brown, turn back over on the grill. Spread the blue cheese paste on the chops, and continue to cook until the paste melts into the meat. Then they're ready. Serve with a little mint jelly, baked potatoes, and a salad.

Note: This recipe can be used with pork chops, too, and can be done in a Dutch oven rather than on a grill. If using lamb chops in the Dutch oven, the fat rendered from browning the chops can be drained off to enhance the flavor of the chops prior to applying the blue cheese paste.

More Cee Dub's Dutch Oven and Other Camp Cookin'

Old World Onion Supper

4 medium onions	2 (12-ounce) bottles beer
(Idaho-Eastern Oregon)	1 tablespoon caraway seeds
1/4 cup butter	Mustard-Horseradish Sauce
2 pounds spicy German sausage	

Peel onions and slice thinly. Sauté onions in butter in large heavy skillet over medium heat. Slice sausage diagonally in 2-inch pieces. Add to pan with onions and brown for 3–4 minutes. Pour beer over onions and sausage. Sprinkle with caraway seeds and simmer uncovered for 25 minutes. Remove onions and sausage from skillet and place in serving dish. Keep warm. Over high heat, reduce beer to 2 cups. Pour over onions and sausage. Serve with Mustard-Horseradish Sauce. Serves 8.

MUSTARD-HORSERADISH SAUCE:

1 cup sour cream	2 teaspoons cream-style
2 tablespoons prepared mustard	horseradish

Blend ingredients well.

Onions Make the Meal Cookbook

Sausage, Potato, Cabbage Dish

4 mild Italian sausages	Seasoned salt and pepper
2 tablespoons oil	3 cups shredded cabbage
6 medium potatoes, sliced	1 cup chicken broth
1 medium onion, sliced	

Slice sausage into 2-inch slices. Heat oil in large skillet on medium heat; place sausage in skillet. Add sliced potatoes and onions to skillet, and cook for 30 minutes, stirring once or twice. Season with seasoned salt and pepper. Add cabbage and pour chicken broth over top; stir, cover, and let cook for about 15 more minutes or until vegetables are tender. Serves 8.

Mackay Heritage Cookbook

24 Hour Salami

3 pounds hamburger
1/3 cup water
1 1/2 teaspoons liquid smoke
1 1/2 teaspoons seasoned pepper

1 1/2 teaspoons garlic salt
1 1/2 teaspoons mustard seed
3 tablespoons Morton Tender
  Quick mix

Mix all ingredients together. Form into 6 rolls and wrap individually in foil. Chill 24 hours. Bake at 350° for 1 hour. Refrigerate.

Spragg Family Cookbook

Brats, Beer, and Onion Packet

2 medium onions, cut into thin
  wedges
1/3 cup beer

5 smoked, cooked bratwurst
5 hot dog buns, split

Heat grill. Cut 18x18-inch piece of heavy-duty foil; spray with non-stick cooking spray. Place onions in shallow layer on center of foil; sprinkle with beer. Top with bratwurst. Wrap packet securely using double-fold seals, allowing room for heat expansion. When ready to grill, place packet, seam-side-up, on gas grill over medium heat, or on a charcoal grill 4–6 inches from medium coals. Cook 30 minutes or until onions are tender. To serve, open packet carefully to allow steam to escape. Place bratwurst in buns and top with onions.

The Miracle Cookbook

The Scott Ski Pole was invented by Sun Valley's Edward Scott in 1958. Scott's invention of the first tapered aluminum ski pole immediately replaced the bamboo and steel poles.

Bratwurst

Bratwurst, a favorite of the old-world wurstbacher's is an excellent all-around sausage. Its mildly spiced flavor compliments any food fare.

7 pounds lean meat	**1¼ teaspoons white pepper**
1½ pounds pork butt	**1¼ teaspoons black pepper**
1½ pounds pork fat	**1 teaspoon nutmeg**
4 tablespoons salt	**1 teaspoon mace**
3 tablespoons sugar	**1 teaspoon ginger**
4 tablespoons chopped fresh	**1 cup cold water**
** parsley**	**2 cups whey, or nonfat dry milk**
2 whole eggs	**Prepared 33–36mm hog casings**

Grind meats and pork fat together through medium plate (of grinder) one time. In a large mixing bowl, combine ground mixture with all remaining ingredients except casings; mix/knead thoroughly for up to 3 times or until mixture is mixed well.

Stuff a portion of the seasoned mixture into prepared casings and twist into 6-inch links; refrigerate. Shape remaining mixture into 6-inch diameter patties; refrigerate. Cook, fry, bake, or broil as you would any fresh pork sausage.

Note: True venison lovers can eliminate the pork butt and substitute 8½ pounds venison and 1½ pounds beef fat in place of the above meat/pork/fat proportions. Sausage that isn't eaten within 2 or 3 days should be double wrapped and frozen.

Sausage & Jerky Handbook

Pepper-Style Jerky

Because jerky is virtually fat free, it makes a great snack food.

5 pounds lean meat	1 teaspoon cayenne pepper
4 tablespoons salt	2 teaspoons coriander
1 teaspoon curing salt	2 teaspoons garlic powder
1 teaspoon smoke flavoring	5 cups cold water
1 teaspoon white pepper	Coarsely ground black pepper
1 teaspoon chili powder	

Cut away as much fat/tallow as possible from the jerky meat. Place trimmed meat in freezer for 2–3 hours, or until meat is slightly frozen; remove from freezer. Slice the meat into ¼- to ⅜-inch-thick slabs (at this point, a protective glove is advised to help prevent accidents). Slice the meat slabs into ¼- to ⅜-inch-thick strips.

Combine meat strips and all remaining ingredients, except coarsely ground black pepper, in an ample-size, nonmetallic brining vessel; stir/mix well. Refrigerate mixture overnight (about 8 hours) to cure; continue to stir occasionally.

Next day, spread the cured jerky strips evenly on drying racks. Do not rinse strips! Sprinkle each piece generously with coarsely ground black pepper. Dry at 150°–170° in oven, smoker or dehydrator (check occasionally for doneness) until jerky reaches desired degree of dryness, 5–24 hours, depending on drying method used.

Note: Jerky is ready to eat when there is very little moisture left on the inside of the strips and slightly sticky on the outside, yet still flexible enough to bend without snapping.

Sausage & Jerky Handbook

Game

With more than 60% of Idaho designated as public land, hunters have ample opportunity to bag the big one. This hunter waits for his chance as he peers out over the beautiful Owyhee Plateau near Battle Creek.

PHOTO © WILLIAM H. MULLINS OUTDOOR PHOTOGRAPHY

Burger Pot Pie

When I think of old-fashioned meat pies like Grandma used to make, the first thing that comes to mind is her renowned potato pie crust. The following is a close rendition of her best.

2 pounds hash browns
1 egg, beaten
1 tablespoon granulated onion
$1/2$ teaspoon salt
1 tablespoon olive oil
1 pound lean ground venison
1 (16-ounce) can whole-kernel corn, undrained
1 (16-ounce) can green beans, undrained

1 (10-ounce) can tomato soup, undiluted
$1/3$ teaspoon oregano
$1/3$ teaspoon black pepper, table ground
1 tablespoon sugar
1 cup grated Monterey Jack cheese

Combine hash browns, egg, granulated onion, and salt in mixing bowl; toss lightly. Press hash brown mixture into greased 9-inch-deep pie plate to form crust; bake crust in preheated 400° oven for 15–20 minutes; remove and set aside.

Heat olive oil in skillet; add lean ground venison. Cook over medium-high heat until venison is browned, stirring frequently to crumble; drain and set aside.

Combine corn, green beans, tomato soup, oregano, pepper, and sugar in mixing bowl; stir well; add browned venison. Pour filling mixture into hash brown pastry; bake in preheated 400° oven for 20 minutes. Remove, top with sprinkling of Monterey Jack cheese, and bake an additional 5 minutes or until cheese is melted and light golden brown. Cool slightly and cut into 6 pieces. Makes 6 servings.

98 Ways to Cook Venison

Stuffed Peppers

8 large bell peppers	1 teaspoon garlic salt
1/4 teaspoon salt	1 1/2 teaspoons coarse black pepper
1 pound lean ground venison	2 tablespoons minced onion
2 cups cooked white or brown rice	2 (14 1/2-ounce) cans Italian stewed tomatoes, undrained, divided
1 teaspoon chili powder	1 cup grated mozzarella cheese

Cut the top out of each bell pepper; remove seeds and rinse. In a large saucepan, add 1/4 teaspoon salt and enough water to cover bell peppers. Parboil for 6 minutes; drain and set aside.

Combine venison, cooked rice, chili powder, garlic salt, pepper, minced onion, and 1 can Italian stewed tomatoes in large skillet; stir well. Simmer until venison is mostly cooked through; drain. Spoon mixture evenly into parboiled bell peppers; arrange peppers in a lightly oiled shallow baking dish. Top with 1 can tomatoes and mozzarella cheese; bake in preheated 375° oven for 25 minutes. Makes 8 servings.

98 Ways to Cook Venison

Stroganoff

2 tablespoons butter	1/4 teaspoon pepper
1 pound lean ground venison	1 (10 3/4-ounce) can cream of chicken soup
1 cup diced onion	
1 (8-ounce) can mushroom stems and pieces, drained	1 cup sour cream
	Fresh parsley
2 tablespoons flour	4 cups cooked noodles
2 teaspoons garlic salt	

Heat butter in large skillet; add ground venison, onion, and mushrooms. Cook over medium heat until venison is browned, stirring frequently to crumble; drain. Stir in flour, garlic salt, pepper, and cream of chicken soup; cook over medium-low heat 8 minutes, stirring frequently. Stir in sour cream; heat through. Garnish with fresh parsley sprigs and serve over hot cooked noodles. Makes 4 servings.

98 Ways to Cook Venison

Chicken Fried Venison Steak

1 elk or moose round steak, or	1/2 teaspoon pepper
2 deer round steaks	1 or 2 cloves garlic, crushed
1 cup flour	1/4 cup olive oil
1 teaspoon dried thyme	1 large onion, sliced or diced
1 teaspoon dried oregano	Water to cover
1 teaspoon salt	

Cut all fat and sinew from the steak. Cut steak into serving sizes. Mix flour, thyme, oregano, salt and pepper together. Coat both sides of steak pieces with the flour mixture.

In a large skillet, sauté the garlic in oil over medium heat. Turn the heat up to medium high, and brown the flour-covered steak. When browned, add leftover flour to oil. Mix together. Add onion. Cover meat and onion with water. Cover skillet. Turn heat on low and cook for 45 minutes or until tender. You may need to thin gravy a little before you serve it. It is good served over potatoes, noodles, or rice. Serves 4–6.

Cookin' in Paradise

Country Hash

2 tablespoons olive oil	1/4 teaspoon black pepper, table
1 medium onion, diced	ground
3 cups leftover venison roast,	1 1/2 cups milk
chopped	3/4 cup Italian bread crumbs
4–5 medium potatoes, diced	6 large eggs
1/2 teaspoon salt	

Heat olive oil in large skillet; add onion, venison roast, potatoes, salt and pepper. Cook, uncovered, over medium heat 20 minutes, turning frequently, until potatoes are cooked through. Drain. Reduce heat, then break eggs over hash mixture; cover. Cook additional 2–3 minutes, or until eggs reach desired degree of doneness. Makes 6 servings.

98 Ways to Cook Venison

Sweet & Sour Meatballs

1 pound lean ground venison
3 slices white bread, crumbled
1 egg, beaten
$\frac{1}{3}$ teaspoon salt
$\frac{1}{3}$ teaspoon marjoram
2 tablespoons olive oil
4 green onions, including tops, diced
1 medium red pepper, diced

1 ($15\frac{1}{2}$-ounce) can pineapple chunks, undrained
$\frac{1}{3}$ cup apple cider vinegar
$\frac{1}{3}$ cup catsup
$\frac{1}{3}$ cup sugar
2 tablespoons soy sauce
2 tablespoons cornstarch
4 cups hot cooked rice

Combine lean ground venison, bread, egg, salt, and marjoram in a large mixing bowl; mix/knead thoroughly. Shape mixture into 1-inch meatballs. Place meatballs on cookie sheet in preheated 375° oven; bake 30 minutes or until meatballs are cooked through; set aside.

Heat olive oil in large skillet; add onions and bell pepper. Cook over medium heat until onions are crisp-tender, stirring frequently; drain. Stir in pineapple chunks with juice, vinegar, catsup, sugar, soy sauce, cornstarch, and meatballs. Bring mixture to a boil; reduce heat and simmer 7 minutes, or until meatballs are heated through. Serve over hot cooked rice. Makes 4 servings.

98 Ways to Cook Venison

Apple Cider Chops

¹/₄ cup flour	2 cups apple cider
¹/₂ teaspoon dry mustard	2 tablespoons brown sugar
¹/₂ teaspoon salt	3 apples, peeled and quartered
¹/₄ teaspoon cayenne pepper	¹/₃ cup raisins
¹/₄ teaspoon allspice	¹/₄ cup dried currants
¹/₄ teaspoon ground ginger	¹/₃ teaspoon ground cinnamon
8 venison chops, cut 1 inch thick	4 cups hot cooked rice
¹/₄ cup olive oil	

Combine flour, dry mustard, salt, cayenne pepper, allspice, and ginger in small mixing bowl; mix well. Dredge venison chops in flour mixture. Reserve leftover flour. Heat olive oil in Dutch oven and cook dredged chops over medium-high heat until chops are browned on both sides; remove. Drain Dutch oven.

Stir in apple cider, brown sugar, and reserved flour; cook over medium heat 2 minutes, stirring constantly until smooth. Remove from heat. Place chops in cider mixture and top with apple quarters, raisins, currants, and cinnamon. Cover and bake in preheated 350° oven for 1 hour or until chops are tender. Serve over hot cooked rice. Makes 4 double servings.

98 Ways to Cook Venison

Prime Rib of Venison

When you're having friends over for dinner, nothing is more impressive than a properly prepared prime rib of venison.

2 beef bouillon cubes	Salt
2 tablespoons beef soup mix	Garlic pepper
3 cups hot water	Spiced crab apples
1 large onion, chopped	Fresh parsley sprigs
1 (6- to 7-pound) venison	
standing-rib roast	

Dissolve bouillon cubes and beef soup mix in 3 cups hot water; add chopped onion and stir well. Pour into baking dish. Sprinkle sides and back of venison prime rib with salt and garlic pepper, to taste.

Insert meat thermometer into thickest portion of roast. Place roast in preheated 400° oven; cook, uncovered, 30 minutes or until well browned. Baste with onion/soup stock; reduce heat to 325°. Bake, uncovered, for 1½ hours or until meat thermometer reaches 155°–160°, basting often with onion/soup stock. Slice between each rib. Serve with small bowl of stock; garnish with spiced crab apples and parsley twigs.

98 Ways to Cook Venison

Venison North Idaho

2 venison steaks, thick loin	½ bay leaf
½ clove garlic	1 teaspoon Worcestershire sauce
1 tablespoon olive oil	2 tablespoons currant or apple
2 tablespoons butter	jelly
Salt and pepper to taste	¼ cup dry sherry
½ cup chopped mushrooms	½ cup thick cream

Rub the surface of steak gently with the garlic. Heat olive oil and butter until sizzling in frying pan, and sauté steaks quickly in this until both sides are brown. Season with salt and pepper to taste. Combine rest of ingredients and pour over steaks. Bake in 350° oven for 70 minutes.

Recipes Logged from the Woods of North Idaho

Grenadine of Venison

MARINADE:

1½ cups water
½ cup red wine vinegar
1 teaspoon dehydrated onion
    flakes
1 clove garlic, minced

½ teaspoon thyme
4 sprigs parsley
12 whole black peppercorns
½ cup chopped celery
1 teaspoon salt

Place ingredients in saucepan; bring to a boil. Simmer covered for one hour. Cool. Pour over meat and marinate in refrigerator for 24 hours. This Marinade is good for elk as well as venison recipes.

1 (6-ounce) loin of venison,
    marinated
Salt and pepper to taste
¾ cup prepared beef bouillon
¼ cup tomato juice
1 slice white bread, made into
    crumbs

1½ teaspoons red wine vinegar
¼ teaspoon brown sugar
¼ clove garlic, minced
¼ cup evaporated skim milk

Remove meat from Marinade and cut into 1-inch slices. Preheat broiler. Season meat and broil on a rack 4 inches from source of heat. Cook 5 minutes on each side; remove and set aside.

Pour bouillon and tomato juice in skillet; add bread crumbs. Place over low heat and add vinegar, brown sugar, and garlic. Add meat to the sauce and season to taste. Simmer for 5 minutes. Add milk. Reheat and serve.

Tastes from the Country

Kabobs

If you're a kabob lover, you're going to love this recipe. The right combination of herbs and spices transforms venison into a culinary delight guaranteed to please.

1½ pounds venison round steak
½ cup olive oil
½ cup pineapple juice
¼ cup red wine vinegar
3–4 drops hot sauce
2 cloves garlic, minced
½ teaspoon basil
½ teaspoon oregano
1 teaspoon salt

1 large onion, quartered
1 pound medium-size fresh
   mushrooms
1 pound small-size cherry
   tomatoes
2 (8-ounce) cans pineapple chunks
12 (6-inch) wooden skewers,
   soaked in water overnight

Trim tallow from venison; cut venison into 1- to 1½-inch cubes. Place venison cubes in shallow dish; stir in olive oil, pineapple juice, red wine vinegar, hot sauce, garlic, basil, oregano, and salt. Refrigerate 2–3 hours, turning occasionally.

Alternate venison cubes, onion sections, mushrooms, cherry tomatoes, and pineapple chunks on wooden skewers; reserve marinade.

Spray grill rack with light coating of vegetable spray. Place skewered meat and vegetables on rack; grill over medium-hot coals 10–12 minutes or until meat reaches desired degree of doneness, turning and basting as needed with reserved marinade. Makes 6 double servings.

98 Ways to Cook Venison

Teriyaki Elk Kabob

TERIYAKI MARINADE:

¹/₂ cup soy sauce	**2 teaspoons ground ginger**
2 tablespoons molasses	**2 teaspoons dry mustard**
¹/₄ cup oil	**6 garlic cloves, minced**

Combine ingredients. Set aside.

1¹/₂ pounds elk steak, cubed	**Zucchini, cubed**
2 green peppers, cubed	**Cucumbers, cubed**
15 cherry tomatoes	**Pitted olives (whole)**
¹/₂ pound fresh mushrooms	**Red peppers, cubed**
1 medium onion, cubed	

Marinate meat for 15 minutes. Drain. Place ingredients on skewers, alternating meat and vegetables. Grill 5–10 minutes, turning frequently and basting with Teriyaki Marinade.

Cookin' at Its Best

Basic Jerky

¹/₂ cup salt	**5 pounds lean meat (elk, caribou,**
¹/₂ tablespoon garlic salt	**deer, beef, etc.)**
¹/₂ tablespoon pepper	**Garlic powder (optional)**

Make a mixture of salt, garlic salt, and pepper. Cut meat into 2-inch-wide strips, 1 inch thick. Roll strips in seasoning, or "dredge," as the television cooks say. Place meat in a crock and weight down with a plate. Brine this way in refrigerator for 5 days, then remove and rinse. Dry and place in smoker. Smoke about 18 hours or until the meat is a purple color when you cut into it. At this point you can rub garlic powder into it, if you like. Five pounds raw meat makes 1 pound jerky.

Variation: Mix brine ingredients with 1 quart of water, bring to a boil, and place the meat in the boiling mixture for 10 minutes. Remove and place immediately in the smoker.

Don Holm's Book of Food Drying, Pickling and Smoke Curing

Elk Loin with Red Wine Glaze and Morel Mushrooms

4 tablespoons butter, softened, divided
4 large morel mushrooms
1 tablespoon chopped garlic
1/4 cup chopped onion
Salt to taste
Ground pepper to taste
1 tablespoon olive oil

4 (1-inch-thick) elk steaks
1 teaspoon chopped shallots
1/2 cup red wine
Juice of 1/2 lemon
1 tablespoon soy sauce
1 teaspoon chopped ginger
1 tablespoon snipped Italian parsley

You will need 2 skillets. In one skillet, melt 2 tablespoons butter and sauté fresh (or pre-soaked dried) morel mushrooms with garlic and onion. Keep cooking until liquid is absorbed. Salt and pepper to taste. Heat second skillet over medium-high heat, adding 1 tablespoon oil and elk steaks. Cook until medium rare. Remove from skillet and set aside (meat will bleed; reserve juices for later).

To skillet, add chopped shallots, red wine, lemon juice, soy sauce, and ginger. Cook until reduced to syrup. Add reserved meat juices. To finish your glaze, whisk in remaining 2 tablespoons soft butter and taste for salt and pepper. Put meat back into glaze and let flavors mesh for 2 minutes.

To serve, place meat on platter and top with glaze and morel mushrooms. Sprinkle with fresh parsley. Serves 4.

Spaetzle, red cabbage, and lingonberries are a great addition to this dish. B.R. Cohn Cabernet-Sauvignon is a suggested wine.

Ketchum Cooks

The Oregon Trail stretches 510 miles across the southern half of Idaho. For most of the trek across Idaho, the trail follows the Bear or the Snake Rivers.

Antelope in Brie Cream

1 pound antelope steak
  medallions
Salt and pepper to taste
2 tablespoons butter, clarified
1 tablespoon butter
2 tablespoons chopped shallots
$\frac{1}{4}$ cup skinned, seeded, chopped
  tomato

$\frac{1}{4}$ cup sherry
$\frac{1}{2}$ cup heavy cream
1 teaspoon chopped parsley
$\frac{1}{2}$ teaspoon chopped thyme
2 tablespoons mashed roasted
  garlic
$2\frac{1}{2}$ ounces brie, skinned, grated
4 buttermilk biscuits

Cut antelope steaks into $\frac{1}{2}$-inch-thick medallions. Salt and pepper the steaks to taste. Sauté medallions in clarified butter for 2–3 minutes on each side or until desired doneness; hold in warm oven.

In the same pan, melt 1 tablespoon butter; add shallots and chopped tomato, and sauté 2 minutes; deglaze with sherry. Add heavy cream, parsley, thyme, and roasted garlic; bring to a simmer. Add the brie; season to taste with salt and pepper. Place steaks on the buttermilk biscuits and top with the sauce. Yields 4 portions.

Cooking on the Wild Side

Grilled Pheasant Breast with Rosemary Cream Sauce

ROSEMARY CREAM SAUCE:

2+ tablespoons butter
1 tablespoon chopped garlic
1/2 cup chopped shallots
1 pound sliced mushrooms
1 cup chopped leeks
1 cup chopped red onion
1 cup white wine
1/2 cup concentrated chicken
 stock

2 cups heavy cream
2 tablespoons chopped rosemary
1 tablespoon chopped tarragon
1 teaspoon chopped thyme
Flour
2 tablespoons chopped parsley
1/4 cup sliced green onions
Salt and pepper to taste

Sauté in 2 tablespoons butter the garlic, shallots, mushrooms, leeks, and red onion. Deglaze with white wine, and reduce the liquid by three-fourths. Add chicken stock, heavy cream, and herbs. Salt and pepper to taste. Thicken with a little flour and butter roux. Finish with chopped parsley and green onions.

Salt and pepper
4 boneless, skinless pheasant
 breasts
Olive oil
1 pound fettuccine, cooked

Parmesan cheese
Sliced green onions for garnish
Red pepper, cut into spikes for
 garnish

Salt and pepper the pheasant breasts. Brush with olive oil, and grill to just done. Do not overcook. Toss fettuccine in Rosemary Cream Sauce. Top with grilled, sliced pheasant breasts. Garnish with fresh Parmesan cheese, sliced green onions, and red pepper spikes. Yields 4 portions.

Cooking on the Wild Side

Sautéed Duck Breasts
with Roasted Apples on Pasta

4 boneless, skinless duck breasts
Salt and pepper to taste
2 tablespoons clarified butter
2 tablespoons butter
1 pound Granny Smith apples,
  skinned, thickly sliced
1/4 cup chopped shallots

2 teaspoons chopped garlic
1/4 cup apple jack brandy
2 cups heavy cream
Additional salt and pepper,
  if desired
Cooked pasta of your choice
1/2 cup Parmesan cheese

Place duck breasts between plastic wrap and pound out to even thickness. Salt and pepper breasts. In saucepan, sauté breasts in 2 tablespoons clarified butter for 2–3 minutes on each side, or to desired doneness; remove from pan and hold in a warm oven. In same saucepan, add 2 tablespoons butter, apples, shallots, and garlic, and sauté for 2 minutes. Deglaze the pan with apple jack; add cream, bring to a simmer, then adjust flavor with salt and pepper. Toss with pasta. Slice duck breasts and place on pasta; garnish with Parmesan cheese. Yields 4 portions.

Cooking on the Wild Side

Wild Goose a L'Orange

1 wild goose, ready to cook
1 onion, minced
1/4 teaspoon tarragon leaves
2 tablespoons butter or margarine
1/2 cup orange juice
2 tablespoons shredded orange
  peel

1/8 teaspoon salt
1/8 teaspoon dry mustard
1/4 cup currant jelly
2 tablespoons port or cranberry
  cocktail
1 orange, pared and sectioned
1 1/2 teaspoons cornstarch

Preheat oven to 325°. Wash a 6–8 pound goose and pat dry. Skewer neck skin to back, and cross wing tips over back. Place goose breast-side-up on rack in shallow roasting pan in preheated oven. Cook onion and tarragon in butter until onion is tender. Add orange juice, orange peel, salt, mustard, and jelly. Stir constantly over medium heat until jelly melts.

Reduce heat; stir in wine and orange sections. Reserve half of sauce for glaze; baste with remainder during 3 1/2-hour cooking time. If goose gets too brown, place aluminum foil lightly over breast. Bird is done when drumstick meat feels very soft.

Stir cornstarch slowly into reserved sauce until mixture thickens and boils 1 minute; serve with goose. Serves 4.

Idaho's Wild 100!

 Between 1861 and 1866, Idaho's gold output totaled about $52 million—or about 19% of the total discovery for the United States.

Blue Grouse Cacciatore

2–3 cloves garlic, peeled and
  pressed
2–3 tablespoons olive oil
2 blue grouse (or chukars or
  pheasant), cut in serving pieces
2 (12-ounce) cans tomato sauce
2 (12-ounce) cans tomato paste

2+ tablespoons Italian seasoning,
  divided
2 (14½-ounce) cans stewed
  tomatoes
2 small onions, diced
1 (4-ounce) can sliced olives
2 (4-ounce) cans sliced mushrooms

Sauté pressed garlic in olive oil 2–3 minutes until brown. Lightly brown birds in olive oil. While birds are frying, mix tomato paste and tomato sauce together in bowl along with 1 tablespoon Italian seasoning. When birds are lightly browned, transfer them to large casserole dish or Dutch oven. Pour mixture of tomato sauce and tomato paste over them. Then add stewed tomatoes. Place vegetables over the top and sprinkle additional Italian seasoning over the top. Bake at 350°–375° for 1 hour. Serve over rice. Serves 4.

Idaho's Wild 100!

 Idaho has more public land (over 60% of the state) than any state in the lower 48, except Nevada (more than 77% is public). Of that, approximately two-thirds is federal land, most of which is managed by the U.S. Forest Service or the Bureau of Land Management.

Sage Grouse in Gravy

This is a classic camp dinner for sage grouse hunting trips. It works perfectly in a Dutch oven.

1 sage grouse, cut in pieces
Flour
¼ cup olive oil
½ cup blush or white wine
1 package onion soup mix (Lipton)

1 (10¾-ounce) can cream of
   mushroom soup
½–1 (15-ounce) can chicken broth,
   divided

Dredge sage grouse in flour. Brown in olive oil in a large heavy skillet. Remove grouse and deglaze pan with wine. Add soup mix, soup, and about ½ of the broth; stir. Put the grouse back in the pan, cover and simmer for 1 hour or until the meat is tender. Add additional broth, if necessary. Serve over rice or noodles. Serves 3–4.

Note: I prefer to bone and pound the breasts to increase tenderness and reduce cooking time. This recipe can be modified by adding vegetables (mushrooms, carrots, potatoes), either canned or raw. If canned, drain, then add in for the last 20 minutes of cooking time. If raw, add for at least 40 minutes cooking time. This recipe can be used for other birds, but works best with sage grouse.

Idaho's Wild 100!

Sage Hen & Super Wild Rice

3 cups wild rice, cooked in
    chicken stock
2 tablespoons butter
1 cup sliced mushrooms
1 tablespoon flour
1 teaspoon chopped garlic
1 cup milk
1/2 cup grated Cheddar cheese
2 tablespoons white wine

1 tablespoon fresh lemon juice
1/2 teaspoon chopped thyme
1 tablespoon chopped parsley
Salt and pepper to taste
2 cups sage hen body meat,
    cooked, diced
1 cup seasoned bread crumbs
1/2 cup grated Parmesan cheese

Drain wild rice that has been cooked in chicken stock. Place in greased 1 1/2-quart casserole. Melt butter in saucepan; cook mushrooms until browned and liquid is absorbed; blend in flour and garlic. Add milk slowly and stir until smooth and thick. Add cheese, wine, lemon juice, thyme, and parsley, stirring until cheese is melted. Add sage hen meat to sauce. Add sage hen sauce to rice and bake at 350° for 30 minutes or until hot and bubbly. Top with bread crumbs and Parmesan cheese. Yields 6 portions.

Cooking on the Wild Side

Poultry

The Snake River Birds of Prey Natural Area, near Kuna, is home to the largest concentration of nesting raptors in North America. Twenty-four species of predatory birds can be found there such as these juvenile hawks, as well as eagles, falcons, and owls.

PHOTO © WILLIAM H. MULLINS OUTDOOR PHOTOGRAPHY

Beer Can Chicken

I first saw beer can chicken prepared on television. It was a hoot, so I decided to try it. It was fun to prepare and it turned out very good. The beer makes it very moist and the rub gives it a good flavor.

MEMPHIS RUB:

¼ cup paprika
1 tablespoon finely packed
  brown sugar
1 tablespoon sugar
2 teaspoons salt
1 teaspoon celery salt

1 teaspoon freshly ground black
  pepper
1–3 teaspoons cayenne pepper
1 teaspoon dry mustard
1 teaspoon garlic powder
1 teaspoon onion powder

Combine all ingredients in a jar, twist the lid on airtight, and shake to mix. Store away from heat or light for up to 6 months. Makes about ½ cup.

1 large whole chicken (about
  3½–4 pounds)

3 tablespoons Memphis Rub
1 (12-ounce) can beer

Remove fat just inside the body cavity of the chicken. Rinse chicken, inside and out, then drain and blot dry, inside and out, with paper towels. Sprinkle 1 tablespoon of the rub inside the body and neck cavity, then rub another 1 tablespoon all over skin of bird. If you wish, rub another ½ tablespoon of mixture between the flesh and the skin.

Preheat the grill. Pop the tab on the beer can. Use a "church key" style can opener. Make 6 or 7 holes in the top of the can. Pour out the top inch of beer, then spoon the remaining dry rub through the holes into the beer. Holding the chicken upright, with the opening of the body cavity down, insert the beer can into the cavity.

Stand the chicken up in the center of the hot grate (medium heat). Spread out the legs to form a sort of tripod, to support the bird.

Cover the grill and cook the chicken until fall-off-the-bone tender, 1½–2 hours. Using tongs or oven mitt, lift the bird to a platter. Be careful not to spill hot beer on yourself. Let stand for 5 minutes before carving the meat off the upright carcass.

Another Cookbook

Beck's Honey Mustard Roasted Chicken

My pard, ex-roommate from college days, river-running nut, Tom Beck, provided this quick and tasty recipe. While your chicken is roasting in a 12-inch Dutch oven, get a pot of rice going in your 10-inch Dutch oven for a quick 2-pot supper. Tom, aka, "Catfish," first used honey mustard for this dish, but you can substitute barbeque sauce, sweet and sour sauce, or something similar to suit yourself.

1 frying chicken, cut into pieces
½ cup prepared honey mustard
¾ cup water or white wine

Salt, pepper, or other seasonings to taste

"Catfish" uses a circular, wire rack which just fits in the bottom of a 12-inch Dutch. (He found his at a yard sale.) If you can't find something similar, you can use several rings from canning jars placed in the Dutch.

Brush the honey mustard on the chicken and let set for a few minutes while the charcoal gets going. Put your rack in the bottom of the Dutch and add water and/or wine. Arrange chicken pieces skin-side-up on the rack and season with salt and pepper. (I like to use something along the lines of Mrs. Dash, which adds a little color as well.) Set the Dutch in your firepan with 4 or 5 briquets going underneath. Line the outside of the lid with 18 to 22 briquets, with 3 or 4 over the center of the lid. Roast for about 45 minutes to 1 hour. If you want, set your 10-inch Dutch on top of your 12-inch Dutch and let the charcoal cook in 2 directions. Serves 4–6.

Cee Dub's Dutch Oven and Other Camp Cookin'

Real Fried Chicken

This method was handed down from a former slave who had come west following the Civil War, and had cooked for an outfit out of Texas. Folks from down south have told me that this is still the best way to do it.

2 cups flour	1 (2- to 3-pound) chicken, cut up
Salt and pepper to taste	Shortening or lard

Mix the flour, salt and pepper in a sack. Shake a few pieces of the chicken in the sack at a time. Starting with the largest pieces, place in a heavy cast-iron skillet in hot grease that is ½–1 inch deep. Cook 5–10 minutes, turning frequently so they don't burn. Reduce heat and continue to cook and turn until golden brown, 20–30 minutes.

The secrets here are: grease, not oil; cast-iron cookware; and not covering chicken while cooking. The only spices are salt and pepper.

Sowbelly and Sourdough

Easy Company Curry Chicken

2 tablespoons butter	1 (10¾-ounce) can cream of
3 tablespoons curry powder	mushroom soup
1 apple, chopped fine	Salt
1 onion, chopped fine and	Paprika
sautéed	2½–3 pounds fryer, cut up
2 cups cream or canned milk	

Melt butter in pan. Add curry powder. Sauté apple and onion in butter. Add cream and soup. Salt and paprika fryer. Spread out in greased shallow glass pan in 1 layer. Pour sauce over and bake at 350° for 1½ hours, uncovered. Serve with couscous or rice.

Generations "Coming Home"

Extra Good Chicken

8 boneless, skinless chicken
  breast halves
8 thin slices Swiss or mozzarella
  cheese
1 (10¾-ounce) can cream of
  chicken soup

Dash Kitchen Bouquet
¼ cup water
1 (6-ounce) package stuffing mix
¼ cup butter, melted

Place breasts in greased 9x13-inch pan and top each with a slice of
cheese. Combine soup, Kitchen Bouquet, and water. Pour over chick-
en. Toss stuffing mix and seasoning packet with butter. Sprinkle over
chicken breasts. Cover and bake at 350° for 40 minutes. Remove
cover; continue to bake an additional 20 minutes.

Idaho Cook Book

Red Chicken

1 (8-ounce) can tomato sauce
1 can water
2 tablespoons brown sugar
2 tablespoons mustard
2 tablespoons Worcestershire
  sauce

¼ cup vinegar
Salt and pepper to taste
Dash of garlic powder
Dash of oregano
1 tablespoon chopped onion
1 chicken, halved or cut up

Mix all ingredients, except chicken. Place chicken in greased 9x13-
inch baking dish; pour mixture over. Bake at 350° for 1½ hours.

Down Home Country Cookin'

Dog Bark Park near Cottonwood is home to the world's two biggest beagle sculptures:
Toby, 12 feet tall and Sweet Willy Colton, 30 feet tall.

Chicken Marrakesh with Lentils

Lentils absorb the flavors of aromatic spices and dried fruits in this deliciously fragrant preparation from Morocco.

2 tablespoons canola oil
8 chicken thighs (2½ pounds),
   skin removed and fat trimmed
¾ cup all-purpose flour
1 cup dry lentils, rinsed
6 large scallions, chopped
6 tablespoons minced cilantro,
   divided
12 whole dried apricots (about 3
   ounces), quartered
⅔ cup golden raisins
¼ cup minced parsley

1½ teaspoons minced fresh ginger
¼ teaspoon ground allspice
¼ teaspoon ground cinnamon
¼ teaspoon ground cumin
⅛ teaspoon ground nutmeg
¼ teaspoon cayenne pepper
1¾ cups low-sodium chicken
   broth
¼ cup water
Salt and freshly ground black
   pepper to taste

Preheat oven to 350°. In a large, deep, oven-proof skillet with a lid, heat oil over medium heat.

Coat chicken with flour and shake off the excess. Add chicken to the skillet in batches and cook until browned, about 5 minutes per batch. Set chicken aside.

Drain fat from skillet. Add lentils, scallions, 4 tablespoons cilantro, apricots, raisins, parsley, ginger, allspice, cinnamon, cumin, nutmeg, and cayenne to the skillet. Cook 1 minute, stirring. Place chicken and its juices atop lentil mixture. Add broth and water and bring to a boil. Cover skillet and place it in the oven. Bake 30 minutes, then uncover and bake 20 minutes longer, or until chicken and lentils are tender.

Before serving, season to taste with salt and pepper and sprinkle with remaining cilantro. Serves 6–8.

The Pea & Lentil Cookbook

St. Joe River is the world's highest navigable river at a 2,128-foot elevation. It runs 66.3 miles.

Chicken Chalupas

Best if made a day in advance.

2 (10¾-ounce) cans cream of
  chicken soup
1 pint sour cream
1 (4-ounce) can green chiles
1 (4-ounce) can chopped ripe
  olives

¼ cup chopped green onion
¾ pound grated Jack cheese
4 large chicken breasts, cooked,
  deboned, and chopped
12 flour tortillas
¾ pound grated Cheddar cheese

Combine soup, sour cream, chiles, olives, and green onion. Mix and add Jack cheese. Remove 2 cups of mixture and set aside. Add chopped chicken to remaining mixture; fill 12 tortillas and roll up. Place tortillas in a 9x13-inch pan, seam-side-down. Pour remaining mixture on tortillas. Spread evenly and top with grated Cheddar. Bake at 350° for 40 minutes.

Cooking with Cops, Too

Chicken Enchiladas

1 (16-ounce) can tomatoes
1 (4-ounce) can chopped green
  chile peppers
¼ teaspoon ground coriander
½ teaspoon salt
1 cup dairy sour cream
2 cups cooked, finely chopped
  chicken

1 (3-ounce) package cream cheese,
  softened
¼ cup finely chopped onion
12 flour tortillas
1 cup Monterey Jack cheese

Place tomatoes, chile peppers, coriander, and salt in blender; blend until smooth. Add sour cream, and blend just until smooth. Set aside.

Mix chicken, cream cheese, and onion, and spread on tortillas. Roll up and place in 7½x12x2-inch baking dish. Pour tomato mixture over rolled-up tortillas. Cover with foil. Bake about 30 minutes at 350°. Sprinkle with cheese and return to oven until cheese melts. Serves 6.

A Taste of Heaven

Creamy Chicken Enchiladas

$^{1}/_{2}$ pound skinless, boneless
  chicken breasts, steamed or
  baked
1 (10-ounce) package frozen
  chopped spinach, thawed and
  well drained
$^{1}/_{4}$ cup thinly sliced scallions
1 cup sour cream
$^{1}/_{4}$ cup plain yogurt
2 tablespoons unbleached
  all-purpose flour

$^{1}/_{4}$ teaspoon ground cumin
Salt to taste
$^{1}/_{4}$ cup milk
1 (4-ounce) can diced green chiles,
  drained
6 (7-inch) flour tortillas
3 ounces ($^{1}/_{3}$ cup) Monterey Jack
  cheese, grated
Salsa and chopped scallions for
  garnish

Shred cooked chicken into bite-size pieces. Combine chicken, spinach, and scallions; set aside.

In a separate bowl, combine sour cream, yogurt, flour, cumin, and salt. Stir in milk and chiles. Divide sauce in half.

Combine chicken mixture and half the sauce. Divide this filling among the tortillas and roll them up. Place rolled tortillas in the bottom of a Dutch oven or baking pan. Spoon the remaining sauce over the enchiladas.

Bake in a Dutch oven for 25–30 minutes, or in 350° conventional oven for 30 minutes. Sprinkle with cheese and let stand for 5 minutes. To serve, garnish with salsa and additional chopped scallions. Yields 6 servings.

The Outdoor Dutch Oven Cookbook

Yummy Chicken Tortillas

1 (16-ounce) carton sour cream
1 (10¾-ounce) can cream of
  chicken soup
4–6 chicken breasts, boiled
  and cut up
1 (4-ounce) can diced black olives

1 (4-ounce) can diced green chiles
1 (16-ounce) jar mild salsa
1 (10-count) package large flour
  tortillas
2 cups shredded Cheddar cheese

Mix together sour cream and soup. Set aside. Mix chicken, olives, chiles, and salsa together. Put small amounts in middle of tortillas. Roll up and place in baking dish, seam-side-down. Spread sour cream mixture over tortillas. Sprinkle with cheese. Bake at 350° for 25–30 minutes.

Cookin' at Its Best

Jalapeño Chicken

1½ pounds chicken breast fillets
1½ cups water
2 tablespoons butter
1 box chicken-flavored stuffing
  mix
1 teaspoon ground cumin
  (optional)

1 cup mild or medium salsa
2 cups shredded Monterey Jack
  cheese with jalapeño peppers
¾ cup sour cream
1 chopped jalapeño pepper, or
  to taste

Preheat oven to 325°. Cook chicken breasts as desired, and slice into thin strips. Bring water and butter to boil in a saucepan; add stuffing mix and cumin. Mix and spread evenly into a greased 7x12-inch baking dish. Layer with chicken, salsa, and cheese. Bake for 30 minutes and serve with sour cream and chopped jalapeño.

Centennial Cookbook

Smoked Chicken and Idaho Morel Mushroom Crepes

CREPES:

²⁄₃ cup whole milk
²⁄₃ cup water
3 large eggs

1 cup all-purpose flour
5 tablespoons clarified butter,
  divided

Place milk, water, and eggs in mixing bowl and beat vigorously. Slowly sift in flour while continuing to whisk, then whisk in 3 tablespoons clarified butter. Refrigerate mixture for 1 hour.

Heat a nonstick 6- to 8-inch pan over medium heat till very hot, then coat with ¹⁄₂ teaspoon clarified butter. Add 2 ounces of batter and spread evenly around bottom of pan. Cook until the crepe is formed, then flip with a high-heat rubber spatula. Remove from pan and repeat process with remaining 11 crepes. Separate crepes with wax or parchment paper till needed.

STUFFING:

2 teaspoons butter
1 tablespoon chopped shallots
12 ounces smoked chicken breast,
  cut julienne
3 cups heavy cream
1 cup chicken stock
¹⁄₂ teaspoon salt

¹⁄₄ teaspoon ground white pepper
2 cups sliced morel mushrooms
1 tablespoon cornstarch, dissolved
  in water
¹⁄₂ teaspoon fresh thyme leaves
  (dried is okay if fresh is not
  available)

In a 4-quart saucepan, heat butter and sauté shallots till translucent. Add chicken and sauté for an additional 2 minutes. Add cream and stock and season with salt and pepper. Taste and adjust with more salt and pepper, if needed. Cook for 3–5 minutes, then add sliced morels.

Strain morels and chicken off sauce and return sauce to pan. Place chicken and mushrooms in a glass bowl with plastic wrap over it, so that it can be reheated in a microwave when it is time to stuff the crepes. Bring sauce back to a boil on the stove, and slowly whisk in dissolved cornstarch till sauce resembles a thin gravy. Add thyme leaves to sauce and keep warm till crepes are ready to serve.

Place a crepe on work surface. After warming Stuffing, place about 3 ounces across center of crepe. Roll crepe and place it on a warm entrée-size plate (1 crepe is sufficient for an appetizer, but 2 will make a nice entrée). Ladle about 2 ounces of sauce over crepe; sprinkle with chopped parsley or garnish with a sprig of fresh thyme and serve.

The Idaho Table

Tarragon Chicken Pot Pie

3 chicken breast halves, skinless
   and boneless
4 cups water
1 teaspoon coarsely ground
   pepper
1 teaspoon dried tarragon leaves
1 sweet onion, coarsely chopped,
   divided
1/2 cup flour

1/2 cup fat-free liquid nondairy
   creamer
1/2 teaspoon each salt and
   pepper
2 1/4 cups reserved chicken broth
2 cups chopped carrots
1 cup frozen green peas
1 (4 1/2-ounce) can low-fat
   refrigerated biscuit dough

Poach chicken breasts in water, pepper, tarragon, and 1/2 the onion for 20 minutes. Remove chicken with slotted spoon and shred into bite-size pieces. Strain and reserve the broth.

Combine flour and 1 cup broth in jar. Shake until well blended. In a small saucepan, bring 1 cup broth to a boil. Gradually pour in flour mixture, stirring constantly. Cook until thickened, approximately 5 minutes. Slowly stir in creamer, salt and pepper. Pour into Dutch oven.

Meanwhile, place 1/4 cup broth in small sauce pan. Add remaining onion and carrots and cook over high heat until carrots are just slightly soft. Add to Dutch oven along with frozen peas and chicken. Mix thoroughly.

Bake at 375° for 30 minutes or until chicken mixture is hot and bubbly. Separate biscuit dough into 12 rounds; arrange biscuits on top of chicken mixture and bake for 10–12 minutes or until biscuits are golden brown. Serves 6.

Note: You may substitute your favorite biscuit recipe for the refrigerated dough.

Northern Lites: Contemporary Cooking with a Twist

Smoking Large Birds

Large birds mean turkeys or geese—there is no known way to smoke an ostrich. A 10–15 pound turkey, however, fits nicely into one of those portable aluminum home smokers, and the result is superb.

BRINE:

4 quarts water	**1¹/₂ cups curing salt**
¹/₂ cup brown sugar	**3 cups cider**
¹/₂ teaspoon ginger	**4 tablespoons black pepper**
¹/₂ cup lemon juice	**¹/₂ ounce maple flavoring**

If more brine is needed, the same proportions should be used. Mix thoroughly in a nonmetallic container in which the entire bird can be submerged. Simmer over medium heat for 5 minutes per pound. Remove bird from brine and air-dry for an hour. Rub skin with additional brown sugar. Place bird in smoker, which has been preheated, and smoke for 1 hour per pound. Every hour, baste bird with melted butter or sauce.

Remove bird from smoker and finish off in the kitchen oven at 300°. The bird should then have a rich golden brown color with free-moving joints.

Don Holm's Book of Food Drying, Pickling and Smoke Curing

Seafood

The South Fork of the Snake River is considered one of the best fly fishing rivers in North America with its large population of trout. One-fourth of Idaho residents own a fishing license. Another 200,000 non-residents also buy licenses.

PHOTO © WILLIAM H. MULLINS OUTDOOR PHOTOGRAPHY

Rainbow Trout Roulade with Crisp Potato Cake

POTATO CAKES:

2 large russet potatoes
1 tablespoon chopped shallot
1 teaspoon chopped fresh dill
1/2 teaspoon freshly ground black pepper

Kosher salt to taste
2 egg whites, beaten
1 cup cornmeal
1 cup canola oil

Wash potatoes; bake at 350° for 50 minutes or until cooked through. Remove potatoes from oven and allow to cool for 20 minutes. Cut potatoes in half lengthwise and grate white meat out of skin into a mixing bowl; combine with shallot, dill, black pepper, salt, and egg whites. Pack batter into 4-ounce balls, and press on a counter into 3/4-inch-thick cakes. Coat cakes with cornmeal. In a nonstick pan, heat oil till hot, but not smoking. Cook cakes for 1 minute or until golden brown. Flip cakes and place pan in oven for 3–4 minutes or until other side is golden brown. Remove cakes from pan and blot with a paper towel in preparation for serving.

TROUT ROULADE:

2 tablespoons + 2 teaspoons butter, divided
1 tablespoon shallot, finely diced
1/2 pound crawfish tail meat
2 cups fresh spinach leaves
2 teaspoons finely chopped fresh dill

1 teaspoon kosher salt, divided
1/2 teaspoon white pepper (fresh ground)
4 rainbow trout
1 cup Pinot Blanc

Preheat oven to 400° and butter an 8-inch-square baking dish. In a nonstick sauté pan, heat 2 tablespoons butter and add shallot. Sauté for 45 seconds or until shallot becomes translucent. Add crawfish tail meat and cook briefly. Once crawfish tails begin to turn red, toss with spinach, dill, 1/2 teaspoon salt, and 1/4 teaspoon freshly ground pepper and remove stuffing from pan into a bowl.

Locate and remove pin bones from trout by making a slice on top and bottom of the row of bones and pulling the strip out with your fingers (most respectable fish markets will do this for you). Use a flexible fillet knife to slide the fillet off the skin. After skin is removed from the 4 trout, place fillets 2 on top of each other, each in 4 stacks,

(continued)

(Rainbow Trout Roulade with Crisp Potato Cake continued)

skin-side-up on a work surface. Sprinkle fillets with remaining kosher salt and white pepper. Divide spinach and crawfish stuffing into 4 even piles and place in the center of the stacks of trout fillets. Roll the 2 ends of the fillets around filling and secure ends of fillets with tooth-picks. Place stuffed trout in greased baking dish so stuffing is showing on top and bottom. Pour ¼ cup of wine and a small flake of remaining butter over each roulade and bake for 12–15 minutes or until crawfish tails are just barely cooked through.

The Idaho Table

Papa's Favorite Trout

Jack Hemingway says, "This was Papa's favorite trout recipe. Mmmmm!"

**1 dozen (6- to 8-inch) little
brookies, filleted, but leave the
blood line along backbone**

**Salt and pepper
1 stick butter
Juice of 2 lemons**

Salt and pepper trout inside and out. Melt butter in a large skillet until it froths. Add trout and brown on both sides. Add lemon juice prior to turning trout over with spatula. Baste continuously until butter and trout are browned. Eat right away! Serves 6–8.

Ketchum Cooks

Famous Idaho authors: The poet Ezra Pound was born in Hailey, just 11 miles south of where Ernest Hemingway is buried. Vardis Fisher, born in Annis, authored many novels, including *Children of God, Tale of Valor,* and *Mountain Man* (later made into the Hollywood film "Jeremiah Johnson").

Sugar-Cured Rainbows

Rainbow trout are delicious when sugar-cured.

Split and open fish. Rub each with a handful of salt, then a handful of brown sugar. Place in layers in wooden barrel or crock, skin-side-down. Sprinkle each layer with black peppercorns. The top layer should be skin-side-up. Place in a cool spot overnight. Then wash in cool, fresh water for 20 minutes. Stack and press out moisture. Blot dry with towels.

Smoke for 2–3 hours at about 85° until a nice pellicle (thin skin or film) is formed. Smoke another hour at 110°, then an hour at 120°, and longer, if necessary.

Don Holm's Book of Food Drying, Pickling and Smoke Curing

Stream-Side Salmon

1 (2- to 3-pound) salmon fillet   ½ cup sour cream
Salt and pepper   1 onion, sliced into rings
Lemon pepper   1 lemon, sliced into rings
Fresh or dried dill weed

Arrange enough aluminum foil to be double wrapped and have a closed seam for cooking. Lay the salmon fillet on the aluminum foil. Dust the fillet with salt and pepper. Lemon pepper works well, too. Sprinkle fresh or dried dill on the fillet. Brush sour cream on the fillet abundantly. Place thin slices of onion and lemon over the fillet. Wrap up the fillet in the aluminum foil. Place directly over briquets or on the coals of your campfire on a low fire. Turn fillet over after about 20 minutes and cook for approximately 20 more minutes. Depending on how hot your coals are, cooking time can be reduced to 15 minutes per side.

Cee Dub's Dutch Oven and Other Camp Cookin'

Baked Salmon with Sour Cream

4 salmon fillets
4 tablespoons chopped onion,
  sautéed

1 tablespoon parsley flakes
Salt and pepper
1 cup white wine

Place salmon in a single layer in greased baking pan. Sprinkle with onion, parsley, salt and pepper. Pour wine over fish. Bake uncovered at 375° for 15 minutes. Remove and pour off liquid.

SOUR CREAM SAUCE:

1 cup sour cream (regular or
  fat free)
$^1/_2$ teaspoon dill weed

$^1/_2$ teaspoon sautéed onion
Salt and pepper
Paprika

Mix all ingredients and spread over salmon. Sprinkle with paprika and return to oven 10 minutes or just until fish is tender. Do not overcook. Serves 4.

Another Cookbook

Grilled Salmon
with Avocado Corn Chutney

$^1/_2$ cup olive oil
2 tablespoons fresh lime juice
1 teaspoon lime zest
1 teaspoon chopped garlic

$^1/_4$ teaspoon salt
$^1/_8$ teaspoon pepper
6 (6- to 8-ounce) salmon fillets,
  skin removed

Combine olive oil, lime juice, zest, garlic, salt and pepper. Wash and pat the fillets dry. Place fillets in marinade for 20 minutes while you make the chutney. Grill the fillets to your taste; top with the chutney to serve. Yields 6 portions.

AVOCADO CORN CHUTNEY:

$1^1/_2$ cups coarsely chopped
  avocado, firm, but ripe
$1^1/_2$ cups corn kernels
$^1/_2$ cup julienne sliced jicama
$^1/_4$ cup chopped red onion

2 tablespoons fresh lime juice
2 tablespoons fresh chopped
  cilantro
2 tablespoons sour cream
Salt and pepper to taste

Combine all ingredients; refrigerate.

Cooking on the Wild Side

Thai-Dyed Salmon Kabobs

MARINADE:

1 onion, minced
5 cloves garlic, minced
1 cup olive oil
2 teaspoons sesame oil
1/3 cup soy sauce

3/4 cup bourbon whiskey
1/4 cup firmly packed brown
  sugar
Cayenne pepper to taste

Combine ingredients in blender or food processor and blend until smooth. Marinate salmon and mushrooms overnight.

3 pounds salmon fillets, cut into
  2-inch cubes
1 pound shiitake mushrooms,
  cleaned

1 bunch green onions, cut into
  1-inch slices

Skewer all ingredients on 6–8 metal skewers, alternating salmon, mushrooms, and onions. Grill or broil approximately 4 minutes, turning often to cook all sides. Serves 6–7.

Ketchum Cooks

Smoked Florentine Salmon

1 pound smoked salmon
1 cup cooked, drained spinach
4 tablespoons butter or
  margarine, divided
Dash nutmeg
1/4 teaspoon pepper
2 tablespoons chopped onion
1 clove garlic, chopped fine

3 tablespoons flour
1/4 teaspoon salt
1 1/4 cups milk
2 tablespoons sherry
1/4 cup grated Parmesan cheese
3 hard-cooked eggs, sliced for
  garnish
Watercress for garnish

Mash salmon and chop spinach. Mix spinach with 2 tablespoons butter, nutmeg, and pepper. Spread the mixture in a greased 8-inch-round baking dish, 2 inches deep. Cook onion and garlic in 2 tablespoons butter. Blend in flour and salt. Mix with milk and cook until thick, stirring. Add sherry and salmon. Spread over spinach mixture in baking dish. Sprinkle with cheese. Bake at 350° for 20–25 minutes. Garnish with egg slices and watercress. Serves 6.

Don Holm's Book of Food Drying, Pickling and Smoke Curing

Dutch Oven Halibut

3 tablespoons olive oil
6–8 cloves garlic, minced
4 tablespoons chopped fresh
  tarragon
1/4 cup lemon juice

2 cups white wine or cooking
  liquid
4–5 pounds halibut, cut into
  chunks, or fillets

Heat olive oil in 12-inch Dutch oven. Add garlic, and sauté for a few minutes, stirring constantly. Add fresh tarragon, lemon juice, and white wine or cooking liquid. Stir to blend all ingredients. Add halibut chunks or fillets; mix to coat the halibut with all the flavors. Cover and put Dutch oven into firepan. Put 6–8 briquets under the Dutch oven and 15 briquets on the lid. Cook 20–30 minutes depending upon the size of the chunks or fillets. When done, take off fire and remove halibut. Serve the juice as a sauce to be poured over halibut, or as an excellent dip for bread.

More Cee Dub's Dutch Oven and Other Camp Cookin'

Halibut with Tarragon Cream

1 1/2 pounds halibut (skinless
  fillets, cheeks or steaks)
1/2 cup nonfat yogurt cheese
1 tablespoon low-fat mayonnaise

1 teaspoon dry tarragon
3/4 cup grated low-fat mozzarella
  cheese

Rinse and dry halibut. Place in a baking pan just large enough to hold fish. Mix all other ingredients together and spread over halibut. Bake at 400° for 15–30 minutes or just until fish flakes when tested with a fork (time will vary depending upon thickness). Place under broiler until top is puffy and browned, approximately 2 minutes. Serve immediately. Serves 4.

Note: Fresh fish is always best for flavor and texture; however, flash-frozen halibut is an excellent substitute. The key is to allow adequate thawing time.

Northern Lites: Contemporary Cooking with a Twist

Idaho Catfish Stew

2 pounds skinned catfish fillets,
  fresh or frozen
5 slices bacon
1½ cups chopped onions
1 (28-ounce) can tomatoes,
  undrained
⅛ teaspoon pepper, freshly
  ground

1 (8-ounce) can tomato sauce
3 cups diced Idaho potatoes
2 tablespoons Worcestershire
  sauce
2 teaspoons salt
¼ teaspoon hot pepper sauce

Thaw fillets, if frozen. Cut in 1½-inch pieces. Fry bacon in Dutch oven over low heat until crisp. Drain on absorbent paper; crumble and set aside. Add onions to Dutch oven; cover and cook 5 minutes or until tender. Stir in remaining ingredients, except bacon and catfish. Bring to a boil; simmer 30 minutes. Add bacon and catfish. Cover and simmer 8–10 minutes or until fish flakes easily when tested with a fork. Serves 6.

Idaho's Wild 100!

Herbed Crab Cakes with a Cucumber-Dill Sauce

The unofficial University of Ketchum Prom has been in existence for 17 years, and is always a good party with some really wild outfits. Held in the spring, with a pink flamingo theme, I started serving these at my pre-prom warm-up parties.

1 pound fresh crab, flaked and shelled	1 tablespoon lemon juice
3 tablespoons finely diced celery	Pinch of cayenne pepper
2 tablespoons finely diced red bell pepper	1 teaspoon dry mustard
1 teaspoon each minced fresh rosemary and chives	3 tablespoons mayonnaise
2 teaspoons low-sodium soy sauce	1 teaspoon Worcestershire sauce
	Dash Tabasco
	3 cups bread crumbs (more for breading)

Combine all ingredients, except bread crumbs, in a large bowl and mix well. Form into small balls, if an appetizer; large patties as a dinner entrée. Pat in bread crumbs and fry in oil, about 3 minutes per side. Serve with lemon wedges or Cucumber-Dill Sauce. Makes 4–6 large patties or 10–12 small patties.

Note: Can be made a day in advance and kept in refrigerator until ready to cook. Freezes well.

CUCUMBER-DILL SAUCE:

1 large cucumber, peeled, seeded, and finely minced	2–3 tablespoons finely chopped fresh dill
1/3 cup sour cream	1/8 teaspoon salt
1/3 cup unflavored low-fat yogurt	Dash freshly ground pepper
2 tablespoons reduced-calorie or regular mayonnaise	Dash hot pepper sauce

Combine all ingredients. Chill thoroughly. Serve with hot or cold fish. Can be blended for a smoother consistency. Spoon 4 tablespoons on a plate and lay crab cake on top. Makes 2 cups.

Ketchum Cooks

Sea Scallops
with Fresh Pineapple Salsa

Scallops are best if cooked very quickly over high heat. They should have a rich golden brown crust and be moist and tender inside.

1¹/₂ pounds sea scallops
1 tablespoon olive oil
2 garlic cloves, minced

2 tablespoons Sauterne wine
Salt and pepper to taste

Discard tough, crescent-shaped membrane at side of each scallop. Rinse scallops with cold water; drain and pat dry. Heat olive oil in large sauté pan to very hot. Add scallops, garlic, Sauterne, salt and pepper to taste. Sauté until golden brown, 3–4 minutes.

FRESH PINEAPPLE SALSA:
2 cups chopped fresh, ripe
  pineapple
¹/₃ cup chopped sweet onion
¹/₃ cup chopped cilantro (fresh)
1 tablespoon seeded, chopped
  jalapeño pepper

1 tablespoon lemon juice
1 tablespoon tarragon vinegar
¹/₂ teaspoon salt

Place all ingredients in food processor fitted with metal blade. Process until chopped, but not puréed. Salsa may be made several hours before serving.

Note: Pineapple should be very ripe, or it may make the salsa bitter. Serves 4.

Northern Lites: Contemporary Cooking with a Twist

Nearly 85% of all the commercial trout sold in the United States is produced in the Hagerman Valley near Twin Falls.

Maxwell Bar Shrimp

MARINADE:

1 clove garlic, pressed
$^1\!/_4$ cup Sauterne wine
$1^1\!/_2$ tablespoons parsley and
  basil

$^1\!/_8$ teaspoon lemon pepper
$^1\!/_2$ cup olive oil
$^1\!/_8$ cup lemon juice
$^1\!/_2$ teaspoon salt

Mix all ingredients together in medium-size bowl. Marinate shelled shrimp for an hour or so.

8 jumbo shrimp

Shell and devein shrimp; marinate for 1 hour or so. Grill for about 10 minutes, careful not to scorch. Baste with Marinade. (Shrimp are like salmon—they don't take long to cook, and are easy to overcook). While you are grilling the shrimp, make Sauce. Serves 4.

SAUCE:

1 stick butter, clarified
$^1\!/_2$ teaspoon lemon juice

$^1\!/_2$ tablespoon parsley
1 clove garlic, pressed

Melt butter in lemon juice with garlic and parsley for the sauce.

Recipes Stolen from the River of No Return

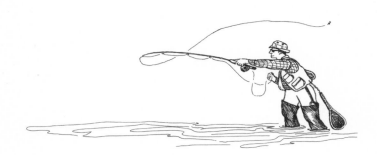

Feta Shrimp Bake

This is always a favorite dish on Rocky Mountain River Tours' Middle Fork float trips.

1¹/₄ cups chopped onion
4 garlic cloves, minced
¹/₈ cup olive oil
6 fresh tomatoes, chopped
¹/₂ cup chopped fresh parsley
1 tablespoon chopped fresh basil
2 teaspoons fresh marjoram
2 teaspoons grated lemon peel

Salt and freshly ground pepper
  to taste
1 teaspoon allspice
3 pounds shrimp, peeled and
  cleaned
1¹/₂ pounds feta cheese, crumbled
1 pound linguini pasta, cooked

In a Dutch oven or skillet, sauté onion and garlic in oil. Add tomatoes, parsley, basil, marjoram, and lemon peel. Simmer about 10 minutes. Season with salt, pepper, and allspice. If preparing conventionally, pour mixture into 2-quart casserole dish.

Put the shrimp on top of mixture. Sprinkle with feta cheese. Bake in Dutch oven for about 20 minutes, or in 350° conventional oven for 30–40 minutes, until the shrimp is done. Serve on top of linguini. Yields 8 servings.

The Outdoor Dutch Oven Cookbook

Cakes

Built in 1892, the Old Schoolhouse Museum exhibits Silver City's history. The Silver City area, in the Owyhee Mountains, was a major silver and gold producer, mining more than 60 million dollars worth of the precious metals.

Potato Cake

This recipe is about 140 years old. It's so moist, you don't need to frost it.

²/₃ cup butter or shortening
2 cups flour
¹/₂ cup milk
2 teaspoons baking powder
¹/₄–1 teaspoon ground cloves
¹/₂–1 teaspoon cinnamon
¹/₂ teaspoon salt
¹/₂ cup cocoa (or 2 squares chocolate, melted)

2 cups sugar
1 cup hot mashed potatoes
4 eggs (beat yolks and whites separately, add whites last)
¹/₄–1 teaspoon nutmeg
1 teaspoon vanilla
1 cup chopped nuts

Combine all ingredients; mix well and bake in greased 9x13-inch cake pan at 375° for 40 minutes.

Idaho's Wild 100!

Fresh Tomato Cake

7 medium-size tomatoes
¹/₂ cup butter, softened
1 cup packed brown sugar
2 eggs
¹/₂ cup raisins
¹/₂ cup chopped dates
3 cups flour

2 teaspoons baking powder
1 teaspoon baking soda
¹/₂ teaspoon salt
1 teaspoon allspice
¹/₂ teaspoon ground ginger
³/₄ teaspoon grated orange rind

Skin tomatoes; cut into quarters and remove seeds. Chop. Measure 3 cups. Drain well in sieve. Set aside.

Cream butter and brown sugar until light and fluffy. Add eggs, one at a time, beating well after each. Stir in raisins, dates, and drained tomatoes (mixture may appear curdled). Combine dry ingredients; gradually add to creamed mixture. Turn in to greased 9x5-inch loaf pan. Bake at 350° for 1 hour and 10 minutes, or until tests done. Cool in pan 5 minutes. Remove from pan and complete cooling on wire rack. Sprinkle with powdered sugar before serving, if desired.

Cookin' at Its Best

Oatmeal Cake

My mother often baked this moist and yummy cake when I was growing up.

CAKE:

1¼ cups boiling water
1 cup rolled oats
1 cup white sugar
1 cup brown sugar
½ cup butter or margarine
2 eggs

1⅓ cups unbleached all-purpose
  flour
1 teaspoon baking soda
½ teaspoon ground cinnamon
½ teaspoon salt
1 teaspoon vanilla extract

Grease and flour a 12-inch Dutch oven or 9x13-inch pan and set aside.

Pour boiling water over oats and let stand while mixing the rest of the cake. Cream together the sugars and butter or margarine. Add eggs and mix well. In a separate bowl, sift together flour, soda, cinnamon, and salt. Add to sugar mixture. Stir in oatmeal mixture and vanilla. Pour batter into Dutch oven or pan.

Bake in Dutch oven for 30 minutes, or in 350° conventional oven for 30–40 minutes.

TOPPING:

1 cup brown sugar
3 tablespoons melted butter
6 tablespoons cream

1 cup shredded coconut
1 cup chopped nuts

Mix brown sugar, melted butter, cream, coconut, and nuts. Pour Topping over partly cooled cake and place under broiler for a few minutes until brown and bubbly. Yields 12 servings.

The Outdoor Dutch Oven Cookbook

Genuine Idaho potatoes are deep brown and have a rounded, somewhat elongated shape. They have very few eyes and the eyes are shallow. When purchasing, look for clean, smooth, firm-textured potatoes that have no cuts, bruises or discoloration.

Camas Creek Carrot Cake

Camas is a blue flower which grows in meadows on the upper reaches of this stream on the Middle Fork of the Salmon River.

2 cups unbleached all-purpose flour	1¹/₂ cups vegetable oil
1¹/₂ teaspoons baking soda	4 eggs
2 teaspoons baking powder	2 cups grated carrots
1 teaspoon salt	1 (8-ounce) can crushed pineapple, drained
2 teaspoons ground cinnamon	1 cup flaked coconut
2 cups sugar	¹/₂ cup chopped walnuts

Lightly butter a 12-inch Dutch oven or 9x12-inch baking pan.

In a large bowl, combine flour, baking soda, baking powder, salt, and cinnamon. Stir in sugar, vegetable oil, eggs, carrots, pineapple, coconut, and walnuts. Pour batter into Dutch oven or pan.

Bake in Dutch oven for 30–40 minutes, or in 350° conventional oven for 45–55 minutes. Let cool and frost with Cream Cheese Frosting (recipe follows). Yields 12–15 servings.

CREAM CHEESE FROSTING:

8 ounces cream cheese, softened	1 teaspoon vanilla extract
¹/₂ cup unsalted butter, softened	¹/₃ cup confectioners' sugar

Combine cream cheese, butter, and vanilla; beat until fluffy. Gradually add the confectioners' sugar. Beat again until smooth.

The Outdoor Dutch Oven Cookbook

Eggless, Milkless Spice Cake

1 cup water or beer
2 cups raisins
1 cup brown sugar
$1/3$ cup margarine
$1/2$ teaspoon cinnamon
$1/2$ teaspoon allspice

$1/8$ teaspoon nutmeg
$1/2$ teaspoon salt
2 cups flour
1 teaspoon baking powder
1 cup chopped walnuts or pecans

Grease and flour a 9x13-inch pan. In medium saucepan, bring to boil water or beer, raisins, brown sugar, margarine, cinnamon, allspice, nutmeg, and salt. Boil for 3 minutes and remove from heat and let cool. Gradually add remaining ingredients to cooled liquid mixture. Pour batter into cake pan. Bake at 350° for 35–45 minutes. If center bounces back when pressed, it's done.

Cool; ice with your favorite icing or top with brown sugar, coconut, and margarine, then place back in oven on broil; remove when brown. Can be served hot or cold. Makes 10–12 servings.

Variation: Makes great fruit cakes by adding 1 cup of candied fruit and chopped dates. For best results, bake in loaf pans.

Grandma Jane's Cookbook

Hootenholler Whiskey Cake

$1/2$ cup butter, softened
1 cup sugar
3 eggs, beaten
1 cup flour
$1/2$ teaspoon baking powder
$1/4$ teaspoon salt
$1/2$ teaspoon nutmeg

$1/4$ cup milk
$1/4$ teaspoon baking soda
$1/4$ cup molasses
1 pound raisins
2 cups chopped pecans
$1/4$ cup bourbon

In a large bowl, cream butter with sugar and add eggs. Combine flour, baking powder, salt, and nutmeg. Add butter mixture and mix well. Add milk.

Combine baking soda and molasses. Mix well and add to batter. Stir in raisins, nuts, and bourbon. Pour batter into a greased and floured 9x5x3-inch loaf pan. Bake at 300° for 2 hours. Makes 1 loaf cake.

Note: This cake, wrapped in foil, keeps for weeks.

Bound to Please

Burnt Sugar Candy Bar Cake

2¹/₄ cups granulated sugar,
  divided
³/₄ cup hot water
3 cups all-purpose flour
¹/₂ teaspoon baking powder
¹/₄ teaspoon baking soda
²/₃ cup butter, softened

2 eggs, separated
2 teaspoons vanilla
1 recipe Brown Butter Frosting
1¹/₂ cups coarsely chopped candy
  bars (Hershey's, Mars, Nestle's
  Crunch, etc.)

Grease and flour 2 round baking pans. In a large skillet, cook ³/₄ cup sugar over medium-high heat until sugar just begins to melt. Reduce heat; cook until sugar is golden brown, about 1–3 minutes more, stirring mixture constantly. Carefully stir in hot water (syrup will form lumps). Bring to a boil; reduce heat. Continue stirring until mixture is free of lumps. Remove from heat. Pour syrup into a large measuring cup. Add additional water to equal 1³/₄ cups liquid. Set aside to cool.

Preheat oven to 350°. In a large mixing bowl, stir together flour, baking powder, and baking soda. In a separate bowl, beat together the 1¹/₂ cups sugar, butter, egg yolks, and vanilla with an electric mixer on medium speed for 1 minute, until smooth. Alternately add flour mixture and sugar syrup to egg mixture, beating on low speed after each addition just until combined. Clean beaters thoroughly.

In a medium mixing bowl, beat egg whites until stiff peaks form. Fold into batter; divide batter into baking pans; spread evenly. Bake for 25 minutes or until toothpick inserted in center comes out clean. Cool in pan; transfer to wire racks; cool completely. Prepare Brown Butter Icing.

BROWN BUTTER ICING:

¹/₂ cup plus 3 tablespoons butter
  (no substitute), divided
2 (3-ounce) packages cream
  cheese, softened

6¹/₂ cups sifted powdered sugar,
  divided
1 teaspoon vanilla
2–3 teaspoons milk

In a small saucepan, heat and stir ¹/₂ cup butter over low heat until melted. Continue heating until butter turns a nut-brown color. Remove from heat; cool for 5 minutes.

In a large mixing bowl, beat together cream cheese with 3 tablespoons butter until combined. Beat in about 2 cups sifted powdered sugar.

(continued)

(Burnt Sugar Candy Bar Cake continued)

Beat in the browned butter and vanilla. Gradually beat in remaining powdered sugar and milk until frosting is of spreading consistency.

Spread 1/2 cup frosting over bottom cake layer. Sprinkle layer with 1/2 the chopped candy. Put on top layer, rounded side up, and frost sides and then top. Garnish with the rest of the coarsely chopped candy bar pieces, if desired.

Be Our Guest

Idaho Chocolate Cake

This cake is dark, dense and wonderfully fudgy.

1 (4-ounce) Idaho russet potato,
   peeled and grated
2 cups sour cream
1 3/4 cups cake flour
1 3/4 cups sugar
3/4 cup unsweetened cocoa

1/2 cup unsalted butter
2 large eggs
1 1/2 teaspoons baking soda
1 teaspoon vanilla
1/2 teaspoon salt

Position rack in center of oven and preheat to 350°. Butter a 9x13-inch baking pan and dust with flour. Place grated potato in work bowl. Combine all remaining ingredients and add half of the mixture to potato. Mix for 3 minutes, scraping bowl once. Transfer mixture to a larger bowl, add the balance of sour cream mixture, and beat an additional 3 minutes. Scrape sides of bowl once. Pour into prepared pan. Bake 35–40 minutes or until cake tester inserted in middle comes out clean. Cool completely in pan on rack. Invert onto cake dish and frost, if desired.

Idaho Cook Book

Did you know that Idaho has a seaport? The Port of Lewiston lies 465 miles inland from the Pacific Ocean along the Columbia/Snake River systems and facilitates the exportation of millions of bushels of grain down the Snake and Columbia Rivers for overseas shipment.

Chocolate Zucchini Cake

¹/2 cup butter or margarine, softened
¹/2 cup vegetable oil
1³/4 cups sugar
2 eggs
1 teaspoon vanilla
¹/2 cup sour milk
2¹/2 cups flour
¹/2 cup cocoa

¹/2 teaspoon baking powder
1 teaspoon baking soda
¹/2 teaspoon cinnamon
¹/2 teaspoon ground cloves
2 cups shredded zucchini (or carrots)
2 bananas, sliced
³/4 cup chopped nuts (optional)

Cream together butter or margarine with oil and sugar. Add eggs, vanilla, and sour milk (add 1¹/2 teaspoons lemon juice to milk, wait 10 minutes) and mix well. Sift together and add flour, cocoa, baking powder, baking soda, cinnamon, and cloves. Stir in the shredded zucchini (or carrots), bananas, and nuts, if desired.

Put 16–18 coals on the lid around the rim, 4 in the middle of the lid, 4 directly under the oven, and 6 around the bottom outside edge. Pour batter in greased 12-inch Dutch oven; after 15 minutes of baking, remove the 4 coals from the middle of the lid and continue cooking for about 30 minutes. You don't have to frost this cake unless you really want to, because it is already very moist.

Hey Ma! Come Quick! The Hog's in the Garden Again!!

Editor's Extra: Can bake in 375° oven for 45–50 minutes in greased Bundt pan.

Cherry Chocolate Dump Cake

2 (21-ounce) cans cherry pie filling
1 chocolate cake mix, with
  pudding in the mix

1 (20-ounce) bottle cherry-flavored
  carbonated soda

Place pie filling in the bottom of a greased 12-inch Dutch oven. Sprinkle dry cake mix over the fruit filling. Gently pour carbonated soda over the cake mix. Cover and bake, using 5 or 6 briquets under the Dutch oven, 20 on the outside rim of the lid, and 3 or 4 in the middle of the lid. Bake 35–45 minutes. Top with ice cream or whipped cream for an added treat.

More Cee Dub's Dutch Oven and Other Camp Cookin'

Editor's Extra: Can bake in 375° oven for 35–45 minutes, uncovering for the last 10 minutes. Serve as you would cobbler.

Rhubarb Upside-Down Cake

5 cups chopped rhubarb
1 cup sugar
1 (3-ounce) package raspberry
  Jell-O

3 cups mini-marshmallows
1 white or yellow cake mix,
  prepared according to package
  directions

Spread rhubarb in a greased 9x13-inch cake pan. Sprinkle with sugar and Jell-O. Top with marshmallows. Mix the cake mix as directed, then pour over the rhubarb. Bake at 350° for 45–55 minutes. Let sit for 5 minutes; when done, turn upside-down into a cookie sheet.

Cookin' in Paradise

The 3.5 million-year-old sediments at the Hagerman Fossil Beds National Monument contain about 200 horse skeletons, 20 of which are complete. The more than 200 vertebrate, invertebrate, and plant species preserved there represent the last vestiges of animals that existed prior to the Ice Age and the earliest appearances of modern flora and fauna.

Pineapple Upside-Down Cake

¹/₄ cup butter or margarine
1 cup packed brown sugar
1 (20-ounce) can sliced pineapple,
  drained and juice reserved
1 (16-ounce) jar maraschino
  cherries, drained

1 package yellow cake mix
Oil and eggs as recommended on
  cake mix package

Preheat oven to 375°. Melt butter in 12-inch Dutch oven. Sprinkle brown sugar evenly over butter. Arrange pineapple slices and cherries over top; press gently. Add enough water to pineapple juice to measure 1¹/₄ cups. Make cake batter as directed on package, except use pineapple juice mixture instead of water. Pour batter gently over pineapple and cherries. Bake 40–45 minutes or until toothpick inserted in center comes out clean. Immediately turn pan upside-down onto lid or plate; leave Dutch oven over cake 1 minute. Serve warm or cool. Store loosely covered.

Potatoes Are Not the Only Vegetable!

Pen's Pineapple Upside Dump Cake

¹/₄ pound (1 stick) butter
1 cup brown sugar
1 (20-ounce) can crushed
  pineapple

1 white or yellow cake mix
1 (20-ounce) bottle carbonated
  lemon-lime soda

Melt butter and brown sugar in the bottom of a 12-inch Dutch oven, and spread evenly over the bottom of the Dutch oven. Spoon in evenly the undrained pineapple. Sprinkle dry cake mix over the pineapple. Gently pour carbonated soda over cake mix. Cover and bake, using 5 or 6 briquets under the Dutch oven, 20 on the outside rim of the lid, and 3 or 4 in the middle of the lid. Bake 40–50 minutes.

More Cee Dub's Dutch Oven and Other Camp Cookin'

Editor's Extra: Can bake in 375° oven for 40–50 minutes, uncovering for the last 10 minutes. Serve in bowls like cobbler.

Georgia Apple Cake and Topping

2 cups sugar
1/3 cup fresh or bottled lemon
  juice
1 cup oil
2 teaspoons vanilla

2 eggs, beaten
3 cups flour
1¼ teaspoons baking soda
1 teaspoon salt
3 cups chopped apples

Preheat oven to 350°. Grease a 9x13-inch baking pan. In mixing bowl, combine sugar, lemon juice, oil, vanilla, and eggs; beat well. Add flour, soda, and salt; mix well. Fold in apples. Bake at 350° for 45 minutes.

TOPPING:
1 cup brown sugar
¾ stick butter or margarine

¼ cup milk
2 tablespoons vanilla

Mix brown sugar, butter or margarine, milk, and vanilla in saucepan. Boil 3½ minutes (it will be like a soft-ball stage). Prick holes in warm cake; pour Topping over the warm cake.

Quilter's Delight, Busy Day Recipes

Apple Crisp Cake

¹⁄₃ cup milk	1 package dry yeast
¹⁄₄ cup sugar	1 egg, beaten
¹⁄₂ teaspoon salt	1¹⁄₂ cups sifted flour
2 tablespoons butter	3 apples, pared and thinly sliced
¹⁄₄ cup very warm water	

Scald milk; stir in sugar, salt, and butter; cool to luke warm. Measure very warm water into large mixing bowl. Sprinkle in yeast, stirring until dissolved. Add lukewarm milk mixture. Add beaten egg and flour. Stir until blended; spread batter in well-greased 9x13x2-inch baking pan. Arrange apple slices on top.

TOPPING:

¹⁄₄ cup soft butter	1 teaspoon cinnamon
¹⁄₂ cup brown sugar	¹⁄₂ teaspoon nutmeg
¹⁄₂ cup sifted flour	

Cut butter into mixture of brown sugar, flour, and spices. Sprinkle over apples; cover. Let rise in warm place until double in bulk, about 1 hour. Bake at 400° for 30 minutes.

Recipes Logged from the Woods of North Idaho

Apple Pound Cake

3 cups flour
1 teaspoon baking soda
1 teaspoon salt
1½ cups oil
2 cups sugar

3 eggs
2 teaspoons vanilla
2 cups finely chopped apples
  (4 or 5)
1½ cups chopped walnuts

Sift flour, soda, and salt. In large bowl, beat oil, sugar, eggs, and vanilla until well blended. Gradually add flour mixture and blend until smooth. Fold in apples and walnuts. Pour batter into a greased and floured Bundt pan. Bake in preheated 325° oven for 1 hour and 20 minutes. Delicious plain, but even better with Topping spooned over warm cake.

TOPPING:
¼ cup butter
¼ cup light brown sugar

2 teaspoons milk

In small saucepan, combine all ingredients; bring to a boil over medium heat. Continue boiling for about 2 minutes, stirring constantly. Let cool some before putting on cake.

Tastes from the Country

Poppy Seed Cake

4 eggs
2 cups sugar
1½ cups vegetable oil
3 cups flour

1½ teaspoons baking powder
½ teaspoon salt
12 ounces evaporated milk
½ cup poppy seeds

Mix eggs, sugar, and oil in a large bowl. Then add the rest of the ingredients. Pour into a greased and floured Bundt pan. Bake at 350° for 1 hour; watch closely for doneness. Glaze (powdered sugar with water to thin) while warm, if desired.

Down Home Country Cookin'

Sugar-Free Banana Split Cake

FIRST LAYER:

1 (16-ounce) box low-fat vanilla wafers

2 tablespoons butter, melted

Crush vanilla wafers and mix with melted butter. Place in a 9x13-inch pan.

SECOND LAYER:

2 (8-ounce) packages low-fat cream cheese, softened

1 (5-ounce) package sugar-free vanilla instant pudding

1 (12-ounce) carton low-fat Cool Whip, divided

Mix together cream cheese, pudding and ½ carton Cool Whip and spread on cookie crumbs.

THIRD LAYER:

2 large bananas

1 (20-ounce) can crushed pineapple, drained

Chopped nuts (optional)

Slice bananas onto Second Layer and add crushed pineapple. Top with remaining Cool Whip, and sprinkle with nuts, if desired.

Generations "Coming Home"

Lemon Cheesecake

Absolutely needs to be made the day before serving.

CRUST:

1½ cups graham crackers, processed very fine

1½ cups walnuts, processed very fine

9 tablespoons butter, melted

Combine, press into bottom and up sides of a springform pan, and bake 5 minutes at 350°.

FILLING:

3 (8-ounce) packages cream cheese, very soft

1⅓ cups sugar

3 eggs

¼ cup lemon juice

2 teaspoons vanilla extract

Beat together, fill partly baked Crust, and bake 40 minutes at 350°.

TOPPING:

2 cups sour cream

3 tablespoons sugar

1 teaspoon vanilla extract

Stir Topping ingredients together. Spread Topping on cheesecake after it has baked 40 minutes. Continue to bake 15 minutes longer (will not look set). Cool 30 minutes.

GLAZE:

¾ cup water

⅓ cup lemon juice

1 egg yolk

½ cup sugar

1½ tablespoons cornstarch

¼ teaspoon salt

1 tablespoon butter

Combine liquids of Glaze in saucepan. Stir in sugar, cornstarch, and salt. Boil over low heat and stir until thick. Remove from heat and add butter. Cool 20 minutes. Spread Glaze on the cheesecake, then cool and refrigerate until well chilled.

The Hearty Gourmet

Meaghan's Blonde Brownie Torte

¾ cup butter, softened
1¾ cups brown sugar
4 eggs
½ cup milk
1 teaspoon vanilla
1⅔ cups flour
1 teaspoon baking powder
½ teaspoon salt

2 (8-ounce) packages cream
  cheese, softened
2 teaspoons vanilla
⅔ cup sugar
⅓ cup unsweetened cocoa
1½ cups whipping cream
Grated semisweet chocolate

Cream butter and brown sugar. Beat in eggs, milk, and vanilla. Add dry ingredients. Spread in 2 (8-inch) pans and bake at 350° for 25–30 minutes. (Best to grease pan, put in wax paper round, and butter and flour the wax paper, too.)

Beat cream cheese and vanilla with sugar and cocoa, creaming until fluffy. Slice each cake layer in half horizontally and top each with ⅓ of the cream cheese filling. Cover and chill. Just before serving, beat whipping cream to stiff peaks and frost outside of cake. Sprinkle top with grated chocolate.

Wapiti Meadow Bakes

Broiled Coconut Topping

½ cup brown sugar
3 tablespoons soft margarine
2 tablespoons milk

¾ cup shredded coconut
¾ cup chopped nuts

In bowl mix brown sugar, margarine, and milk with electric mixer or beaters. When smooth, spread on warm cake (not hot). Sprinkle coconut and nuts over top. Place in oven on broil for about 3–4 minutes. This will cover a 9x13-inch cake.

Grandma Jane's Cookbook

Cookies & Candies

Carved by the great Snake River, Hells Canyon, North America's deepest river gorge, plunges 8,000 feet below snowcapped He Devil Peak of Idaho's Seven Devils Mountains. There are no roads across the canyon's 10-mile wide expanse.

One Cup Cookies

1 cup butter, softened
1 cup brown sugar
1 cup sugar
3 eggs
1 cup peanut butter
1 cup flour

1 teaspoon baking soda
1 cup oats
1 cup chopped walnuts
1 cup bran
1 cup shredded coconut
1 cup chocolate chips

Cream butter and sugars, then add eggs one at a time. Beat in peanut butter. Add flour and soda. Mix well; add remaining ingredients one at a time. Bake at 350° for 10 minutes.

Sharing Our Best

Chewy Coconut Cookies

1/2 cup butter or margarine,
    softened
1/2 cup packed brown sugar
1/2 cup granulated sugar
1 egg
1/2 teaspoon vanilla

1 1/4 cups unsifted flour
1/4 teaspoon salt
1/2 teaspoon baking powder
1 1/3 cups shredded coconut
1 cup (6 ounces) chocolate chips

Cream together butter or margarine and sugars; beat in egg. Add vanilla, unsifted flour, salt, baking powder, coconut, and chocolate chips; mix until well blended. Dough will be slightly crumbly. Drop onto ungreased cookie sheet by teaspoonfuls. Bake in 375° oven for 9–10 minutes, or just until brown. May appear moist and gooey in centers, but will firm up as they cool off. Makes a small batch.

A Taste of Heaven

The first dog sled race in the Lower 48 was held in 1917 in Ashton. The first race went from West Yellowstone, Montana, to Ashton, Idaho. What was supposed to take six hours to complete took 29 hours, due to blizzard conditions! The race, held in February, features a 100-mile race and a 60-mile race that begins and ends in Ashton.

Swedish Wedding Cookies

1 cup butter, softened
5 tablespoons powdered sugar
1/2 teaspoon vanilla
1 teaspoon salt

2 cups flour
1 cup finely ground pecans
2 pounds powdered sugar

Cream butter and 5 tablespoons powdered sugar together. Add vanilla, salt, flour, and pecans, and mix together well. By teaspoonfuls, roll dough in balls and place on ungreased cookie sheet. Bake at 275° for 45 minutes to 1 hour, or until just golden on bottoms. As they just come out of the oven, shake a few at a time in a brown paper lunch bag filled 1/2 full with powdered sugar. Allow to cool in single layer, then put in sealed container, shaking rest of powdered sugar around them and between each layer.

Wapiti Meadow Bakes

Basque Wedding Cookies

1 cup butter, softened
1 cup sifted confectioners' sugar, divided
1 1/2 tablespoons grated lemon peel

1 tablespoon water
2 1/2 cups sifted all-purpose flour
1/2 teaspoon salt
2/3 cup whole blanched almonds

Cream butter until light and fluffy. Stir in 1/4 cup confectioners' sugar, peel, and water.

Mix flour with salt, and beat into butter mixture. Knead with hands until dough is light. Pinch off heaping teaspoonfuls of dough, press them flat, and wrap around a whole almond to cover completely. Shape like a tiny leaf and place 1 inch apart on greased baking sheet. Bake at 350° for 15 minutes. Take care not to overbake.

Remove from cookie sheet, cool 2 or 3 minutes, then roll in confectioners' sugar. Cool completely, then roll again. Makes 4 dozen.

Basque Cooking and Lore

Banana Spice Cookies

1³/₄ cups flour
1 teaspoon baking powder
¹/₂ teaspoon baking soda
¹/₂ teaspoon salt
¹/₂ teaspoon ground cinnamon
¹/₄ teaspoon ground cloves

1 cup sugar
²/₃ cup shortening
2 eggs, well beaten
1 cup mashed bananas
1 cup chopped nuts

Blend dry ingredients, except sugar, and set aside. Add sugar gradually with shortening, creaming until fluffy. Add eggs gradually, beating well. Add dry ingredients alternately with the bananas, mixing after each addition, until blended. Stir in nuts. Drop by tablespoonfuls onto greased cookie sheet. Bake at 375° for 10–12 minutes. Frost as desired.

Generations "Coming Home"

Lemon Chocolate Chip Cookies

¹/₂ cup butter or margarine,
  softened
1 (18¹/₄-ounce) box lemon cake mix

2 large eggs, slightly beaten
1 (12-ounce) package chocolate
  chips

Cut butter into cake mix until crumbly. Add eggs and chips, incorporating thoroughly. Chill in the refrigerator for 1 hour.

Preheat oven to 375°. Remove from fridge and roll into walnut-sized balls. Place balls on ungreased cookie sheets. Bake in preheated oven 10–12 minutes. Cool on baking rack. Store in air-tight container.

This cookie dough can be rolled into a log, tightly wrapped and frozen, for use at a later date.

Elegant Cooking Made Simple

Chocolate Chip Pudding Cookies

1 cup butter
1/4 cup granulated sugar
3/4 cup brown sugar
2 eggs
1 teaspoon vanilla
2 1/4 cups flour

1 teaspoon baking soda
1 (4-ounce) package chocolate or vanilla instant pudding
1 (12-ounce) package chocolate chips

Soften butter in the microwave, then cream butter, sugars, eggs, and vanilla. Add flour, baking soda, and pudding mix. If you would like chocolate, chocolate chip cookies, use chocolate pudding, otherwise use vanilla pudding mix. Add chocolate chips; mix well. Drop by teaspoon onto a greased cookie sheet. Bake for 8–10 minutes at 350°.

Down Home Country Cookin'

Pudding Sugar Cookies

1 cup butter, softened
1 cup vegetable oil
1 cup sugar
1 cup powdered sugar
2 eggs
1 teaspoon vanilla

1 (3.4-ounce) package instant lemon pudding mix (or flavor of choice)
4 cups flour
1 teaspoon cream of tartar
1 teaspoon baking soda

In a large mixing bowl, cream the butter, oil, and sugars. Beat in eggs, vanilla, and pudding mix. Combine flour, cream of tartar, and soda; gradually add to the creamed mixture. Drop by tablespoons 2 inches apart onto ungreased cookie sheet. Flatten with a glass dipped in sugar. Bake at 350° for 12–15 minutes or until lightly browned. Remove to wire racks. Makes 7 dozen.

Mackay Heritage Cookbook

Applesauce Cookies

1 cup shortening
2 cups sugar (part brown,
   if you like)
Pinch of salt
1 egg
3 cups flour

1 teaspoon cinnamon
$^1/_2$ teaspoon nutmeg
$^1/_2$ teaspoon baking soda
1 teaspoon baking powder
1 cup applesauce
1 cup wheat germ

Cream shortening and sugar with a pinch of salt. Beat in egg, then add sifted dry ingredients. Add applesauce and wheat germ and mix into a stiff batter. (Add more flour if batter is not stiff enough.) Drop spoonfuls onto greased cookie sheet. Bake at 375° for 15–20 minutes.

Spragg Family Cookbook

Oatmeal Cookies

The ol' cookie standby. These have been a favorite in one form or another for 150 years.

1 cup butter, softened
1 cup sugar
2 eggs, beaten
$1^3/_4$ cups oatmeal
1 cup flour

$^1/_2$ teaspoon baking soda
$^1/_4$ teaspoon salt
1 teaspoon cinnamon
1 cup raisins
4 tablespoons milk

Cream the butter and add sugar and eggs. Mix well. Mix in remaining ingredients. If the dough is too stiff, add a small amount of milk to loosen it. Place small dabs on a greased baking sheet and bake at 350° for 8–12 minutes.

Note: Some prefer to throw in some nuts or even a handful of chocolate chips.

Sowbelly and Sourdough

Dainty Waffle Cookie

¹/₄ cup margarine, softened
6 tablespoons sugar
1 egg
¹/₂ teaspoon vanilla

1 square unsweetened chocolate,
  melted
¹/₂ cup flour
Powdered sugar

Cream margarine and sugar; beat in egg and vanilla until light and fluffy. Blend in chocolate. Add flour; mix well. Drop by rounded teaspoon 1 inch apart onto a preheated waffle iron. Bake 1 minute. Remove to wire rack to cool. Dust with powdered sugar.

Cookin' at Its Best

Moon Rocks

No bake!

2 cups sugar
3 tablespoons cocoa (optional)
¹/₂ teaspoon salt
¹/₂ cup butter or margarine
¹/₂ cup water

1 cup peanut butter
4 cups oatmeal
1 cup nonfat dry milk
1 cup raisins
1 teaspoon vanilla

Combine in large saucepan sugar, cocoa (if desired), salt, margarine, water, and peanut butter. Bring to rolling boil on medium heat; stir as needed to prevent sticking. Remove from burner and add oatmeal, powdered milk and raisins; mix well, then add vanilla. Drop by teaspoons onto wax paper or cookie sheet sprayed with nonstick spray. Let stand till cool.

Grandma Jane's Cookbook

Craters of the Moon, at 618 square miles, is the largest young basaltic lava field in the lower 48 states. Sixty distinct lava flows form the Craters of the Moon lava field, each ranging in age from 15,000 to just 2,000 years old. Magma poured from fissures in the earth's crust to form what we see today—uneroded cinder cones, craters, and endless fields of lava that look as if they oozed across the land yesterday.

Oatmeal-Cheesecake-Cranberry Bars

2 cups all-purpose flour
1¼ cups quick-cooking oatmeal
¾ cup packed brown sugar
1 cup butter, softened
12 ounces cream cheese,
  softened
½ cup sugar

2 eggs
2 teaspoons lemon juice
1 teaspoon vanilla
1 (16-ounce) can whole cranberry
  sauce
2 teaspoons cornstarch

In a large mixing bowl, stir together flour, oatmeal, and brown sugar. Add butter and use fingers to blend until mixture resembles coarse crumbs. Reserve 1½ cups of the crumbs. Press remaining crumbs into a greased 9x13-inch pan. Bake at 350° for 15 minutes.

In the same bowl, beat cream cheese and sugar with an electric mixer until light and fluffy. Beat in eggs, lemon juice, and vanilla. Spread over crust.

Stir together cranberry sauce and cornstarch; spoon carefully over cream cheese layer. Sprinkle with reserved crumbs. Bake 40 minutes more or until set. Cool and store in refrigerator. Bring to room temperature to serve. Makes 36 bars.

Another Cookbook

Fudgy Chocolate Cookie Bars

1¾ cups flour
¾ cup powdered sugar
¼ cup Hershey's cocoa
1 cup cold butter
1 (12-ounce) package chocolate
   chips, divided

1 (14-ounce) can sweetened
   condensed milk
1 teaspoon vanilla
1 cup chopped walnuts

Combine flour, sugar, and cocoa; cut in butter until crumbly (can be done in food processor). Press firmly on bottom of a 9x13-inch baking dish. Bake 15 minutes at 350°.

Over medium heat, melt 1 cup chocolate chips in condensed milk and vanilla. Pour evenly over crust. Top with nuts and remaining 1 cup chips. Press down firmly. Bake 20 minutes or until set. Cool. Chill. Cut into bars. Store covered.

Wapiti Meadow Bakes

Coconut Dream Bars

CRUST:
½ cup butter
½ cup brown sugar

1 cup flour

Mix butter, brown sugar, and flour until crumbly. Pat in greased 9x13-inch pan. Bake 10 minutes at 375°. Set aside.

FILLING:
2 eggs
1 cup brown sugar
1 teaspoon vanilla
2 tablespoons flour

½ teaspoon baking powder
¼ teaspoon salt
1½ cups shredded coconut
1 cup nuts (optional)

Cream eggs, brown sugar, and vanilla. Add flour, baking powder, salt, coconut, and nuts, if desired. Pour mixture over Crust. Bake 20 minutes at 375°. Cut when cool.

Generations "Coming Home"

Pumpkin Bars

4 eggs
2 cups sugar
1 teaspoon baking powder
1 teaspoon baking soda
1 cup oil
2 cups flour
1 teaspoon cinnamon

$^1/_4$ teaspoon nutmeg
$^1/_2$ teaspoon ground cloves
$^1/_2$ teaspoon salt
2 cups pumpkin (cooked or canned)
$^1/_2$ cup chopped nuts (optional)

Beat eggs; add sugar, baking powder, baking soda, oil, flour, and spices; mix well. Add pumpkin and nuts, if desired; mix well. Spread on greased cookie sheet and bake at 350° for 20–25 minutes. Frost with Cream Cheese Frosting.

CREAM CHEESE FROSTING:

$^1/_4$ cup margarine, softened
1 (3-ounce) package cream cheese, softened

1 teaspoon vanilla
$2^1/_2$ cups powdered sugar

Mix all ingredients in a small bowl until smooth. Frost cooled pumpkin bars.

The Miracle Cookbook

Bing Bars

1 (12-ounce) package chocolate
  chips
3/4 cup peanut butter
12 ounces Spanish peanuts,
  ground in blender
12 large marshmallows

1 (14-ounce) can sweetened
  condensed milk
1/2 cup butter
2 teaspoons cherry flavoring
1 (6-ounce) bag cherry chips

Melt chocolate chips and peanut butter together. Add ground peanuts. Put 1/2 of mixture in greased 9x13-inch pan. Set aside remainder.

Combine marshmallows, condensed milk, and butter in medium saucepan; bring to boil for 5 minutes. Add cherry flavoring and chips. Spread this mixture over first layer in pan, then spread remainder of chocolate mixture on top. Cut into bars when cool.

Spragg Family Cookbook

Lemon Bars

CRUST:
1 cup butter
2 2/3 cups flour

1/2 cup sugar

Combine in food processor with plastic blade. Pat firmly into 9x13-inch baking dish. Bake at 350° for 15–20 minutes, or until golden at edges.

FILLING:
6 eggs
2 1/4 cups sugar
6 tablespoons flour

3/4 teaspoon baking powder
9 tablespoons lemon juice
Powdered sugar for garnish

Combine Filling ingredients in food processor and pour over baked Crust. Return to oven for 18–20 minutes, or until set. Sprinkle with powdered sugar run through a sieve. Chill, then cut into squares.

Wapiti Meadow Bakes

Cinnamon Brownies

³/₄ cup baking cocoa
¹/₂ teaspoon baking soda
²/₃ cup butter or margarine,
    melted, divided
¹/₂ cup boiling water
2 cups sugar
2 eggs, beaten

1 teaspoon vanilla extract
1¹/₃ cups all-purpose flour
1¹/₂–2 teaspoons cinnamon
¹/₄ teaspoon salt
1 cup (6 ounces) semisweet
    chocolate chips

In a mixing bowl, combine cocoa and baking soda; blend in ¹/₃ cup melted butter. Add boiling water, stirring until thickened. Stir in sugar, eggs, vanilla, and remaining butter. Add flour, cinnamon, and salt. Fold in chocolate chips. Pour into a greased 9x13x2-inch baking pan. Bake at 350° for 30 minutes or until brownies test done. Cool.

FROSTING:
6 tablespoons butter, softened
¹/₂ cup baking cocoa
2²/₃ cups powdered sugar

1–1¹/₂ teaspoons cinnamon
¹/₃ cup evaporated milk
1 teaspoon vanilla

Cream butter in a mixing bowl. Combine cocoa, sugar, and cinnamon; add alternately with milk to creamed butter. Beat to a spreading consistency; add vanilla. Add more milk, if necessary. Spread over the brownies. Yields 3 dozen.

Recipes Logged from the Woods of North Idaho

Idaho Spud Mini Balls

2½ pounds semisweet chocolate
  chips
1 (12-ounce) carton Cool Whip,
  room temperature

1 package unflavored gelatin
Coconut or chopped nuts

Melt chocolate chips with Cool Whip and gelatin. Mix well. Refrigerate at least one hour. Scoop and roll into balls. Roll in coconut or chopped nuts.

Sharing Our Best

Cookies 'n Cream Fudge

16 chocolate cream-filled
  sandwich cookies, broken into
  chunks, divided
1 (14-ounce) can sweetened
  condensed milk

2 tablespoons butter or margarine
2⅔ cups vanilla chips
1 teaspoon vanilla extract

Line an 8-inch-square baking pan with aluminum foil; coat with non-stick cooking spray. Place ½ of the broken cookies in pan. In a heavy saucepan, combine milk, butter, and chips; cook and stir over low heat until chips are melted. Remove from heat; stir in vanilla. Pour over cookies in pan. Sprinkle with remaining cookies. Cover and refrigerate for at least 1 hour. Cut into squares. Yields 3 dozen.

Ashton Area Cookbook

Straddling the Idaho-Utah border, Bear Lake is the only known habitat of the Bonneville Cisco, a pearly, silver fish with an average length of around six inches. There are an estimated nine million of them in the lake.

See's Fudge

My grandmother told me this was the See's Candy original fudge recipe. It is yummy!!

1 cup chopped nuts
1 (6-ounce) package chocolate
  chips
1 stick butter, softened
1 teaspoon vanilla

2 cups sugar
1 (5-ounce) can (^{2}/$_3$ cup)
  evaporated milk
1^1/$_4$ cups miniature
  marshmallows

Using a large bowl, add nuts, chocolate chips, butter, and vanilla. Set aside. Using a large heavy pot, add sugar, canned milk, and marshmallows. Boil 6 minutes, stirring constantly. Pour over chocolate chip mixture and stir until it gets creamy and chocolate chips melt. Pour into buttered flat casserole or platter. Cool, then cut.

Sharing Our Best

Southern-Style Pecan Fudge

6 tablespoons butter or
  margarine
^{1}/$_4$ cup milk
1 pound powdered sugar

^{1}/$_2$ cup unsweetened cocoa
1 tablespoon vanilla
^{1}/$_4$ teaspoon salt
1 cup chopped pecans

In large microwave-safe bowl, place butter and milk. Microwave on HIGH 1^1/$_2$–2 minutes until butter is melted. Stir in powdered sugar, cocoa, vanilla, and salt until smooth, then stir in nuts. Spread mixture quickly in buttered 9x5-inch loaf pan. Cool. Cut into squares.

Quilter's Delight, Busy Day Recipes

Coeur d'Alene boasts the world's longest floating boardwalk, a 3,300-foot-long, 12-foot-wide walkway that features a swinging gate for sailboats.

Two Flavored Fudge

2 cups packed brown sugar
1 cup white sugar
1 cup evaporated milk
$^1/_2$ cup butter
1 (7-ounce) jar marshmallow
  crème

1 (6-ounce) package butterscotch
  chips
1 (6-ounce) package chocolate
  chips
1 cup chopped nuts
1 teaspoon vanilla

In a saucepan, combine brown sugar, white sugar, milk, and butter. Bring to a full boil over medium heat, stirring constantly. Boil for 15 minutes, stirring frequently. Remove from heat. Add marshmallow crème, butterscotch chips, and chocolate chips. Stir until melted and mixture is smooth. Add chopped nuts and vanilla. Pour into a greased 9-inch pan to cool. Cut into squares.

The Miracle Cookbook

Lucy's Peanut Butter Fudge

$^1/_2$ cup sugar
$2^3/_4$ cups sugar substitute
$^1/_2$–$^3/_4$ stick butter or margarine
1 (12-ounce) can evaporated milk
1 teaspoon vanilla

1 (6-ounce) package chocolate
  chips
1 (7-ounce) jar marshmallow
  crème
$^1/_4$–$^1/_3$ cup peanut butter

In a heavy skillet, bring to a boil sugar, sugar substitute (that measures cup for cup like sugar), butter, and canned milk over medium-high heat, and cook about 20 minutes, stirring every 5 minutes. Using cold water test, make sure mixture has reached the hard-ball stage. Turn off heat; quickly add vanilla, chips, and marshmallow crème. Add peanut butter. Stir thoroughly with a wooden spoon. Pour onto buttered cookie sheet and allow to firm before cutting.

Idaho Cook Book

Spud Candy

Tastes like Mounds candy bars.

³/₄ cup instant potatoes, prepared
   per package directions
1 teaspoon vanilla
4 cups powdered sugar, sifted

4 cups flaked coconut
1 (12-ounce) package chocolate
   chips
1/3 bar paraffin

Combine potatoes, vanilla, sugar, and coconut. Mix well and chill overnight. Shape into balls and chill again. Melt chocolate and paraffin in double boiler. Dip candy in chocolate and place on waxed paper to set.

Tastes from the Country

Caramel Popcorn

2 cups brown sugar
¹/₂ cup Karo syrup
1 cup butter
1 tablespoon water

2 cups miniature marshmallows
1 teaspoon baking soda
1¹/₂ cups unpopped popcorn

Combine sugar, syrup, butter, water and marshmallows in heavy saucepan. Bring to boil. When marshmallows are completely melted, the mixture should have been boiling for about 1 minute. If not, continue to cook until mixture has boiled for 1 minute. Remove from heat and add baking soda.

Pop popcorn in hot air popper. When cool, remove all unpopped kernels. Popcorn should fit in an extra large metal bowl. Pour caramel mixture over the top of the popcorn and stir lightly to completely cover popcorn.

Let popcorn cool slightly until you can handle it, and then separate into sandwich bags and seal. Yields about 25 bags of popcorn.

Cooking for a Crowd

A Heavenly Candy Hash

2 cups sugar
1 cup milk

³/₄ cup corn syrup
6–8 cups cornflakes

In large saucepan, boil sugar, milk, and syrup to hard-ball stage. Stir in all the cornflakes it will hold. Then drop on oiled or waxed paper and form into balls. Coconut or nuts may be added.

Note: Work fast when mixing and forming the balls. Also, oil your fingers to keep the hot ingredients from sticking to and burning your fingers.

Idaho's Wild 100!

Sweet Chex Mix

¹/₂ large box Rice Chex Cereal
¹/₂ large box Corn Chex Cereal
¹/₂ box Golden Grahams Cereal
1 cup sweetened shredded
  coconut

1 cup slivered almonds
2 cups light Karo syrup
2 cups sugar
1¹/₄ cups butter

In an extra large metal heat-resistant bowl, combine cereals, coconut, and almonds. Toss well. Meanwhile in a large saucepan, cook the Karo syrup, sugar, and butter. Bring to a boil. Boil for 2 minutes. Pour over top of cereal mixture and stir gently until well coated.

Transfer mix to large roll pans. Spread into a thin layer—you will need 3–4 pans. Continue to stir on pans, breaking up large chunks every 10 minutes until cool. You want the result to be small chunks instead of large balls of the mixture. When cool, you can place in sandwich bags to distribute, or place the mixture into a large serving bowl. Yields 25–30 bags.

Cooking for a Crowd

Fruit Pizza

1 (20-ounce) package refrigerator
   sugar cookie dough
1 (8-ounce) package cream
   cheese, softened
$1/4$ cup powdered sugar
1 (8-ounce) carton frozen
   whipped topping, thawed
2–3 kiwi fruit, peeled and sliced
1 (11-ounce) can mandarin
   oranges, drained

1 cup fresh strawberries, sliced
$1/2$ cup red seedless grapes, halved
$1/4$ cup sugar
$1/4$ cup orange juice
2 tablespoons water
1 tablespoon lemon juice
Pinch of salt
$1^1/2$ teaspoons cornstarch

Pat cookie dough into ungreased, 14-inch pizza pan. Bake at 375° for 10–12 minutes or until brown. Cool. Beat cream cheese and powdered sugar; fold in whipped topping and spread over cookie crust. Arrange fruit on top.

In saucepan, combine $1/4$ cups sugar, orange juice, water, lemon juice, salt, and cornstarch. Bring to a boil; stir constantly for 2 minutes or until thickened. Cool. Brush over fruit. Chill and store in the refrigerator. Yields 16–20 servings.

A Century of Recipes

Pies & Other Desserts

The Appaloosa may be the oldest recognizable horse breed in the world, known for its unique spotted coat pattern. Known for their intelligence and speed, the Nez Perce Indians bred them for warhorses. The breed was essentially "lost" until 1938 when the Appaloosa Horse Club was formed in Moscow, Idaho.

Old-Fashioned Lemon Pie

1 cup sugar
5–6 tablespoons cornstarch
1/8 teaspoon salt
2 cups water
1/3–1/2 cup lemon juice
  (approximately 2 lemons)

2 teaspoons grated lemon rind
3 egg yolks, beaten
2 tablespoons milk
1 (9-inch) pie shell, baked

Combine sugar, cornstarch, and salt in 2 cups cold water in top of double boiler. Place over boiling water in bottom of double boiler. Stir and cook for about 8–10 minutes or until mixture thickens. Add lemon juice and rind; continue cooking about 5 minutes more. (If you want more lemony flavor, add more rind, not juice—juice will only thin the filling). Beat egg yolks with milk. Slowly add eggs to lemon mixture, folding in with spoon. Cook only until mixture clears. (Eggs will curdle if overcooked). Remove from heat; cover with wax paper to cool, stirring occasionally. Place cold pie filling in prebaked pie shell. Cover with Meringue.

MERINGUE:
3 egg whites
1/4 teaspoon cream of tartar
4 tablespoons powdered sugar

1/8 teaspoon lemon extract
  (optional)

Whip egg whites until frothy; add cream of tartar and continue beating until Meringue stands in stiff peaks. Fold in sugar a spoonful at a time. Add extract. Spread over cooled pie filling in shell. Bake in preheated 350° oven for 10–15 minutes until Meringue is lightly browned.

A Taste of Heaven

Located on the North Fork of the Clearwater River in north central Idaho, Dworshak Dam, at a height of 717 feet, is the highest straight-axis gravity dam in North America—which means it is straight from canyon wall to canyon wall and basically held in place by its own weight. It is also the third highest dam in the United States, and twenty-second highest dam in the World.

Lemon Pie

1¼ cups plus 6 tablespoons
  sugar, divided
7 tablespoons cornstarch
½ cup cold water
1½ cups hot water

3 eggs, separated
Grated rind and juice of 1 lemon
1 tablespoon butter
1 (9-inch) pie shell, baked
⅛ teaspoon salt

Combine 1¼ cups sugar, cornstarch, and cold water; add hot water, and cook until thick. Add egg yolks, lemon rind, lemon juice, and butter; cool. Fill pie shell.

Beat egg whites with salt until stiff enough to form soft, rounded peaks. Add 6 tablespoons sugar gradually, 1 tablespoon at a time, beating well after each addition. Continue beating until meringue is very thick and glossy; spread on pie. Bake at 350° for 12–15 minutes.

Be Our Guest

Sour Cream Raisin Pie

1 (3-ounce) package vanilla
  pudding mix (not instant)
¼ teaspoon salt
2 teaspoons lemon juice
½ cup sugar
¾ cup water

1 cup raisins
½ cup water
½ pint sour cream
1 (9-inch) pie shell, baked
¼ teaspoon nutmeg

Mix pudding, salt, lemon juice, sugar, and water; set aside. Combine raisins and water in saucepan. Bring to boil, then add pudding mixture. Mix well. Cook over medium heat, stirring well, until mixture thickens and is clear. Remove from heat and cool 5 minutes. Add sour cream. Blend and turn into cooled baked pie shell. Sprinkle with nutmeg.

Generations "Coming Home"

Perfect Pumpkin Pie

1 (15-ounce) can pumpkin
  (2 cups)
1 (14-ounce) can sweetened
  condensed milk
2 eggs
1 teaspoon cinnamon

1/2 teaspoon ginger
1/2 teaspoon ground cloves
1/2 teaspoon nutmeg
1/2 teaspoon salt
1 (9-inch) unbaked pie shell or
  deep-dish pie shell

For 12-inch Dutch oven, let the coals heat up to about 400°–425°. With wire whisk, beat pumpkin, condensed milk, eggs, spices, and salt. Pour into crust. Bake 15 minutes. Remove enough coals to lower temperature to 350° and continue baking 35–40 minutes, or until knife inserted 1 inch from the crust comes out clean. Cool, if desired. This amount serves 6–8. Double or triple recipe if feeding more people.

STREUSEL TOPPING:
1/2 cup packed light brown sugar
1/2 cup flour

1/4 cup butter
1/4 cup chopped nuts

Combine brown sugar and flour; cut in butter until crumbly. Stir in nuts. After pie has baked for 30 minutes at 350°, sprinkle on top of pie; bake 5–10 minutes longer.

Potatoes Are Not the Only Vegetable!

Walnut Rum Pie

¾ cup sugar
½ cup butter, softened
½ cup flour
2 eggs, beaten

2 tablespoons dark rum
1 cup chocolate chips
1 cup coarsely chopped walnuts
1 (8-inch) pie shell, lightly baked

Combine sugar, butter, flour, and eggs, and beat until smooth. Add rum and beat until blended. Stir in chocolate chips and walnuts. Spoon into pie shell. Bake at 350° for 30–35 minutes, or until set and just golden brown.

Note: This is just enough for a smaller, 8-inch pie. Make 1½ recipes for 9-inch pan and double for 10-inch pan.

Wapiti Meadow Bakes

Green Tomato Pie

4 medium green tomatoes
½ lemon
¾ cup sugar
½ teaspoon salt
¼ teaspoon cinnamon

1½ cups raisins
1½ tablespoons cornstarch
Cold water
1 tablespoon butter
1 (9-inch) unbaked pie shell

Slice tomatoes very thin. Slice lemon thin and add to tomatoes along with sugar, salt, and cinnamon. Cook in saucepan until tomatoes are tender; add raisins. Moisten cornstarch with a little cold water and add to mixture, stirring constantly until thick. Remove from heat and add butter. Cool slightly, then pour into pie shell. Cover with top crust and bake at 400° for 25 minutes.

Caldera Kitchens

Apple-Cranberry Streusel Custard Pie

1 (14-ounce) can sweetened
  condensed milk
1 teaspoon cinnamon
2 eggs, beaten
1/2 cup water
1 1/2 cups fresh or frozen
  cranberries
2 medium apples, pared and
  sliced

1 (9-inch) unbaked pie shell
1/4 cup firmly packed brown
  sugar
1/4 cup sifted all-purpose flour
2 tablespoons cold butter or
  margarine
1/4 cup chopped nuts

Place rack in lowest position of oven and preheat to 425°. In large mixing bowl, combine milk and cinnamon. Add eggs, water, and fruit. Mix well. Pour into pastry shell.

In medium mixing bowl, combine sugar and flour, and cut in margarine until crumbly. Stir in nuts and sprinkle mixture over top of pie. Bake 10 minutes, then reduce heat to 375° and bake 30–40 minutes, until golden.

Idaho Cook Book

Apple Filling for Pies

2 1/2 cups sugar
2 cups brown sugar
1 cup cornstarch
1 1/2 teaspoons salt
1 teaspoon cinnamon

1 teaspoon nutmeg
2 1/2 quarts water
2 tablespoons lemon juice
6 quarts sliced apples

Prepare 6 quart jars. Mix sugars, cornstarch, salt, cinnamon, and nutmeg in 4-quart Dutch oven. Stir in water. Heat to boiling, stirring frequently, then reduce heat. Cook, stirring constantly, until thickened and bubbly, about 5 minutes. Stir in juice. Pack into hot jars, 1/3 full of apple slices. Pour on enough hot syrup to cover slices. Continue filling jars. Seal. Process in boiling water bath 20 minutes.

Ashton Area Cookbook

Idaho Centennial Apple Pie

CHEESECAKE FILLING:

1 (8-ounce) package cream
  cheese, softened
1/3 cup sugar

1 egg
1/2 teaspoon vanilla
Pastry for 2 (9- or 10-inch) pies

Combine cream cheese, sugar, egg, and vanilla in a small bowl with an electric mixer until light. Pour into one unbaked pie crust. (At this point, you can put it in a gallon freezer bag and freeze to make later.)

APPLE FILLING:

1 cup sugar
3 tablespoons cornstarch
1/2 teaspoon cinnamon
1/4 teaspoon salt

6 cups peeled and sliced apples
  (Jonathan when in season)
1/4 cup apple juice
2 tablespoons butter

Combine sugar, cornstarch, cinnamon, and salt in a large saucepan. Add apples, apple juice, and butter. Place on medium heat. Bring to a boil. Reduce heat. Cover and simmer for 2 minutes. Spoon over Cheesecake Filling.

Roll dough for top crust. Lift onto filled pie. Trim 1/2 inch beyond edge of pie plate. Fold under the bottom crust and flute. Decorate with pastry scraps and cut vents in crust. Bake at 400° for 40 minutes or until nicely browned.

Another Cookbook

The white potato belongs to the same family, called Solanaceae, as tomatoes, tobacco, chile pepper, eggplant and the petunia.

Blueberry Banana Pie

1 (16-ounce) can blueberries
2½ tablespoons cornstarch
½ cup sugar
2 tablespoons butter

1 teaspoon lemon juice
2 bananas
1 (8-inch) pie crust, baked
1 cup whipping cream, whipped

Drain blueberries and add juice to cornstarch and sugar. Boil until thick. Add butter, lemon juice, and berries, and cool. Place sliced bananas in the baked pie shell. Add blueberry mixture. Cover with plastic wrap and refrigerate. When cool, cover with sweetened whipped cream.

Another Cookbook

Bing Huckleberry Pie

¾ cup sugar
¼ cup flour
1 tablespoon cornstarch
2 cups ripe Bing cherries, halved
    and pitted

½ teaspoon almond extract
2 cups huckleberries
1 double pie crust
1 tablespoon butter or
    margarine

Mix dry ingredients. Wash, drain, and prepare Bing cherries. Sprinkle almond extract over. Gently combine with huckleberries and the dry mixture. Transfer into bottom crust. Dot with butter or margarine. Cover with top crust. Seal edges, and cut slits near the center. Cover with foil.

Bake at 375° about 20 minutes. Remove foil and bake 25 minutes longer. Cool and serve with whipped cream topping.

Huckleberry Haus Cookbook

Huckleberry-Apple Crisp

2 cups huckleberries
2 cups peeled and sliced tart
  apples
1 tablespoon lemon juice
1/2 cup packed brown sugar
1 cup all-purpose flour

3/4 cup sugar
1 teaspoon baking powder
1 egg, slightly beaten
1/2 cup butter, melted
1/2 teaspoon cinnamon

Butter a 1/2-quart baking dish. Put in huckleberries and apples. Sprinkle with lemon juice and brown sugar. Mix next 3 ingredients; stir in egg and mix until crumbly. Sprinkle over fruit. Top with melted butter and cinnamon. Bake at 350° for 45 minutes. Serve warm or at room temperature.

The Rocky Mountain Wild Foods Cookbook

Apple Crisp with Mint

1 teaspoon softened butter
1 cup sugar
1 cup whole-wheat flour
1/2 teaspoon baking powder
1 large egg
2 tablespoons finely minced
  fresh mint

1 tablespoon ground cinnamon
2 pounds tart apples, peeled,
  quartered, and cut into
  1/4-inch slices
2 cups whipped cream

Butter sides and bottom of an 8-inch-square baking dish. Sift together sugar, flour, and baking powder into bowl. Make well in center and drop in egg. Mix together with 2 knives or pastry cutter until flour has absorbed the egg.

Stir together mint and cinnamon. Add apples and toss to mix well. Arrange slices in buttered pan. Scatter flour mixture over top, pressing it gently into a smooth layer to cover apples completely.

Bake at 350° for 45–50 minutes. Serve at room temperature with whipped cream.

Basque Cooking and Lore

Blackberry Dumplings

| 2 (10-ounce) packages frozen | $^1/_4$ cup sugar |
| blackberries | |

Pour berries into 2-quart saucepan; stir in sugar. Warm over lowest heat setting, stirring occasionally.

DUMPLINGS:

| 1 cup biscuit mix | 1 small egg |
| $^1/_3$ cup milk | 1 tablespoon sugar |

Stir all ingredients together to form soft dough (do not overwork). Increase heat under berries to medium-high, stirring constantly to a full boil. Drop Dumplings in 1 tablespoon at a time; reduce heat, and cook 10 minutes uncovered; cover and cook 10 minutes.

Elegant Cooking Made Simple

Apple Dumplings

This requires some cloth sacks, such as muslin. Since flour no longer comes in cloth sacks, these can be hard to come by unless you make up some of your own. You can use just pieces of cloth, but they are a little harder to handle.

4–6 small apples	$^1/_4$ teaspoon cinnamon for each
1 batch of prepared biscuit	apple
dough	Water for boiling
1 teaspoon sugar for each apple	

Wash, peel, quarter, and core the apples and set aside. Roll out prepared biscuit dough until it is $^1/_4$ inch thick. Put 4 apple quarters back together, and while holding, sprinkle with sugar and cinnamon. Wrap each one in a square of dough and seal at the top. Place each one in a small cloth sack and place in boiling water for 30 minutes. Serve with cream, syrup, or hard sauce.

Sowbelly and Sourdough

Amy Tanner's Apple Crunch

THE CRUNCH:

3/4 cup sugar
1 cup flour
1/8 teaspoon mace

1/4 teaspoon salt
1/3 cup butter

Mix all ingredients in food processor, or cut the butter into the mixed dry ingredients using a pastry cutter.

THE APPLES:

6 apples, peeled, sliced (Granny
  Smith or Northern Spy)
1/2 cup red cinnamon candies (2
  bottles)

1 teaspoon vanilla

Line a 10-inch Dutch oven with aluminum foil. Place apple slices into the Dutch oven and distribute to a fairly flat, even surface. Sprinkle the cinnamon candies evenly over the surface. Sprinkle vanilla evenly over the surface. Top with The Crunch. And again, distribute this over the surface forming a flat, even covering. Bake at 375° for 45 minutes indoors, or outdoors, use about 7 briquets under the Dutch and about 16 on the lid. Topping should barely start to brown. Serve hot with the most decadent vanilla ice cream you can find. Serves 4–6.

Cee Dub's Ethnic & Regional Dutch Oven Cookin'

Peach Cobbler

1 stick butter or margarine,
   softened
1¼–1½ cups sugar, divided
2 cups flour
1 cup milk
4 teaspoons baking powder
½ teaspoon salt
1 (29-ounce) can peaches (reserve
   juice) or 8 fresh peaches
2 cups reserved peach juice,
   or peach nectar

Combine butter, 1 cup sugar, flour, milk, baking powder, and salt. Spread batter in a greased 9x11-inch pan. Spread sliced peaches over dough and pour juice over the peaches. Sprinkle with ¼–½ cup of sugar to taste. Bake at 375° for 45–50 minutes.

The Miracle Cookbook

Basque Blackberry Cobbler

6 ounces cream cheese
2 sticks butter
2½ cups flour, divided
Pinch of salt
4 cups berries
½ cup sugar
½ teaspoon nutmeg
1 teaspoon cinnamon
1 teaspoon lemon or lime juice
2 tablespoons melted butter

For pastry, cut the cream cheese and butter into 2 cups flour and salt. Form soft dough into ball and chill. Pour berries into 12-inch Dutch oven and sprinkle with sugar, nutmeg, cinnamon, and juice. Sprinkle with remaining flour and evenly pour melted butter over the top of fruit. Roll well-chilled pastry dough to about 11-inch circle. Carefully place the crust over the berries. Use 5 or 6 briquets under the Dutch oven, and load the lid with 25 briquets (or use 350° oven). Bake for 45 minutes.

More Cee Dub's Dutch Oven and Other Camp Cookin'

Pear-Cranberry Cobbler

This is a simple, but absolutely delicious Dutch oven dessert.

Butter a 12-inch Dutch oven or 9x12-inch baking pan.

CRUST:

2¹/₂+ cups unbleached all-purpose flour, divided
1 teaspoon salt
10 tablespoons unsalted butter

²/₃ cup chilled vegetable shortening
¹/₂ cup ice water

Mix 2¹/₂ cups flour and salt. Cut butter and shortening into flour with pastry blender or fingers until it forms pea-sized lumps. Add water, working mixture as little as possible until dough is formed. Wrap dough in plastic and chill for 20 minutes.

FILLING:

7 cups cranberries (24 ounces)
8 pears, peeled and diced
1 cup sugar
¹/₂ cup unbleached all-purpose flour

¹/₂ teaspoon ground allspice
¹/₄ teaspoon ground cardamom
6 cups ice cream or whipped cream (optional)

Sprinkle cranberries and pears with sugar, ¹/₂ cup flour, allspice, and cardamom. Mix well. Spread mixture in Dutch oven or pan. Put pastry on a floured board and roll out to ¹/₈-inch thickness, in a round 1-inch larger than pan.

Fold dough in half to place on top of fruit. Unfold carefully and crimp edges decoratively. Cut slits in top.

Bake in Dutch oven for 35–40 minutes, or in 350° conventional oven for 50–60 minutes, until crust is golden brown and bubbly and cranberries have split. Cool 15 minutes and serve with ice cream or whipped cream. Yields 12 servings.

The Outdoor Dutch Oven Cookbook

Filthy Wilma

CRUST:

1¼ cups flour

1 stick butter, melted

1 cup chopped nuts

Combine ingredients and press in bottom of greased 9x13-inch pan. Bake at 375° for 15 minutes.

FIRST LAYER:

1 (8-ounce) package cream cheese, softened

1 cup powdered sugar

1 medium (12-ounce) carton Cool Whip

Combine ingredients, blend well and spread on cooled Crust.

SECOND LAYER:

1 (3-ounce) package vanilla instant pudding

1 (3-ounce) package chocolate instant pudding

3 cups milk (half-and-half)

1 teaspoon vanilla

Mix all ingredients together and spread on top of First Layer.

TOP LAYER:

1 (12- to 16-ounce) carton Cool Whip

1 package slivered almonds

Combine Cool Whip and almonds and spread on top. Refrigerate.

Cooking with Cops, Too

Food of the Gods

1 cup graham cracker crumbs	1 cup chopped nuts
1⅓ cups sugar	1 cup chopped dates
1⅓ teaspoons baking powder	1 pint whipping cream, whipped
4 eggs, separated	

Roll cracker crumbs very fine. Add sugar sifted with baking powder; mix thoroughly. Separate eggs; beat egg yolks until light, thick and lemon colored. Add to first mixture along with nuts and dates. Fold in stiffly beaten egg whites. Pour into greased 9-inch square pan; bake at 325° for 35–45 minutes. When cool, break into pieces and fold in whipped cream.

Mackay Heritage Cookbook

Amaretto Huckleberry Dessert

2 cups frozen huckleberries	2 tablespoons amaretto liqueur
1 cup sugar	Coffee-flavored ice cream
1 tablespoon cornstarch	Whipped cream

Combine huckleberries, sugar, and cornstarch in a saucepan. Bring to boil over moderate heat, stirring. Boil 2–3 minutes. Remove from heat and cool to room temperature. Stir in amaretto.

Place 2 scoops coffee ice cream in serving bowls, pour huckleberry mixture over, and garnish with whipped cream. Makes 8 servings.

Huckleberry Haus Cookbook

The Coeur d'Alene mining district is the richest silver mining district in the world. In 1985, the district mines produced their one billionth ounce of silver. The district has also produced vast amounts of lead, zinc, and copper.

Chocolate Peanut Butter Delight

1 (1¹/₂-ounce) box chocolate
 pudding mix, sugar free
2 cups plus 2 teaspoons skim
 milk, divided
³/₄ cup reduced-fat creamy
 peanut butter

¹/₄ cup powdered sugar, divided
³/₄ cup chocolate graham cracker
 crumbs
6 ounces fat-free whipped topping

Combine pudding mix and 2 cups milk; prepare according to package directions. Cover with plastic wrap and refrigerate until set.

Combine peanut butter and 3 tablespoons powdered sugar. Put peanut butter mixture on a square of wax paper and pat out gently. Sprinkle with remaining ¹/₂ tablespoon powdered sugar. Top with second sheet of waxed paper and roll out mixture until evenly distributed over entire paper.

Spread all but 2 tablespoons of the crumbs over bottom of 8x8-inch pan. Remove top sheet of wax paper and carefully flip over so peanut butter mixture is laid on top of crumbs. Peel off remaining wax paper. Using your fingers or the back of a spoon, press peanut butter gently into crumb layer. Spread pudding evenly over peanut butter layer. Refrigerate until ready to serve.

Just prior to serving, spread whipped topping over pudding. Sprinkle with remaining crumbs and cut into squares.

Northern Lites: Contemporary Cooking with a Twist

Zucchini Dessert Squares

Tastes like apple crisp!

CRUST AND TOPPING:

4 cups flour
2 cups sugar
1/2 teaspoon cinnamon

1/2 teaspoon salt
11/2 cups butter or margarine

Combine dry ingredients. Cut in butter until crumbly. Reserve 3 cups. Pat remainder into greased 9x13-inch pan. Bake at 375° for 12 minutes.

FILLING:

8–10 zucchini, peeled, seeded, and cubed
2/3 cup lemon juice

1 cup sugar
1 teaspoon cinnamon
1/2 teaspoon nutmeg

Bring zucchini and lemon juice to boil in pan. Reduce heat. Simmer, covered, 6–8 minutes. Stir in sugar, cinnamon, and nutmeg. Simmer 5 minutes. Mixture will be thin. Spoon over Crust. Sprinkle with reserved Topping mixture. Bake at 375° until golden brown.

Quilter's Delight, Busy Day Recipes

Caramel Bavarian Cream

1 tablespoon gelatin
3/4 cup water, divided
1 cup sugar, divided
1/2 cup hot water
1 cup hot milk

1/4 teaspoon salt
3 egg yolks, beaten
1 teaspoon vanilla
1 cup cream, whipped

Soak gelatin in 1/4 cup water; set aside. Place 3/4 cup sugar in a large skillet over low heat. Stir until it melts and is a clear brown. Stir in slowly 1/2 cup hot water. Stir and boil this syrup for about 1 minute. Add hot milk, 1/4 cup sugar, and salt. Heat until scalded, then pour this mixture over beaten egg yolks. Return this to skillet. Stir and cook until it coats a spoon heavily. Stir in the soaked gelatin. Stir it until dissolved. Cool the custard. Add vanilla; fold in whipped cream. Place in an oiled mold. Chill thoroughly.

Recipes Logged from the Woods of North Idaho

Bread Pudding

4 cups half-and-half
4 tablespoons butter, melted
2 tablespoons vanilla
1 teaspoon cinnamon
1 teaspoon nutmeg
1 cup raisins (optional)

2 cups sugar
3 eggs
1 cup chopped pecans
1½ (10-ounce) loaves stale French
   bread

Combine all ingredients, except bread. Break bread into pieces (may use 8 cups any type bread). Combine with milk mixture; mixture should be very moist, but not soupy. Pour into lightly oiled Dutch oven. Bake at 350° for approximately 1 hour and 15 minutes, until top is golden brown. Serve warm with Whiskey Sauce. Serves 16–20.

WHISKEY SAUCE:
½ cup butter (1 stick)
1½ cups powdered sugar

1 egg, yolk or whole
¼ cup bourbon, or to taste

Cream butter and sugar over medium heat until all butter is absorbed. Remove from heat and blend in egg yolk. Pour in bourbon gradually to your own taste, stirring constantly. Sauce will thicken as it cools. Serve warm over warm bread pudding.

Recipes Stolen from the River of No Return

Bread Pudding

2 cups scalded milk
2 tablespoons butter
2 cups cubed bread
2 eggs
½ cup sugar

1 teaspoon baking powder
½ teaspoon nutmeg
1 teaspoon vanilla
Raisins to taste

Pour scalded milk and butter over bread cubes and set aside to cool. Beat eggs, sugar, and baking powder. Add nutmeg, vanilla, and raisins. Pour over bread mixture. Bake in slow (300°) oven for 1 hour.

SAUCE:
1 cup brown sugar
1 cup water

1 heaping tablespoon flour
2 tablespoons butter

Cook, stirring until smooth, and serve over bread pudding.

Tastes from the Country

Lemon Mousse
with Raspberry Purée

1 envelope unflavored gelatin	3 eggs, separated
2 tablespoons white wine	1/2 cup sugar, divided
1/3 cup lemon juice	1 cup heavy cream whipped

In double boiler, sprinkle gelatin over wine until soft. Add lemon juice. Stir over simmering water until gelatin is dissolved. Cool. Beat egg yolks with 3 tablespoons sugar until thick, light colored and ribbon-y. Slowly add slightly cooled gelatin mixture and stir, blending thoroughly. Beat egg whites until foamy; add 5 tablespoons sugar and beat until meringue holds soft peaks. Add whipped cream to egg yolks and fold this into the meringue mixture gradually. Chill at least 2 hours.

RASPBERRY PURÉE:

1 (10-ounce) package frozen raspberries, thawed and drained, juice reserved	2 tablespoons sugar
1 tablespoon lemon juice	1 tablespoon Kirsch or cherry brandy (optional)

In blender, combine thawed and drained raspberries, lemon juice, sugar, and brandy. Purée. Strain in smallest holed sieve until only seeds remain in sieve. Add enough reserved raspberry juice to thin to usable consistency.

To serve, drizzle purée over mound of mousse on each dessert plate.

The Hearty Gourmet

The Borah Peak Earthquake of 1983 changed the elevation of Idaho's highest mountain. Before 8:06 am, October 28, 1983, the mountain was 12,655 feet high; a minute or two later, it was almost a foot higher.

Huckleberry Pizza

CRUST:

¼ cup plus 1 teaspoon sugar, divided
1 package active dry yeast
¼ cup lukewarm water
3½ cups flour
½ teaspoon salt

1 teaspoon lemon Jell-O powder
2 sticks (1 cup) margarine, softened
¾ cup milk, room temperature
2 eggs, slightly beaten

To prepare yeast starter, mix 1 teaspoon sugar and yeast; dissolve in lukewarm water and let stand. Sift flour, salt, ¼ cup sugar, and Jell-O powder. Cut in margarine until crumbly. Add yeast starter, milk, and eggs. Mix to make a soft dough. Place in greased bowl, turn greased side up, cover, and let rise in a warm place until doubled in size.

Punch down, knead on a lightly floured surface, and roll out to fit a round pizza pan. Grease pizza pan, and stretch dough over, forming an edge.

TOPPING:

2 (3-ounce) packages cream cheese, softened
½ cup sour cream
½ cup sugar

1 egg
1½ cups huckleberries
½ cup brown sugar
½ teaspoon ground cinnamon

With an electric beater, mix cream cheese, sour cream, sugar, and egg. Spread evenly over Crust. Combine huckleberries with brown sugar and sprinkle over cream cheese mixture. Dust with ground cinnamon. Bake at 375° about 20–25 minutes, until Crust is golden brown.

GLAZE:

½ cup powdered sugar
1 teaspoon pure vanilla extract

1 tablespoon milk

Mix powdered sugar, vanilla, and milk. Drizzle over huckleberry pizza while still warm. Makes 8 generous servings.

Huckleberry Haus Cookbook

Strawberry Broil

2 cups fresh strawberry slices
¼ cup sour cream

¼ cup packed brown sugar

Place strawberries in an ungreased shallow 1½-quart baking dish. Spread sour cream over berries; sprinkle with brown sugar. Broil until bubbly, about 3–4 minutes. Serve warm.

Centennial Cookbook

Mrs. Beall's Lemon Ice Cream

1 quart plus 1⅓ cups whipping cream
1 quart plus 1⅓ cups milk
5 cups sugar

2 tablespoons grated lemon rind (optional)
Juice of 12 lemons
3 teaspoons lemon extract

In a very large bowl, mix cream, milk, and sugar. Grate and squeeze lemons. Add extract. Put in ice cream maker and process according to directions.

Wapiti Meadow Bakes

Easy Huckleberry Ice Cream

1¹/₂ cups huckleberries
¹/₂ cup sugar
1 tablespoon plus 1 teaspoon
  Clear Jel (or cornstarch)

¹/₂ teaspoon almond extract
1 half-gallon vanilla ice cream

Place huckleberries in a blender and process at low speed, in short intervals, just enough to break the berries. In a saucepan, combine berries with sugar and Clear Jel. Cook, stirring constantly, over moderate heat until mixture thickens. Remove from heat and cool. Stir in almond extract.

Put vanilla ice cream in a mixing bowl and let soften just enough to mix. Pour huckleberry mixture over and mix well. Transfer into plastic ice cream pail and freeze overnight.

Huckleberry Haus Cookbook

Catalog of
Contributing Cookbooks

Dutch oven cooking is a popular way to cookout while camping in any of Idaho's national forests, state parks and other public lands.

Catalog of
Contributing Cookbooks

All recipes in this book have been selected from the cookbooks shown on the following pages. Individuals who wish to obtain a copy of any particular book may do so by sending a check or money order to the address listed by each cookbook. Please note the postage and handling charges that are required. State residents add tax only when requested. Prices and addresses are subject to change, and the books may sell out and not be available. Retailers are invited to call or write for ordering information.

ANOTHER COOKBOOK

by Kay Rose
3434 Creekside   Phone 208-522-2038
Idaho Falls, ID 83404   Email krose@ida.net

I've been collecting recipes for over 40 years and have entered many cooking contests and fairs with success. I've also taught classes for community education for the past 12 years. I finally decided to put together a cookbook, and have been pleased on how well it has been received.

$15.00   Retail price
 $.75   Tax for Idaho residents
 $4.25   Postage and handling

Make check payable to Kay Rose

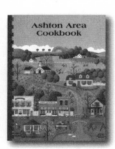

ASHTON AREA COOKBOOK

Ashton Area Development Committee
P. O. Box 508
Ashton, ID 83420   Phone 208-652-3796

Enjoy just good eating? Ashton is full of good cooks, many of whom contributed their family's tried-and-true favorites to help raise money for the Ashton Area Visitor's Center. Includes over 120 pages of delicious recipes along with tips and a special Kids Section. Some old, some new, all good—enjoy!

$8.00   Retail price
$2.00   Postage and handling

Make check payable to Ashton Area Development Committee

BACON IS NOT A VEGETABLE

Idaho State University Outdoor Program
P. O. Box 8128   Phone 208-282-3912
Pocatello, ID 83209   Fax 208-282-4600
                                  Email joycepete@isu.edu

The Idaho State University Outdoor Program has been teaching Dutch oven cooking classes for quite some time. The 131 recipes in this cookbook were compiled from one of these classes. The cookbook offers recipes for breads, vegetables, main dishes, desserts, and helpful tips for cooking in Dutch ovens.

$8.00   Retail price
$4.00   Postage and handling

Make check payable to ISU Outdoor Program

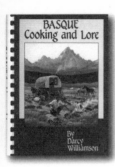

BASQUE COOKING AND LORE

by Darcy Williamson
Caxton Press
312 Main Street
Caldwell, ID 83605

Phone 800-657-6465
Fax 208-459-7450
www.caxtonpress.com

Recipes from the Basque culture plus stories and lore about the Basque people. Southwestern Idaho has the largest Basque population outside of Spain. 176 pages.

$14.95	Retail price	Visa/MC accepted
$.75	Tax for Idaho residents	
$4.00	Postage and handling	

Make check payable to Caxton Press

ISBN 0-87004-346-3

BE OUR GUEST

St. Mark's Episcopal Church
111 S. Jefferson
Moscow, ID 83843

Phone 208-882-2022
Email stmark@moscow.com

Be Our Guest is a collection of recipes that have been shared in our congregation for many years. Among the 450 recipes, we feature full-color divider pages that contain pictures of the beautiful stained glass windows that adorn St. Mark's Episcopal Church.

$15.00 Retail price
$2.50 Postage and handling

Make check payable to St. Mark's Episcopal Church

BOUND TO PLEASE

Junior League of Boise
Boise, ID

Over 2,000 recipes were prepared and tested by Boise Junior League before approving over 700 recipes for *Bound to Please*. Reflecting Idaho cuisine at its finest, from continental to country, this book offers a special ambiance and distinctive style that says "Welcome to Idaho." Currently out of print.

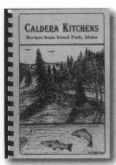

CALDERA KITCHENS

Island Park Library Friends, Inc.
P. O. Box 74
Macks Inn, ID 83433

Phone 208-558-0991

Established by a group of book-loving women in the early 1990s for citizens of Island Park, the library opened with donated books and volunteer time. Now a valued place within the community, fund raising has helped the library to grow, and in 2000, the cookbook was created from that need.

$10.00 Retail price
$2.50 Postage and handling

Make check payable to Island Park Library Friends, Inc.

CEE DUB'S DUTCH OVEN AND OTHER CAMP COOKIN'

by C. W. "Butch" Welch   Phone 208-983-7937
Back Country Press   Fax 208-983-7937
P. O. Box 190   Email ceedub@ceedubs.com
Grangeville, ID 83530   or bcpress@ceedubs.com

A cookbook on Dutch oven and camp cooking, and spiced with humorous and informative stories of Mr. Welch's experience cooking in the back country of Idaho as a game warden. Includes history, selection, and care of Dutch ovens, and many recipes for beginners and more experienced cooks.

$18.95 Retail price   Visa/MC/Discover accepted
$ .95 Tax for Idaho residents
$4.50 Postage and handling

Make check payable to Back Country Press or Cee Dub's   ISBN 0-9672647-1-5

CEE DUB'S ETHNIC & REGIONAL DUTCH OVEN COOKIN'

by C. W. "Butch" Welch   Phone 208-983-7937
Back Country Press   Fax 208-983-7937
P. O. Box 190   Email ceedub@ceedubs.com
Grangeville, ID 83530   or bcpress@ceedubs.com

Cee Dub's latest cookbook contains delicious recipes from many foreign lands, as well as regional favorites of the US of A, which have been adapted for preparation using Dutch ovens. And...of course, the cookbook contains Cee Dub's newest anecdotal stories about his experiences, as only he can tell.

$18.95 Retail price   Visa/MC/Dis accepted
$ .95 Tax for Idaho residents
$4.50 Postage and handling

Make check payable to Back Country Press or Cee Dub's   ISBN 0-9672647-3-1

CENTENNIAL COOKBOOK

Bonners Ferry United Methodist Church
P. O. Box 103
Bonners Ferry, ID 83805   Phone 208-267-2343
    Email bfumc@coldreams.com

From old treasured recipes handed down for generations to up-to-date fast and easy recipes, you're sure to find a favorite in this collection. The good cooks of Bonners Ferry UMC invite you to enjoy their specialties.

$7.50 Retail price
$2.50 Postage and handling

Make check payable to Bonners Ferry United Methodist Church

A CENTURY OF RECIPES

Hospice Visions, Inc.   Phone 208-735-0121
308 Shoshone St. E, Suite 1   Fax 208-735-0661
Twin Falls, ID 83301   Email hospvisi@yahoo.com

Over 400 recipes within this 127-page cookbook make it an unbelievable deal, but the real deal is the unbelievably delicious recipes provided by patients and families served by Hospice Visions, Inc. All proceeds from this cookbook are used to provide quality and compassionate care to the patients.

$10.00 Retail price
$2.00 Postage and handling

Make check payable to Hospice Visions, Inc.

THE COMPLETE SOURDOUGH COOKBOOK

by Don and Myrtle Holm
Caxton Press
312 Main Street   Phone 800-657-6465
Caldwell, ID 83605   Fax 208-459-7450

From the right "starter" to delicious sourdough goodies, this book offers one of the most significant collections of sourdough recipes ever to be tested.

$12.95   Retail price
 $.65   Tax for Idaho residents
$4.00   Postage and handling

Make check payable to Caxton Press   ISBN 0-87004-223-8

COOKIN' AT ITS BEST

New Meadows Senior Citizens Center
P. O. Box 399   Phone 208-347-2363
New Meadows, ID 83654   Fax 208-347-2363

This book was compiled by residents of our beautiful valley and a lot of hard work and love is enclosed. There are 206 pages with approximately 618 recipes. Proceeds help the senior center in our small town to provide meals for our seniors and shut-ins.

$11.00   Retail price
$2.50   Postage and handling

Cookin' at its Best

Make check payable to New Meadows Senior Citizens Center

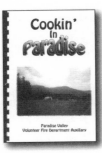

Cookin'
In
paradise

Paradise Valley
Volunteer Fire Department Auxiliary

COOKIN' IN PARADISE

Paradise Valley Volunteer Fire Department Auxiliary
Route 1, Box 519
Bonners Ferry, ID 83805

Home cookin' recipes from members and friends of Paradise Valley Volunteer Fire Department, located in Boundary, Idaho's northernmost county. At the top of the Idaho panhandle, our country is a wildlife paradise of 1300 square miles of mountain beauty. 115 pages, 7 categories.

$7.75   Retail price
 $.39   Tax for Idaho residents
$3.00   Postage and handling

Make check payable to Paradise Valley Volunteer Fire Department Auxiliary

Cooking
For A Crowd

(family reunions, church activities,
community gatherings, farm crews, etc.)

By: Barbara Sanders

COOKING FOR A CROWD

by Barbara Sanders
P. O. Box 205   Phone 208-662-5437
Hamer, ID 83425   Email sanders@directinter.net

This cookbook is full of easy recipes for cooking for large groups of people. It includes tasty main dishes like Porcupine Meatballs, cool side dishes like Orange Jello Salad, and tempting desserts like Caramel Popcorn. Plus Helpful Hints for cooking for any crowd.

$10.00   Retail price   Visa/MC accepted
 $.50   Tax for Idaho residents
$6.00   Postage and handling

Make check payable to Barbara Sanders

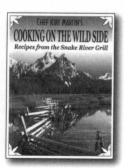

COOKING ON THE WILD SIDE

by Kirt Martin/Snake River Grill
P. O. Box 296
Hagerman, ID 83332

Phone 208-837-6227
Fax 208-837-6081
Email chefkirt@velocitus.net

Chef Kirt Martin is a 3rd generation chef and a graduate of Le Cordon Bleu Easy recipes based on classic French cuisine technique. All recipes are interchangeable with domestic meats. Cookbook was developed in conjunction with "Cooking on the Wild Side" cooking show, now being aired on PBS stations.

$19.85 Retail price
$.99 Tax for Idaho residents
$4.95 Postage and handling

Visa/MC/Discover accepted

Make check payable to *Cooking on the Wild Side*

ISBN 0-9678006-0-9

COOKING WITH COPS, TOO

Pocatello Police Department
P. O. Box 2877
Pocatello, ID 83206-2877

Phone 208-234-6113
Email dmonroe@cityofpocatello.org

Superb collection of recipes, 145 pages, beautiful 3-ring binder, easel included. Delicious, quick and easy, "ingredients-on-hand" recipes collected from all law enforcement agencies in our area. Profits to our local Shop With a Cop program, and dedicated to members of law enforcement—past, present, and future.

$12.00 Retail price
$3.00 Postage and handling

Make check payable to P.P.R.A

DON HOLM'S BOOK OF FOOD DRYING, PICKLING AND SMOKE CURING

by Don and Myrtle Holm
Caxton Press
312 Main Street
Caldwell, ID 83605

Phone 800-657-6465
Fax 208-459-7450

You can learn the easy way to dry, smoke, pickle any meat, fruit or fish with easy-to-follow directions in this food preparation cookbook.

$17.95 Retail price
$.90 Tax for Idaho residents
$4.50 Postage and handling

Make check payable to Caxton Press

ISBN 0-87004-250-5

DOWN HOME COUNTRY COOKIN'

Center for Discovery
P. O. Box 453
Cottonwood, ID 83522

Phone 208-962-5541
Email shears@sd242.k12.id.us

This cookbook contains 70 pages of recipes from several small rural communities in Idaho. There are well over 170 recipes to tempt your taste buds. Come and try some Down Home Country Cookin' from Idaho.

$11.00 Retail price
$.55 Tax for Idaho residents
$2.00 Postage and handling

Make check payable to Center for Discovery

ELEGANT COOKING MADE SIMPLE

by Sandra S. Corey
2205 Wyoming Avenue   Phone 208-455-2323
Caldwell, ID 83605   Email corsand2@aol.com

Elegant Cooking Made Simple contains 200 recipes suitable for casual, formal or buffet dining. The majority of these recipes can be prepared in advance, frozen and reheated. And no one will ever guess you haven't slaved all day.

$6.00   Retail price
$.30   Tax for Idaho residents
$2.00   Postage and handling

Make check payable to Sandra Corey

GENERATIONS "COMING HOME"

Samaria Recreation District   Phone 208-766-4697
4645 S. 4500 W.   Fax 208-766-4118
Samaria, ID 83252   Email cookbook@maladidaho.org

Samaria, Idaho, is known for its generations of wonderful cooks. This cookbook's 311 pages are a compilation of over 1000 recipes dating back to the late 1800s when ingredients were sparse. It features many delicious "from scratch" recipes that will have your family believing Grandma has been in the kitchen.

$19.95   Retail price   Visa/MC/Discover/Amex accepted
$4.00   Postage and handling

Make check payable to Samaria Recreation District

GRANDMA JANE'S COOKBOOK

by Jane Ross
1200 Artesian Road #8   Phone 208-938-2882
Eagle, ID 83616   Email sjanero@msn.com

Updated recipes dating back from the early 1900s. Recipes from women who cooked both at home and professionally. By combining the techniques, you can make home-cooked meals in less time. For today's busy woman, good cooking does not have to be sacrificed for lack of time.

$17.95   Retail price   Visa/MC/Discover/Amex accepted

Make check payable to Jane Ross

THE HEARTY GOURMET

by Diana Swift, Wapiti Meadow Ranch   Phone 208-633-3217
H. C. 72   Fax 208-633-3219
Cascade, ID 83611   Email wapitimr@aol.com

A six-day gourmet stay at Wapiti Meadow Ranch including menus and the recipes to serve special guests elegant dinner-party style. With 100 recipes in plastic sleeves in a looseleaf spiral binder, it's easy to keep the book clean and the recipes portable. Pen and ink drawings adorn each page.

$29.95   Retail price
$1.50   Tax for Idaho residents
$3.00   Postage and handling

Make check payable to Diana Bryant

HEY MA! COME QUICK! THE HOG'S IN THE GARDEN AGAIN!!

Idaho State University Outdoor Program
Dutch Oven Cookbook
P. O. Box 8128
Pocatello, ID 83209

Phone 208-282-3912
Fax 208-282-4600
Email joycepete@isu.edu

The Idaho State University Outdoor Program has been teaching Dutch oven cooking classes for quite some time. These 117 recipes were compiled from one of these classes. The cookbook offers recipes for breads, vegetables, main dishes, and desserts, as well as helpful tips for cooking in Dutch ovens.

$8.00   Retail price
$4.00   Postage and handling

Make check payable to ISU Outdoor Program

HUCKLEBERRY HAUS COOKBOOK

by Reverend Stan Simonik
1933 Davis Avenue
Kingman, AZ 86401

Phone 928-753-7916 or 888-219-5999
Fax 928-753-7133
Email simonik@citlink.net

Huckleberry Haus Cookbook has 162 pages with over 170 easy-to-follow huckleberry recipes and a section of huckleberry picking humor. 5½ x 8½ inches, wire bound. Reverend Stan Simonik is a well-known huckleberry enthusiast and one of the organizers of the Priest Lake Huckleberry Festival.

$10.95   Retail price
$ .86   Tax for Arizona residents
$2.00   Postage and handling

Make check payable to Reverend Stan Simonik   ISBN 0-9715051-0-1

IDAHO COOK BOOK

Janet Walker
Golden West Publishers, Inc.
4113 N. Longview Avenue
Phoenix, AZ 85014-4949

Phone 800-658-5830
Fax 602-279-6901
Email goldwest1@mindspring.com

Idaho Cook Book features delectable potatoes and beans, juicy berries and flavorful fruits, meats, wheat and dairy products found in the great state of Idaho. Collected from some of Idaho's best cooks, as well as from bed and breakfast inns, these recipes are sure to please your taste buds!

$6.95   Retail price
$3.00   Postage and handling

Make check payable to Golden West Publishers   ISBN 1-885590-23-7

THE IDAHO TABLE
A TASTE OF THE INTERMOUNTAIN WEST

by Jonathan R. Mortimer
Holdthebaby Publishing
1207 E. Lexington Ct.
Boise, ID 83706

Phone 208-338-6550
Fax 208-424-0475
Email mortimersidaho@att.net

A collection of unique recipes to please the most discerning palates. Using the foods of Idaho and techniques of the world, *The Idaho Table* will teach you how to get the most out of foods from the Intermountain West.

$22.95   Retail price   Visa/MC/Diners/Amex
$1.15   Tax for Idaho residents
$2.88   Postage and handling

Make check payable to Holdthebaby Publishing   ISBN 0-9724333-2-5

IDAHO'S FAVORITE BEAN RECIPES

Idaho Bean Commission　　　　　　　　　　Phone 208-334-3520
P. O. Box 2556　　　　　　　　　　　　　　　Fax 208-334-2442
Boise, ID 83701-2556　　　　　　Email bean@bean.state.id.us

What's small, dry, generally kidney shaped, packed with protein, carbohydrates, fiber, vitamins, minerals, inexpensive, shelf stable, and delicious? It's an Idaho dried bean! More earth-conscious, health-conscious, and taste-conscious people are turning to dried beans to add variety and interest to a healthy diet.

　$6.50　Retail price
　$.39　Tax for Idaho residents
Make check payable to Idaho Bean Commission

IDAHO'S WILD 100!

Idaho Department of Fish & Game　　　　Phone 208-334-3700
P. O. Box 25 (IDFG)　　　　　　　　　　　　Fax 208-334-2148
Boise, ID 83707　　　　　　　Email swatson@idfg.state.id.us

Dutch oven and camp cooking recipes are featured with emphasis on wild game and fowl. Don't hunt or fish? All recipes can be prepared at home, also.

　$10.00　Retail price
　　$.50　Tax for Idaho residents
　$2.50　Postage and handling
Make check payable to IDFG

KETCHUM COOKS

by Dee Dee McCuskey
Graphic Arts Center - Portland, Oregon
P. O. Box 1838　　　　　　　　　　　　Phone 208-726-4500
Sun Valley, ID 83353　　　　Email gardeningnerd@aol.com

Historical cookbook with illustrations and history of our region. Recipes from the community, restaurants, and author. Portion of proceeds to benefit the Hospice of the Wood River Valley in memory of the author's husband. Hardcover photo courtesy of renowned photographer, David Stoecklein.

　$19.95　Retail price
　$5.00　Postage and handling
Make check payable to *Ketchum Cooks*　　　　ISBN 0-9651469-0-1

MACKAY HERITAGE COOKBOOK

Charlotte McKelvey for South Custer Historical Society
Charlotte McKelvey
Box 90　　　　　　　　　　　　　　　Phone 208-588-3356
Mackay, ID 83251　　　　　　　　Email Char@atcnet.net

The *Mackay Heritage Cookbook* is a 240-page collection of recipes and pictures celebrating Mackay's Centennial in 2001. The book reflects our Idaho heritage with recipes from the early 1900s to the present. It includes many recipes using our famous Idaho potatoes.

　$15.00　Retail price
　　$.75　Tax for Idaho residents
　$3.00　Postage and handling
Make check payable to *Mackay Heritage Cookbook*

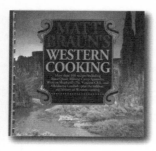

MATT BRAUN'S WESTERN COOKING

by Matt Braun
Caxton Press
312 Main Street   Phone 800-657-646?
Caldwell, ID 83605   Fax 208-459-745(

Western novelist Matt Braun brings home the hearty flavors, traditions and lore of western cooking. 186 pages.

$17.95   Retail price   Visa/MC accepted
  $.90   Tax for Idaho residents
$4.40   Postage and handling

Make check payable to Caxton Press   ISBN 0-87004-374-9

THE MIRACLE COOKBOOK

The Boise Courtyard by Marriott   Phone 208-331-2700
222 Broadway Avenue   Fax 208-331-3296
Boise, ID 83702   Email lisa.benjamin@ihrco.com

A fund raiser for Children's Miracle Network, this 254-page collection of 650 favorites submitted by Courtyard employees, including Marriott's 75th anniversary original Hot Shoppe's recipes. All money raised benefits St. Luke's Children's Hospital in Boise.

$20.00   Retail price

Make check payable to Children's Miracle Network

MORE CEE DUB'S DUTCH OVEN AND OTHER CAMP COOKIN'

by C. W. "Butch" Welch   Phone 208-983-7937
Back Country Press   Fax 208-983-7937
P. O. Box 190   Email ceedub@ceedubs.com
Grangeville, ID 83530   or bcpress@ceedubs.com

A "continuation" of Cee Dub's Dutch Oven: 150 new recipes, new photos, and new stories. Recipes have been contributed by others who enjoy Dutch oven cooking and the outdoors. Included are history, selection and care of Dutch ovens, with information for beginners and experienced camp cooks.

$18.95   Retail price   Visa/MC/Discover accepted
  $.95   Tax for Idaho residents
$4.50   Postage and handling

Make check payable to Back Country Press or Cee Dub's   ISBN 0-9672647-2-3

98 WAYS TO COOK VENISON

by Eldon R. Cutlip
HC 75 Box 113 A2   Phone 800-352-9453
Kooskia, ID 83539   Fax 208-926-4383

One-hundred-twelve pages of down-home cooking for wild game along with tips for game care. Includes recipes for steak, roasts, stews, ribs, ground meat, and soups, and illustrations and charts that are helpful in wild game preparation.

$11.95   Retail price
  $.56   Tax for Idaho residents
$5.00   Postage and handling

Make check payable to Eldons Products   ISBN 0-9644922-3-7

NORTHERN LITES
CONTEMPORARY COOKING WITH A TWIST

by Rose Chaney and Connie (Berghan) Church   Phone 208-263-2940
Lites Ltd.   Fax 208-265-8407
431 Lakeshore Blvd.   Email rrchaney@imbris.com
Sandpoint, ID 83835   or steve.connie7@verizon.net

Northern Lites recipes are incredibly rich in flavor with a minimum of fat and
calories. Recipes are organized in complete menus and are displayed with their
nutritional values. The handcrafted cedar TwistTable holds the cookbook so that
you see all recipes in an entire menu without turning a page.

$24.95   Retail price
 $1.25   Tax for Idaho residents
 $5.00   Postage and handling
Make check payable to Lites Ltd.   ISBN 0-9662467-0-5

OLD-FASHIONED DUTCH OVEN COOKBOOK

by Don Holm
Caxton Press
312 Main Street   Phone 800-657-6465
Caldwell, ID 83605   Fax 208-459-7450

This cookbook specializes in old-fashioned Dutch oven cookery and sourdough
recipes. Includes information on sourdough starters and dried meat.

$14.95   Retail price
 $.75   Tax for Idaho residents
 $4.00   Postage and handling
Make check payable to Caxton Press   ISBN 0-87004-133-9

ONIONS MAKE THE MEAL COOKBOOK

Idaho-Eastern Oregon Onion Committee
P. O. Box 909
Parma, ID 83660

An onion-shaped cookbook with 96 Idaho-Eastern Oregon onion recipes,
including the recipe for the famous onion bloom. This unique cookbook covers
everything from traditional onion soups and onion rings to onion salsa and onion
sandwiches.

$6.00   Retail price
$4.00   Postage and handling
Make check payable to Idaho-Eastern Oregon Onion Committee

THE OUTDOOR DUTCH OVEN COOKBOOK

by Sheila Mills
Ragged Mountain Press/McGraw-Hill   Phone 800-262-4729
P. O. Box 552   Fax 614-759-3641
Blacklick, OH 43004   Email customer.service@mcgraw-hill.com

After 30 years of feeding river runners, Sheila Mills knows what hungry outdoors people like to eat. In this cookbook, she uses a traditional cooking tool to
create new dimensions of contemporary, innovative recipes for everything from
salads to desserts. This is camp cooking as you've never tasted it!

$16.95   Retail price
 $9.00   Postage and handling
Make check payable to McGraw-Hill   ISBN 0-07-043023-3

THE PEA AND LENTIL COOKBOOK
FROM EVERYDAY TO GOURMET

USA Dry Pea and Lentil Council   Phone 208-882-302?
2780 W. Pullman Road   Fax 208-882-640(
Moscow, ID 83501   Email pulse@pea-lentil.com

Appealing to both the novice or professional cook, this wonderful collection o palate-pleasing recipes overflows with basic facts about lentils, split peas, an(chick peas. Features include hardcover with fully concealed wire-o binding color photography; and complete nutritional information for each recipe.

$24.95   Retail price   Visa/MC/Amex
$1.25   Tax for Idaho residents
$4.00   Postage and handling

Make check payable to USA Dry Pea and Lentil Council   ISBN 0-97-00436-0-0

POTATOES ARE NOT THE ONLY VEGETABLE!

Idaho State University Outdoor Program   Phone 208-282-3912
P. O. Box 8128   Fax 208-282-4600
Pocatello, ID 83209   Email joycepete@isu.edu

The Idaho State University Outdoor Program has been teaching Dutch oven cooking classes for quite some time. These 105 recipes were compiled from one of these classes. The cookbook offers recipes for breads, vegetables, main dishes, and desserts, as well as helpful tips for cooking in Dutch ovens.

$8.00   Retail price
$4.00   Postage and handling

Make check payable to ISU Outdoor Program

QUILTER'S DELIGHT, BUSY DAY RECIPES

Lemhi Piece Makers
Salmon, ID

Our cookbook is a product of our enjoyable quilting-day lunches and potluck dinners where we have sampled favorite recipes, and wish to share them with each other and the public. 60 pages, 146 recipes. This cookbook is currently out of print.

RECIPES LOGGED FROM THE WOODS OF NORTH IDAHO

Friends of the West Bonner Library
P. O. Box 1047   Phone 208-448-2207
Priest River, ID 83856   Email prpl@ebcl.lib.id.us

Originally published in 1948, this collection of nearly 700 recipes has been updated with additional recipes and historic photos. Sprinkled with excerpts from library club minutes dating back to 1922, this piece of Idaho history is a must for any cookbook collector.

$12.00   Retail price
 $.60   Tax for Idaho residents
$2.00   Postage and handling

Make check payable to Friends of the Library

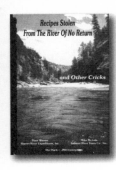

RECIPES STOLEN FROM THE RIVER OF NO RETURN

by Dave Warren
Warren River Expeditions, Inc.
Box 1375
Salmon, ID 83467

Phone 800-765-0421
Fax 208-756-3910
Email salmonriver@raftidaho.com

Dutch and outdoor cooking recipes written by the folks who live and work in Idaho's wilderness... for home and camping. 146 pages.

$10.00   Retail price   All Major Cards accepted
  $.50   Tax for Idaho residents
 $2.00   Postage and handling

Make check payable to Warren River Exp., Inc.   ISBN 0-9670445-0-2

RECIPES TRIED AND TRUE

by Diana Swift, Wapiti Meadow Ranch
H. C. 72
Cascade, ID 83611

Phone 208-633-3217
Fax 208-633-3219
Email wapitimr@aol.com

This collection of favorite recipes was tried on a family of two boys and guests from every corner of the country. This 86-page book featuring recipes from breakfasts to dinners, cookies, candies, and specialty sauces is contained in a spiral notebook with plastic-sleeved pages.

$29.95   Retail price
 $1.50   Tax for Idaho residents
 $3.00   Postage and handling

Make check payable to Diana Bryant

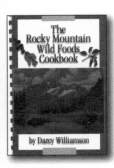

THE ROCKY MOUNTAIN WILD FOODS COOKBOOK

by Darcy Williamson
Caxton Press
312 Main Street
Caldwell, ID 83605

Phone 800-657-6465
Fax 208-459-7450

Easy-to-recognize wild foods are abundant in the west. Darcy Williamson describes 28 plants common to the region, and provides an extensive selection of recipes. 252 pages.

$17.95   Retail price   Visa/MC accepted
  $.90   Tax for Idaho residents
 $4.50   Postage and handling

Make check payable to Caxton Press   ISBN 0-87004-367-6

SAUSAGE & JERKY HANDBOOK

by Eldon R. Cutlip
HC 75 Box 113 A2
Kooskia, ID 83539

Phone 800-352-9453
Fax 208-926-4383

One-hundred-twelve pages for the home sausage and jerky maker; 50 sausage recipes (fresh and smoked); 30 jerky recipes including fish jerky, slim jim, and ground jerky. Includes information about fat-to-meat ratio, cures, and a smoke cooking chart with times and temperatures to follow for perfect sausage.

$11.95   Retail price   Visa/MC/Discover accepted
  $.60   Tax for Idaho residents
 $5.00   Postage and handling

Make check payable to Eldon's Products   ISBN 0-9644922-1-0

SHARING OUR BEST
BICS CONTRACTOR'S COOKBOOK

by Lalia Wilson
722 Cypress
Pocatello, ID 83201

Phone 208-234-0641
Fax 208-238-5149
Email laliawilson@aol.com

An enjoyable easy-to-use cookbook with a wide variety of recipes provided by contributors from Idaho and several states from Hawaii to Virginia. This 3-ring binder of over 400 pages and 750 recipes with helpful tips and hints, also has a book stand and recipe pocket for your use.

$20.00   Retail price

Make check payable to Lalia Wilson

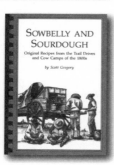

SOWBELLY AND SOURDOUGH
ORIGINAL RECIPES FROM THE TRAIL DRIVES AND COW CAMPS OF THE 1800s

by Scott Gregory
Caxton Press
312 Main Street
Caldwell, ID 83605

Phone 800-657-6465
Fax 208-459-7450

Filled not only with authentic chuck wagon cuisine, but with history and anecdotes, this book conjures up visions of mealtimes at chuck wagons in dusty cow camps. *Sowbelly and Sourdough* returns to a simpler way of living, and brings back the savory goodness of hearty meals built from scratch.

$12.95   Retail price   Visa/MC accepted
 $.65   Tax for Idaho residents
$4.00   Postage and handling

Make check payable to Caxton Press   ISBN 0-87004-369-2

SPRAGG FAMILY COOKBOOK

by Karen Spragg
Ashton, ID

Filled with wonderful family recipes passed down through the generations, *Spragg Family Cookbook* is full of tasty treats that will keep you coming back for more. It contains everything from appetizers to desserts, and is sure to please even the pickiest of eaters. This cookbook is currently out of print.

A TASTE OF HEAVEN

Hospice of Salmon Valley
506 Van Dreff
Salmon, ID 83467

Phone 208-756-6122
Fax 208-756-6126
Email hsv@salmoninternet.com

Tried-and-true recipes by some of the finest cooks in the valley. Many little wisdoms and hints from people who have lived in our valley over 50 years. Proceeds go to support the continued support given to terminally ill people and their families. Hospice of Salmon Valley is a nonprofit organization.

$8.00   Retail price
 $.40   Tax for Idaho residents
$2.00   Postage and handling

Make check payable to Hospice of Salmon Valley

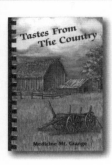

TASTES FROM THE COUNTRY

Medicine Mt. Grange
31146 South Highway 3
Medimont, ID 83842   Phone 208-689-3385

Wonderful recipes from this rural area of Northern Idaho. Old stand-bys, yummy desserts, and unusual recipes for elk and venison as well.

$8.00   Retail price
$2.00   Postage and handling

Make check payable to Medicine Mt. Grange

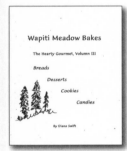

WAPITI MEADOW BAKES

by Diana Swift, Wapiti Meadow Ranch   Phone 208-633-3217
H. C. 72   Fax 208-633-3219
Cascade, ID 83611   Email wapitimr@aol.com

Over 90 sweet-tooth recipes beloved by our guests from back-country Idaho to every corner of the country. Sketches of woodland plants and creatures and guest ranch activities decorate the 54 plastic-sleeved pages in a looseleaf spiral binder.

$29.95   Retail price
 $1.50   Tax for Idaho residents
 $3.00   Postage and handling

Make check payable to Diana Bryant

A Little about the Dutch Oven

There are many theories of how this remarkable cooking pot got its name; one strong theory relates to the purchase of Manhattan Island from Native Americans by Dutch traders. Probably the old traders had a name for them, now long forgotten, but was replaced by a satisfied customer as the "Dutchman's Oven." Now shortened to "Dutch Oven," the cast iron cookware has changed little since the settling of this country. One change is that some are now being made of aluminum, and this cookware is lighter and easier to transport. But the cast iron, three-leg version is the standard.

Cee Dub's Dutch Oven and Other Camp Cookin'

The Dutch oven accompanied pioneers west in the chuck-wagon and was noted by Lewis and Clark as one of their most valued pieces of equipment. This remarkable cooking pot remains an efficient way to prepare food on an open fire, and is considered essential by paddlers, car campers, RV-ers, and even backpackers.

With its snug-fitting lid, it becomes an oven when heated with charcoal briquettes and can be used for baking, braising, stewing, or roasting. With the lid removed, the oven becomes a kettle for boiling, deep-fat frying, or heating food quickly over a fire. The lid, turned upside down on the coals, can be used for frying.

Cast iron requires more cooking time than aluminum, but the number of coals on top and bottom remains the same. Either the cast iron or aluminum Dutch oven can be permanently damaged by pouring cold water into a hot oven; by uneven heating when putting coals on only half the oven or lid; by careless packing while traveling (the legs can be broken off or pushed up through the bottom by too much jamming); and by rust and corrosion.

The Outdoor Dutch Oven Cookbook

Index

Introduced to Idaho in the late 1800s, California quail, with a distinctive teardrop-shaped head plume called a top-knot, generally inhabit valleys and foothills. As ground dwelling birds, their short and powerful legs are well adapted for terrestrial locomotion. They can fly rapidly, but only for short distances.

INDEX

INDEX

INDEX

INDEX

INDEX

INDEX

INDEX

INDEX

INDEX

Collect the Series!
Best of the Best State Cookbook Series

Over 3.5 million copies sold! Cookbook collectors love this Series! The forty-two cookbooks, covering all fifty states (see previous page for listing), contain over 15,000 of the most popular local and regional recipes collected from approximately 3,000 of the leading cookbooks from these states.

To assist individuals who have purchased copies of the BEST OF THE BEST STATE COOKBOOKS and wish to collect the entire Series, we are offering a special **Collect the Series Discount.** You get:

- 25% discount off the list price ($16.95 minus 25% = $12.70 per copy).
- To order online, enter coupon code 25OFF.
- ONLY $5.00 shipping cost for any number of books ordered (within contiguous United States).
- Order the entire 42-book Series for $395.00 plus $25.00 shipping. This represents another 10% savings off the Series discount.

Recipe Hall of Fame Cookbook Collection
Over 3 million copies sold!

The Recipe Hall of Fame Cookbook	**The Recipe Hall of Fame Cookbook II**	**Quick & Easy Cookbook**	**Dessert Cookbook**
6x9 • 304 pages • Index Comb-bound • $16.95	6x9 • 304 pages • Index Comb-bound • $16.95	6x9 • 304 pages • Index Comb-bound • $16.95	6x9 • 240 pages • Index Comb-bound • $16.95

Special Offer! Four-book collection for $40

Collect the Series discounts (see above) also apply to the RECIPE HALL OF FAME COLLECTION. These cookbooks can be ordered for $12.70 per copy (25% discount) or $40.00 for four-book set (40% discount). Shipping is only $5.00 for any number of books ordered. To order online, enter coupon code 4FAME.

Individuals may order cookbooks by phone, mail, or online. All major credit cards accepted. Be sure to mention **Collect the Series** special discount.

QUAIL RIDGE PRESS
P. O. Box 123 • Brandon, MS 39043 • 1-800-343-1583
info@quailridge.com • www.quailridge.com
www.facebook.com/CookbookLadies • www.twitter.com/CookbookLadies

BEST OF THE BEST STATE COOKBOOK SERIES

ALABAMA
ALASKA
ARIZONA
ARKANSAS
BIG SKY
Includes Montana, Wyoming
CALIFORNIA
COLORADO
FLORIDA
GEORGIA
GREAT PLAINS
Includes North Dakota, South Dakota, Nebraska, and Kansas

HAWAII
IDAHO
ILLINOIS
INDIANA
IOWA
KENTUCKY
LOUISIANA
LOUISIANA II
MICHIGAN
MID-ATLANTIC
Includes Maryland, Delaware, New Jersey, and Washington, D.C.

MINNESOTA
MISSISSIPPI
MISSOURI
NEVADA
NEW ENGLAND
Includes Rhode Island, Connecticut, Massachusetts, Vermont, New Hampshire, and Maine
NEW MEXICO
NEW YORK
NO. CAROLINA
OHIO
OKLAHOMA

OREGON
PENNSYLVANIA
SO. CAROLINA
TENNESSEE
TEXAS
TEXAS II
UTAH
VIRGINIA
VIRGINIA II
WASHINGTON
WEST VIRGINIA
WISCONSIN

All BEST OF THE BEST COOKBOOKS are 6x9 inches, are comb-bound, contain approximately 400 recipes, and total 264–352 pages. Each contains illustrations, photographs, an index, and a list of contributing cookbooks, a special feature that cookbook collectors enjoy. Interesting information about each state is scattered throughout the cookbooks, including historical facts and major attractions along with amusing trivia.
Retail price per copy: $16.95.

See previous page for special **Collect the Series Discounts**.

To order by credit card, call toll-free **1-800-343-1583**, visit **www.quailridge.com**, or use the Order Form below.

Order Form

Send check, money order, or credit card info to:
QUAIL RIDGE PRESS • P. O. Box 123 • Brandon, MS 39043

Name _____

Address _____

City _____

State/Zip _____

Phone # _____

Email Address _____

☐ Check enclosed

Charge to: ☐ Visa ☐ MC ☐ AmEx ☐ Disc

Card # _____

Expiration Date _____

Signature _____

Qty.	Title of Book (or State) (or Set)	Total

Subtotal _____

Mississippi residents add 7% sales tax _____

Postage (any number of books) + $5.00

TOTAL _____